For Dan Aaron —
In memory of that summer
at Rye Beach
[illegible]
October 1952

THIS WAS PUBLISHING

Donald Sheehan

THIS WAS PUBLISHING

A *Chronicle of the* BOOK TRADE *in the Gilded Age*

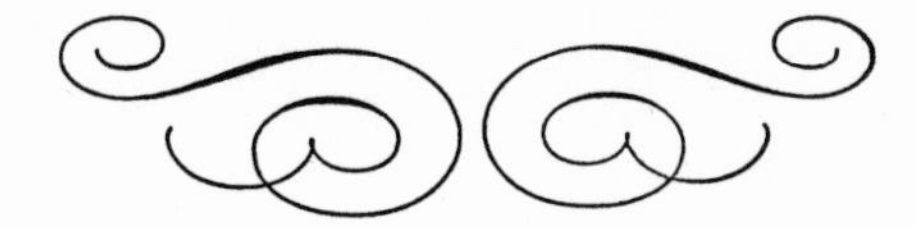

INDIANA UNIVERSITY PRESS
1952 BLOOMINGTON

to

KIT, KERRY, AND JEFF

Acknowledgments

The kindness of many people made the task of writing this book both pleasurable and rewarding.

I am particularly grateful to the publishers who permitted me to search their files for historical materials. Among the many, the late Mr. Charles Scribner must be singled out for his patience and interest. The extensive records of Charles Scribner's Sons—now augustly lodged in the board of directors' room—proved to be a stimulating and indispensable point of departure. The path to the archives of Harper and Brothers led from the desk of the equally cooperative Mr. Frank S. MacGregor to a warehouse, then back to the company's editorial offices. To Mr. A. C. Edwards, I am indebted for a courteous invitation to examine the records of the old and notable firm, Henry Holt and Company. This served to introduce me to another warehouse, where I was able to view the voluminous correspondence of the company's founder written during the first half-century of its existence. The present representative of a distinguished publishing family, Mr. Edward H. Dodd, Jr., graciously placed at my disposal the historical files of a company started by his great-grandfather over a century ago.

I trust I have not betrayed the confidence which the granting of my requests for assistance necessarily involved. The device of using materials only for the period before the First World War was designed to prevent any incidental indiscretions. For those passages of this volume which may seem more like "muckraking" than scholarship, my defense can be only that I believe the record honorable enough to be revealed fully.

A special word of gratitude should be reserved for the editors of *Publishers' Weekly* and its predecessors, who have left the richest storehouse of information on American publishing which can be found. From Frederick Leypoldt and R. R. Bowker to Frederic Melcher, they have combined objective reporting and constructive thinking in a manner which has won the respect both of the trade and the historians of the trade.

It is also a privilege to join the large company who have had reason to be grateful for the help of Professor Allan Nevins of Columbia University. As a guide to the often maligned "Gilded Age," he has offered an indispensable corrective to the youthful impulse to identify the whole of historical truth with the least attractive portion of it.

Among the many who have shared their special knowledge with me at crucial points in the narrative, I am particularly indebted to the following: Mr. Chris Gerhardt, whose experience in New York's book trade goes back to 1884, when he joined the auction house of Bangs and Company; Mr. Oscar Weglin, the distinguished bibliographer, who entered the business in 1893; Mr. William Gleason of the Colonial Press, who assisted with many details on book manufacture; Mr. Roger Kafka, who shared with me his extensive knowledge of editing and book distribution; and Mr. Robert Kennedy, who was able to clarify many points concerning retail operations.

For permission to quote brief passages of copyrighted materials I wish to thank the following authors and publishers: Henry Walcott Boynton, *Annals of American Bookselling, 1638–1850,* John Wiley and Sons, Inc., 1932; R. H. Duffus, "Printing and Publishing" in *Encyclopedia of the Social Sciences,* The Macmillan Co.; Herbert Hungerford, *How Publishers Win,* Ransdell, Inc., 1931; Gustavus Myers, "Preface" in *History of the Great American Fortunes,* Random House, 1936; Walter H. Page, *A Publisher's Confession, 1905,* Doubleday, Page and Co., 1923; George H. Doran, *Chronicles of Barabbas,* Harcourt, Brace and Co., 1939; O. H. Cheney, *Supplementary Report of the Economic Survey of the Book Industry for Bookbinding Executives,* American Book Publishers Council, 1932; Frederick S. Crofts, "Textbooks are not Absolutely Dead Things," Alfred Harcourt, "Publishing Since 1900," Frederick A. Stokes, "A Publisher's Random Notes, 1880–1935" and Frank E. Compton, "Subscription Books," in *The Bowker Lectures on Book Publishing,* First Series, R. R. Bowker and Co., 1943.

Finally, in common with most married authors, I must conclude by reserving the deepest thanks of all for my wife, Kit.

Contents

Introduction

Among the notable studies of the book industry, there is none that deals in any comprehensive manner with the crucial years between the Civil War and the World War when the foundations were laid for modern publishing. The reason for this deficiency is not difficult to discover. Beyond the charming but not especially informative memoirs of publishers in retirement there has been very little material to reveal these origins.

A number of publishers whose histories extend back into the nineteenth century have now made such a study possible. This book owes its appearance to the generous cooperation of Henry Holt and Company, Harper and Brothers, Dodd, Mead and Company, and Charles Scribner's Sons. No one of these firms has anything resembling a complete archive. But taken together, and used in conjunction with the indispensable *Publishers' Weekly,* their records reveal the essential patterns.

It is a commendable and, in many ways, a surprising story. The ruthlessly competitive days at the dawn of the modern industrial period were scarcely a congenial atmosphere for the encouragement of gentlemanly business ethics. Jay Gould and the notorious Jim Fisk suggest the degradation which has been made synonymous with the "Gilded Age." But these pirates should be taken to represent not the whole but only the most disagreeable part. The same years produced another group of business men who found deceit and fraud as repugnant then as we should find them now. Among the latter must be included the leading book publishers—Charles Scribner and Frank Dodd, Joseph Harper, George Brett, William Appleton, Henry Holt, and George Putnam in New York, and an equally distinguished coterie in Philadelphia, Boston, and the other publishing centers.

The availability of materials has to a great extent determined the heroes of the story. Charles Scribner and Henry Holt appear most often because they left behind them a considerable body of correspondence. But probably the trade would not regret being represented by men to whom they so often turned for leadership during their own lifetimes. When these two commented on conditions in the industry, they spoke for the regular book trade from coast to coast.

To the limitations imposed by the nature of the materials should be added the predilections of the author, whose further acquaintance with the publishers of trade books has served to increase a long-standing respect and admiration for them. If the results of this study have thereby been tinctured, the reader is forewarned. But it should be said also that the reading of tens of thousands of letters written by their predecessors provides small reason for thinking that that affection is misplaced.

THIS WAS PUBLISHING

The Philosophy of Publishing

chapter 1

Throughout the years of publishing between the close of the Civil War and the outbreak of fighting in 1914, there ran a constant undercurrent of complaint. In each decade the national economy floundered for at least a little while in the mire of a depression, causing a chorus of wails in which the publishers' voices were easily distinguishable. The years between were beset with special problems, solvable the trade thought, but persistent enough to disturb the pleasures of prosperity. But even beyond the difficulties posed by business cycles and the strain of adjusting to a new industrial age, publishers worried about an inherent quality of their business which would prevent its becoming prosperous under any circumstances.

When a leading publisher at the turn of the century wrote an article describing publishing as the "worst business in the world," the authoritative *Publishers' Weekly* blandly recommended the article to the trade, "however well accepted the conclusions" it contained.[1] This sentiment was scarcely a novelty to a trade organ which had previously printed editorials with such titles as: "Is the

Book Trade 'A Doomed Calling'?" [2] and "Is Bookselling Dead?" [3] The latest survey of publishing, brought out in 1949, testifies to the persistence of this sentiment by devoting its opening paragraphs to denying that the book industry "is chronically sicker than other industries." [4]

Basic to this pessimism, which has survived too long to be ignored, is the belief that whatever its other compensations, publishing is among the least profitable of business enterprises. Walter Page expressed the views of most of the trade when he said: [5]

> Every successful publisher—really successful mind you—could make more money going into some other business. I think that there is not a man of them who could not greatly increase his income by giving the same energy and ability to the management of a bank, or of some sort of industrial enterprise. Such men as Mr. Charles Scribner, Mr. George Brett, Mr. George H. Mifflin, could earn very much larger returns by their ability in banks, railroads or manufacturing, than any one of them earns as a publisher; for they are all men of conspicuous ability. . . . Not one of them has made a colossal fortune.

Among the many adding their assent to Page's diagnosis was William Ellsworth, who retired from the presidency of the Century Company in 1915: "If one wants to make money, let him go into the steel business or into something in which there is money to be made." [6]

Although there is little point in lingering over the failure of successful publishers to gather personal fortunes of tens of millions rather than tens of thousands, it is significant that a sense of monetary sacrifice conditioned the outlook of trade leaders. Few were content to regard themselves as "mere businessmen." More often than not, they liked to believe they were members of a profession requiring special scholarly training and a sense of dedication which rose above material gains. "Publishing, as publishing," wrote Page, "is the least profitable of all the professions, except preaching and teaching, to each of which it is a sort of cousin." [7] What gave publishing its special quality was, of course, its connection with literature, and those who did not truly love books were admonished to stay clear of it. There is something appropriately rhapsodic about Page's description of this devotion, although most of the older publishers would have exercised more restraint in expressing their agreement: "A good book is a Big Thing, a thing to be thankful to heaven for. It is a great day for any of us when we can put our imprint on it. Here is a chance for reverence, for something like consecration." [8]

Since there was no certainty that a particular manuscript would become a profitable investment, this sentiment was available both as an incentive to its publication and as a comfort in the event of its failure. Although most unsuccessful books were not published with the anticipation of certain loss, a substantial number of them owed their presence to the literary enthusiasm of the publisher rather than to his business judgment. Speaking of the "notable publishers" who applied to their work the standards of a profession, the New York *Evening Post* editorialized, "They have felt a compulsion to seek good books regardless of immediate return." [9] The articulate Walter Page added: "Every one of them every year invests in books and authors that they know cannot yield a direct or immediate profit, and they make these investments because they feel ennobled by trying to do a service to literature."[10]

While this zest for cultural philanthropy influenced the trade's attitude, there are a number of indications—one of them being the large number of second-rate novels and the small number of volumes of poetry on any given list—that it was not the major determinant in the decision to publish. As often as publishers expressed their moral superiority over other business men, they asserted that they were business men. The possession of this wider vision did not, they felt, involve any sacrifice of the energy, common sense, and financial astuteness necessary for lesser trades. Rather, it required more of these qualities. If a simple man of commerce was unfit for the unique role of publisher, neither was a "literary man," an unsuccessful author, capable of filling more than the humble position of reader.[11]

As intermediaries between "the immortals and the ordinary world," the guardians of the trade's morality were on constant watch against the incursion of "commercialism," which would divest the business of its character of public service. "We fear," said *Publishers' Weekly* in 1897, "that it is becoming a trade."[12] Ten years later such prominent publishers as Henry Holt and John Murray were certain that the evil day had arrived, and the scolding of *Publishers' Weekly* became more insistent.[13] The fact that these complaints first arose in the 1890's seems to imply that the decades before, when Fisk tilted with Vanderbilt over the carcass of the Erie Railroad and Standard Oil brought a stern order out of the chaos of the Pennsylvania oil fields, were a time of special sobriety and high idealism in the publishing business. This is precisely what the leaders of the trade would have us believe. Recalling the days immediately after the Civil War when he was attempting to establish his own firm, Henry Holt said: [14]

All those old publishers—Putnam, Appleton, Harper and Scribner—were incapable of petty or ostentatious things, and were much more inclined to friendly co-operation and mutual concession than to barbarous competition. The spectacle of a crowd of other men making fools of themselves exercised upon them no temptation to do as the herd did. . . . They were wonderfully kind to me as a young fellow. . . . The idea of any knowledge that I might glean from them being used in rivalry against them, was too small for any of them to think of. In fact, any notion of the contemptible kinds of business rivalry, was too petty to find a place in their minds.

Even if allowance is made for the mist in the eyes of an old man looking back over a half-century to his vigorous and successful youth, the statement contains a substantial truth. Holt himself would be the first to deny that this restraint implied an absence of abuses or that it characterized every member of the trade. Nevertheless, because of the importance of the firms represented in his list, and the dominating position of these individuals within the firms, there can be little question that the character of the business as a whole was affected by a morality higher than that which is customarily associated with the era.

Perhaps this situation was merely fortuitous, arising from the chance presence of a few strong-minded individuals in an industry highly dependent upon personalities. More probably, it was intrinsic to the nature of the business that men like Charles Scribner, Moses Dodd, the original

Harper brother, George Palmer Putnam, and Daniel Appleton should be drawn to it. To this group of New York publishers could be added men of similar stature in the other chief publishing centers of Philadelphia and Boston —William Ticknor and James T. Fields, James Osgood and Joshua Lippincott.

It was this generation of pre-Civil War publishers who laid at the same time the foundations of modern publishing and the groundwork for the firms which were to lead the trade in the fifty year interval between Appomattox and Sarajevo. Most of them had started as retail booksellers. William Ticknor's association with the Old Corner Book Store began as early as 1832,[15] but Daniel Appleton had entered the trade in New York some seven years before, and by 1831 had grafted a publishing business onto a retail store.[16] Before the decade ended, Moses Dodd established himself in the Old Brick Church Chapel building in what is now downtown Manhattan.[17] Another short span would pass before Baker and Scribner moved in next door.[18] Although most of the publishers were recruited from retail book stores, there were other courses of development. George Palmer Putnam had served an apprenticeship in the retail and publishing firm of Wiley and Long, but his first independent effort, made in 1848, was concerned chiefly with the importation of books from England.[19] The publishing activities of Harper and Brothers rested on the foundation of a printing business started by the two eldest of the four brothers in 1817.[20]

Thus, the traditions for the "Gilded Age" were set in quieter years, and at a time when literature was identified more with gentility, scholarship, and instruction, than with popular entertainment. When ill health prevented Moses Dodd from completing a course at the Princeton Theological Seminary, he could turn to a career in the book trade without greatly changing the scope of his interests. A large proportion of his early publishing ventures were volumes of sermons.[21] If a sense of piety was common among the members of this group of founding fathers, so were they characterized by a public interestedness of an unusual vitality. Occasionally, their extra activities were a direct outgrowth of business problems—witness George Palmer Putnam's devotion to the cause of an international copyright law.[22] James Harper's term as Mayor of New York may be taken as a tribute either to his personal ambition or to good citizenship, but in either case it indicates a horizon not confined to the four corners of a profit and loss statement.[23]

It was under these men that the ethics of the trade and the conditions of competition took form. Some died before the Civil War and others bridged the conflict to make their mark felt in the new era. But what insured that their influence would continue to be felt was the remarkable predominance of their own sons among their successors. Although many of the industrial leaders of the postwar period were self-made individualists who felt few restraints in adapting themselves to the churning expansiveness of new conditions, the publishing business came to be dominated by a group of men highly conscious of their past—the heirs, if not of large fortunes, at least of a business tradition they had been taught to respect. John D. Rockefeller matched his young wits with the produce merchants of Cleveland, but Charles Scribner, Jr. contested with a professor of Greek at Princeton and contemplated the day when he would enter his father's firm.[24]

One by one this second generation took their places. When Daniel Appleton retired in 1848, he left five sons to carry on the firm. Of these the outstanding was easily William Henry Appleton, who became his father's partner in 1838 [25] and remained the active head of the business up to his death in 1899.[26] His length of service gave him the distinction of belonging to both the original coterie of publishers and its successors. During the confusing years of the last quarter of the century when many other businesses divested themselves of one morality and seemed not greatly interested in finding another, he provided the publishing trade with standards of dignity and public responsibility which were as commendable as his example was constant. The last of the original Harpers died in 1877, but seven cousins had already completed their apprenticeships and were standing by to take the place of the four brothers. If a fondness for family names is any indication of a concern for family traditions, the Harpers were as dynasty-conscious as the House of Bourbon. Commented *Publishers' Weekly:* [27]

The surnames of the original brothers are continued with religious accuracy, so that there are several Josephs, two or three Fletchers, two or more Johns, etc., who are distinguished in the familiar language of their own counting-room by such titles as "Brooklyn Joe" (because he lives in Brooklyn), "Joe 22" (because of his residence in Twenty-second Street), "Joe Abner", the "Colonel's John" (son of Colonel John Harper, so-called, to distinguish him from "Fifth Avenue Jack", since dead), and "Fletcher, Jr." and "Fletcher 2d", son and grandson of "the Major" who is never called Fletcher at all. There are several other distinctive nicknames which we do not recall.

Among the many, Joseph Wesley Harper, Jr. was perhaps the best of the family's second generation, a man whose sensitivity and charm sometimes obscured his hard-headedness. Although the firm rather took to rough-and-tumble competition, Henry Holt recalled "Brooklyn Joe" as an advocate of higher trade ethics rather than as an opponent: [28]

Joe Harper . . . must have become head of the old house in the seventies. The first time I remember talking with him was when I went down to Franklin Square to tell him that after he had bought the magazine and book-right of one of Hardy's novels, trade courtesy required him to turn over the book-right to me. . . . Joe nearly tired me out by talking all over Robin Hood's barn—a favorite trick of his—and then ended up doing exactly what I wanted, and what the notions of honor then prevalent among publishers of standing required. Imagine in *these days* [1910] a youngster not a dozen years in the trade going to the head of the largest house, and calling him down, and the big man coming down on a point of honor!
. . . Prolixity was not Joe Harper's only weapon when he did not know his man; he used to affect pigheadedness and imbecility. Thus if there was anything rotten in his opponent's case, Joe would lead him to give it away. But if the case turned out sound, nothing could be more candid and generous than Joe's final treatment of it.

Two more of the early stalwarts made their departure when Moses Dodd retired in 1870 and Charles Scribner died a few months later in Lucerne, Switzerland. While the trade mourned the passing of two men who had contributed much to its growth and sense of dignity, the half-century ahead was to demonstrate that it had gained in Frank H. Dodd and the second Charles Scribner more than it had lost. Dodd had entered the business in 1859, and was well prepared to join his cousin, Edward Mead, in a partnership which proved durable. He was among the most attractive of the post-war publishers. A capable and successful business man, he found no difficulty in reconciling the needs of his own house with the best interests of the trade as a whole. When the turn of the century brought fiercer and, to Dodd, less gentlemanly competitive practices to the fore, he could deplore the new conditions with an assurance that nothing in his own record would indicate less than a steady devotion to his professed ideals.

The gap left by the death of the first Charles Scribner was filled by his eldest son, Blair Scribner, who became a partner in the short-lived firm of Scribner, Armstrong and Company.[29] The second Charles Scribner did not become active until his graduation from college in 1875; but the death of Blair Scribner and Edward Seymour and the retirement of Andrew Armstrong deprived the firm of all of its members, and left Charles in 1879 to carry on alone.[30] In the fifty-one years that followed, the steady growth of the House of Scribner was paralleled by the personal esteem which its head enjoyed among the members of the trade. George H. Doran's estimate of his ability is not among the most extravagant which could be cited: [31]

Under the second Charles [Scribner] this house forged to the forefront. He was a truly great publisher. . . . When I first ventured into the ranks of New York publishers in 1908 his was the most generous and cordial of welcomes. There was always a certain magnificent tranquillity to the House of Scribner; always the sense of great reserve of power and genius lay behind their progressive conservatism. The publishing world was somewhat astounded to discover the Princetonian calm of Scribner's rather violently disturbed by those two stormy moderns, Scott Fitzgerald and Ernest Hemingway, but if there were to be departure from habit and tradition, why not celebrate and lead in this movement as they had so successfully led in many others?

Other families were similarly fortunate in finding able sons to succeed able fathers. The trade lost the mainstay of its fight for an international copyright when George Palmer Putnam died in 1872,[32] but the equally devoted George Haven Putnam brought it to a successful conclusion in 1891. A scholar as well as a business man, the second Putnam was both the leading crusader and the foremost historian of his trade. The formidable list of titles credited to him includes: *Books and their Makers during the Middle Ages, The Question of Copyright,* and *Authors and Their Public in Ancient Times.* "There is no name in the annals of the American Book Trade," wrote *Publishers' Weekly,* "more justly honored than that of Putnam." [33]

This recital of virtue could easily be extended until it would become both tedious and unbelievable. Perhaps those accustomed to see in these years the nadir of business morality, are already incredulous. Were the evidence to sustain the reputations of these men limited to obituaries, testimonial dinners, and the fond reminiscences of patriarchs in retirement, the case would be less than proved. But the considerable extant commercial correspondence of the period seems to confirm the view that the philosophy and the practice of publishers were remarkably alike. Such customs as paying honorariums and royalties for uncopyrighted materials and respecting existing relationships between authors and publishers [34] were the products of self-interest, but of a self-interest that sought its salvation in self-restraint rather than in cut-throat competition and illegalisms.

The apparent disparity between the ethics of the day and those of the publishing business requires some further examination. Although the presence of notable families is pertinent, it can scarcely be offered as the primary cause. One thinks immediately of men like Henry Holt, John Macrae, and Frederick Leypoldt who were no less honorable in their dealings for having entered the trade without benefit of interested antecedents. Neither can it be assumed that a birthright carried with it a guarantee of good behavior.

Further, it is entirely possible that the mores of the publishing trade were less exceptional than they appear to be. While the most spectacular figures of the "Gilded Age" have been subjected to considerable investigation, comparatively little is known about the average business man. The writing of business histories, especially industry studies, has not progressed far enough for dogmatic generalizations to be made about "typical" business ethics; but there is at least substantial doubt that the conspicuously discreditable episodes in our commercial history are accurately representative of the whole. The gentlemanliness of a Frank Dodd becomes more plausible when one ceases to equate business morality with the habits of Jay Gould. Conversely, it would be less than exact to consider Dodd as the average publisher. The piracy of foreign books, the bribery of school boards to secure adoptions, were unquestionably part of the trade, even though Dodd disapproved of them. The publishing business shared in the delinquencies of the era and the problems which arose with it. But what seems remarkable is that the larger and more successful firms succumbed least to these practices. Among the regular trade publishers—as opposed to the reprint houses—there existed a code of etiquette which was honored far more often than it was ignored. The leadership of the industry was composed of its most scrupulous men rather than its most grasping.

The nature of the business accounts as well for the actions of these leaders as for their philosophy. While growth in other industries resulted in the gradual removal of the managerial class from the scene of elementary business operations, the publisher could not divorce himself from the authors who lay at the base of his business. Perhaps the difference between a writer—whether novelist, scientist, historian, or theologian—and a factory operative was not greater than the difference between a book and a bag of flour or a bale of cotton. Both in the process of securing his product and in the nature of the product itself, the publisher was confronted with values which could not be placed in a scale of physical needs. A book was worth, intrinsically, what the reader could get out of it. To the publisher was assigned the difficult job of translating the inspiration, the knowledge, or the entertainment it contained into a price which the public would be willing to pay. "As a rule," wrote Henry Holt to Carolyn Wells, "gilded youths don't seek publishing." [35] Neither did business men who measured their success solely by the size of the pot of gold awaiting them. Publishers were certainly not above the pursuit of wealth, but they fancied that the rainbow which led them also had its attractions.

Walter Page once asked Charles Scribner to define publishing.

"Can you call it a business?" he demanded.

"Yes," said Scribner doubtfully; "but that doesn't define it—it is much more than a business."

"Is it a profession, then?"

"No; certainly not, but it is certainly professional."

He thought for a moment, reported Page, and said, smiling: "Publishing is neither a business nor a profession. It is a career." [36]

The Business of Publishing

chapter 2

Although publishers took pride in the intrinsic worth of their product, they were quick to acknowledge their commercial handicaps in competing for the consumer's dollar. Meeting in the centennial summer of July, 1876, the Executive Committee of the American Book Trade Association reported gloomily: [1]

> When a man cuts down his private expenses, this attempt at economy is almost sure to be where it is least likely to be known. The first saving is not in house, furniture, dress, or even jewelry —it is in *books!* Books are largely a luxury.

Not even the trade in textbooks offered much comfort, because the necessity for their use did not imply the replacement of old and battered copies. The "Gilded Age" had its esthetic pretentions, but *Publishers' Weekly* concluded that books were not one of them. Occasionally the search for bric-a-brac, china, and properly academic paintings would turn towards some fragile first editions, but private libraries seemed "almost to have ceased to exist." [2]

However, less concern was felt over the cultural delinquencies of millionaires than over the popular entertainments which arose from time to time to compete for the leisure of the middle class. If a business may be known by the competitors it keeps, the general publisher had less in common with teachers and ministers than with the operators of excursion steamers. In 1896, *Publishers' Weekly* reported that the bicycle craze was "demoralizing the equilibrium of the trade," [3] although it scoffed at the proposal of a bookseller to meet the challenge by adding an inventory of bicycles to his stock. Fifteen years later the threat of automobiles loomed large on the publishers' horizon.[4] The eve of the First World War brought sobering fears of the new motion picture industry, which was already reported to be making large inroads into the circulation of books at the public libraries.[5] Sunday newspapers, bridge, "the post-card deluge," raised the same questions in the trade before 1914 [6] that radio, then television, were to suggest in the modern period.

Taken together, these competitors proved formidable. Fads such as bicycles and post cards came and went, but distractions providing more excitement and requiring less mental effort than books seemed constantly available. Even those who liked to read were lured away in increasing numbers by the popular magazines which made their debut near the turn of the century.

During the slower days of the pre-Civil War years, the attraction of books appears to have been greater. As early as 1850, the value of books manufactured and sold in America annually exceeded $10,000,000. The figures given below are the closest approximations which the Bureau of Census could furnish on the basis of incomplete records.

	1820	1830	1840	1850
School Books	$750,000	1,100,000	2,000,000	5,500,000
Classical Books	250,000	350,000	550,000	1,000,000
Theological Books	150,000	250,000	300,000	500,000
Law Books	200,000	300,000	400,000	700,000
Medical Books	150,000	200,000	250,000	400,000
All Others	1,000,000	1,300,000	2,000,000	4,400,000
Total	$2,500,000	3,500,000	5,500,000	12,500,000

No separate figure was given in the Census of 1860 for book manufacture, but the value of the products in a general category which included newspaper and job printing as well, was $31,063,898.

In subsequent censuses down to 1914, the value of books produced continued to be listed with that of job printing. The totals for the classification were as follows:

1869	$ 41,076,000	1899	$121,798,000
1879	90,970,000	1904	182,612,000
1889	93,909,000	1909	250,926,000
1914	$307,331,000		

Unfortunately, these figures have no validity as an indication of the size of the book business, and are misleading as a reflection of its growth. When, in 1914, books were separated from job printing, it was found that the latter accounted for more than 80 per cent of the total value. The books were appraised at about $56,000,000, which is 448 per cent of the estimated book sales of 1850. But meantime the value of all American manufactures had grown from slightly over one billion dollars to more than twenty-four billion dollars, a rate of increase five times that of the book trade. While book publishing accounted for one per cent of the manufactured wealth in 1850, it represented less than .25 per cent in 1914.[7]

The increase in the value of books produced was roughly proportionate to the growth of population between 1850 and 1910, but there was considerable room for discouragement. The country found other uses for its expanding wealth, even though such developments as the multiplication of educational institutions and the decline in the number of working hours beckoned in the direction of book-buying.

The incompleteness of census returns and business records makes it almost impossible to do more than speculate as to the number of firms and the relative importance of each house within the publishing industry. To these obstacles may be added the question of definition. An author producing his own book, or an iron manufacturer issuing an anniversary volume, performs the function of a publisher, but obviously would not properly be included in that category.

It is customary to point to the difficulty of distinguishing among publishers, printers, and booksellers during the early years of the nineteenth century. Yet the expansion of the book trade and the more frequent separation of its various functions among specializing companies did not necessarily solve the question of practical definition. Much bad feeling, for example, was aroused in the 1890's among local retailers by the increasing sales made by the publishers directly to the consuming public. Basic to the controversy, which was prominently featured in the trade journals, was a question of definition: was it within the province of the regular publisher to engage in the retail trade? [8]

The relation between the manufacture and the publishing of books was a problem for the individual company to settle as its finances and business policy dictated. While it was evident that publishing did not require a printing establishment, many of the larger firms, such as D. Appleton and Company, Harper and Brothers, and J. B. Lippincott, owned factories. The Riverside Press affiliated with Hurd and Houghton and the Knickerbocker Press of G. P. Putnam's Sons were as distinguished in their own right as the publishers who spawned them. Probably a majority of the houses did not at any time after the Civil War do their own printing. Approximately 18 per cent of those listed in the Census of 1914 had plants, and these accounted for 31 per cent of the total production.

The desirability of this vertical integration remained questionable to many publishers. J. Blair Scribner was convinced that Harper and Brothers gained a large advantage by having a manufacturing concern of its own, being thus enabled to produce and sell more cheaply.[9] Yet despite the resources provided by a successful business and the ample purse of Charles Scribner's grandfather, the industrialist John I. Blair, the firm had been in existence a half century before it built its own factory in 1905.[10] Others, among them Henry Holt, continued to feel that such an enterprise was not profitable.[11] If a discernible trend was evident at all, it was in the direction of a separation of these two parts of the business. Apparently, the potential advantage which might be gained by a manufactory was offset by a number of practical difficulties. In addition to the formidable investment required, the tastes of the average publisher were more literary than industrial, and he was inclined to begrudge the additional effort of supervising his own productions. The problem of gearing a publishing house to a printing establishment often resulted in the publication of mediocre and commercially worthless books, selected to keep the presses busy. A few such "fill-ins" could destroy whatever gain had been made in the production cost of the successful titles.[12] There are more than sufficient reasons why, then and now, the manufacturing publisher has been the exception rather than the rule.

In any event, it may safely be concluded that estimates of the number of publishers existing at any given time after 1850 included both those who were their own printers and those who depended on others. When the Riverside Press of Hurd and Houghton manufactured books for Charles Scribner's Sons, there was no doubt as to which firm was the publisher.[13]

The authoritative *Trübner's Bibliographical Guide to American Literature*, compiled in 1859, computed the number of American publishers at more than four hundred, about three-quarters of them located in New York, Philadelphia, Baltimore, and Boston. The giant was Harper and Brothers, with sales of over two million volumes a year; [14] but J. B. Lippincott's quick surge to leadership, symbolized by an enormous factory constructed in 1861, put it not far behind.[15] A general trade sale in New York during the spring of 1864 brought together 125 publishers from all parts of the country. New York was represented by 44, Philadelphia by 25, and Boston sent 24. Although the attendance was truncated by the war in progress, the number of firms participating probably included a large majority of the regular trade publishers.[16] Thirty-seven years later, *Publishers' Weekly* printed a directory of the 1,000 firms which had issued books during 1900,[17] but the list expanded to 1,512 names in 1913. Among these were a number of individual authors, and organizations such as the American Gas Institute and the Eighty-third Ohio Volunteer Infantry Association which scarcely qualified as commercial book houses.[18] The special report of the Bureau of the Census on printing and publishing prepared in 1914 shows a total of 819 book publishing establishments, a better indication of the size of the industry than the much larger figure furnished by *Publishers' Weekly*.[19]

The limited evidence available tends to show that publishing was not susceptible to the monopolistic trend evident in other industries during the last quarter of the nineteenth century. Harper and Brothers had a commanding position in the decade of the 1850's which no firm was able to duplicate in the field of trade publishing up to the eve of the First World War. The same company was among the largest in 1914, but its sales of slightly more than $1,000,000 [20] amounted to less than 2 per cent of the industry's total.[21] A more typical house, Henry Holt and Company, recorded gross sales of $494,222 two years before.[22] Another reflection of the relatively small size of publishing firms is seen in their predilection for the partnership form of business organization. Even after incorporation took place, a number of the leading houses continued to be closely controlled by the original family interests. Henry Holt, for example, capitalized his firm for $250,000 in 1904, but up to the First World War owned four-fifths of the outstanding shares.[23] Charles Scribner was no less the head of Charles Scribner's Sons after its incorporation in 1904 than he had been for the twenty-five years before, the change being made to safeguard the family interests while retaining its authority.[24] The establishment of Macmillan and Company, Inc., in 1896, naturally brought to the second George Brett even more grasp of the business than he, or his father, had enjoyed as the American participant in a predominately English partnership.[25]

Harper and Brothers and, to a lesser extent, D. Appleton and Company offer two conspicuous exceptions to this continued dominance by family interests. The reorganization of Harper and Brothers in 1899 was precipitated by the fact that the family appears to have been, according to its own chronicler, more productive of quantity than of quality in its progeny. A first generation of four, a second of seven, and eleven grandsons of the founders all had been awarded "liberal salaries" and then left "largely to their own devices to display their business capabilities, a policy not always conducive to hard work." [26] The company went through a receivership and emerged in 1900 as a new corporation with George B. Harvey as its head and J. P. Morgan & Company, thanks to a loan of $850,000,[27] as the temporary successor to the Harper interest. Even before Harper and Brothers could recommence its career under new auspices, the trade received a second shock when

D. Appleton and Company applied for receivership. Unlike Harper and Brothers, which failed because of family demands on its assets, D. Appleton and Company became insolvent because of a more extensive experiment into installment sales than the available capital could finance. A new corporation emerged under the guidance of banking interests. William Worthen Appleton continued as head of the firm, but the control of the family thereafter declined.[28]

Although the number of best sellers published by a firm is less than conclusive evidence of its significance in the trade, the fact that the publication of the most successful books was distributed among a comparatively large number of houses is a good indication of the diffuseness of the industry and of the difficulty of concentrating control. Defining a "best seller" as a book whose sales equalled one per cent of the total population of the United States during the decade it was published, Frank Luther Mott listed 111 titles for the half century between 1865 and 1914. These were produced by forty-seven different companies. Harper and Brothers' nine publications were sufficient to secure it first position, but was less than the eleven books which it placed on the list during the single decade of the 1850's. The bulk of the older houses—Scribner, Macmillan, Holt, D. Appleton, and Fields and Osgood—were represented by from four to seven titles. Equally significant is the fact that over 70 per cent of the companies appear only once, many of them being rescued from obscurity by a brief moment of commercial glory. Whatever head-start might be gained by the larger houses with impressive financial resources and extensive sales facilities could be overcome by a small firm possessed of one sufficiently attractive title.[29]

While the highest peaks of best-sellerdom appear to have been reserved for appealing books rather than for outstanding firms, the lower and more crowded elevations reveal the concentrated strength of the commercial leaders of the day. If for Mott's highly selective collection of spectacular successes is substituted an annual list of ten best sellers, the predominance of the larger houses becomes greater. For example, the publication of the two hundred most popular novels of the two decades prior to the First World War was shared by twenty-eight firms, an average of more than seven books for each house. Mott's listing for the same years yields an average of only one book per company. Yet even at this level, the degree of concentration in the industry was not great. No company produced one of the ten best-selling novels for each year of this period, and only six of them appeared on the list as often as every other year.[30]

Incomplete as they are, these statistics concerning the value of books produced, the number of active firms, the typical business structure, and the distribution of outstanding titles, suggest a number of important characteristics of the publishing industry. But the figures indicating the frequent separation of the printing and publishing functions are perhaps the most helpful to anyone attempting a definition of the business. Whatever its essence, it did not consist of the manufacture of books. The distinctiveness of publishing was associated rather with what took place before the manuscript reached the printer, and what had to be done after the finished copies were delivered from the bindery.

Both the editorial and the distributive aspects of the business were made enormously complicated by the fact that a large number of titles were handled by each house. The total book production not only showed a constant absolute increase, but outran population growth as well. The new titles published each year reached about a thousand when Jackson became president in 1829. By the time of the Reconstruction, the total exceeded three thousand. The depression years of the early 1890's brought forth approximately five thousand new publications annually, while the turn of the century saw the total approach six thousand. Within these seventy years, the number of new books published for each million inhabitants increased from forty-five to 143.[31] Harper and Brothers boasted that in the sixty years of its existence before 1878, it alone had produced 3,291 works.[32] In 1880, the moderate-sized houses of Charles Scribner's Sons and G. P. Putnam's Sons published forty-nine and thirty titles respectively, omitting new editions.[33]

Each new book represented not only the labor of making arrangements with an author and obtaining a satisfactory manuscript; it entailed the even more difficult task of marketing a new product. Wrote Alfred Harcourt: [34]

> The publisher's problem, and the tooth paste manufacturer's problem are quite different. During the course of a year some publishers issue several hundred new books, and many issue at least one hundred—that is, one every three business days. And

besides there are already on their lists from several hundred to several thousand older titles, each requiring cataloguing and detailed attention. The cosmetic manufacturer would throw up his hands at the idea of a new product every three days.

Occasionally, the trade got excited about the thousands of books competing in the market. An editorial in *Publishers' Weekly* in 1901 on the "Remedy for the Evils of the Book Trade" asserted that the current trade depression—which existed in the midst of a general prosperity—resulted from a maladjustment of supply and demand. It added: [35]

> In this country alone during the last year there were issued something over nineteen hundred novels, and of that number not more than one hundred reached a sale of ten thousand copies. The chances are that fifty of them did not sell that many.

But twelve years later the same publication brought a different set of arguments to bear in a piece called: "The Flood of New Books—A Defence." [36] While the quantity of titles was lamented from time to time, industry spokesmen associated an increasing number of publications with prosperity and interpreted a decline as a symptom of approaching trouble. This observation was perfectly valid; but the dilemma posed by finding encouragement in the questionable practice of diluting prosperity to spread it over a greater area of titles was never resolved.

Not only did the marketing of books become proportionately more difficult as the number of titles increased; it was also true that the cost of a number of small editions was much greater than that of a lesser number of large editions. Publishing became profitable only when the non-recurring cost of the composition of the type and the making of plates could be spread over a large number of copies. "We have just been reading," wrote Robert Burdette in the *Brooklyn Eagle,* "about the distribution of the profits on a $1.50 book. On the first thousand, the stereotyper loses six cents per copy, the publisher loses eighteen cents, the author loses ten cents, the printer loses his time, and the reader his patience." [37] However facetious, this statement contained an essential truth. Actually the "break-even" point at which a publisher began to make money in the 1880's was about one thousand copies. It rose to at least 1,500 copies by 1914. On the eve of the Second World War, it stood at approximately 2,500 copies; [38] but first costs have now risen to an extent that the point of first returns is variously estimated at between five and ten thousand copies.

The history of thirteen books published by Charles Scribner in 1880 for which complete records are available may be used to illustrate this basic problem. The total net profit on the first editions, which averaged 1,288 copies, was $151. All but two registered a gain, but the most successful of them showed a profit of only $90. However, the nine sets of plates paid for by the publisher cost over $4,000, which meant that on a second printing of equal size the net profit would be that much greater. Typical of the list was Charles Robinson's *Studies in the New Testament,* the manufactured cost of which was 32¢ a copy. To this may be added an author's share of 15¢ a copy based upon a 10 per cent royalty of the retail price of $1.50. Yet, when the expense of making plates was distributed among the thousand copies, it added 38¢ to the cost of each—more than doubling the expense of manufacture. On an edition of ten thousand, the amount chargeable to plates would have been less than 4¢ a copy, and would have permitted a much larger profit margin.

The same ledger which provides these figures lists the size of the first editions for 138 books published between 1880 and 1882. Only 28 per cent of these exceeded 1,500 copies. About 15 per cent were 2,500 or more, and the maximum printing, reserved for Palfrey's *Antietam* and other titles in the *Campaign Series,* was 6,000 copies. What lends poignancy to this record is the indication that only two of the 138 titles were reprinted.[39]

An interview held with William Lee of Lee and Shepard in 1885 furnishes even more discouraging testimony: [40]

> A book of four hundred pages is considered an edition at 1000, and the total cost, including advertising, copyright, books to the press for review and all incidentals is about $1250. This first edition, if all sold, will bring a net return of only $675, leaving $550 unaccounted for. A second edition will cost only $450, as the plates are on hand, and there is no expense on that score; and on that edition the return will again be $675, leaving still $225 of the original expenditure to be gotten out of the work. On the next edition, if it can be disposed of, this shortage is cleared up and a very small profit remains. So it can be seen that to be a slightly profitable investment, there must be at least three editions of 1000 copies of every book published. How can publishers be blamed for their extreme caution?

Of course, the most profitable part of the business, then and now, consisted not in the current books, but rather in older titles still in demand whose plates had already been paid for. The financial stability of a house was largely dependent on the extent and activity of its "back-list." It is commonly assumed that the commercial life of the average book has shortened perceptibly in modern times. O. H. Cheney in his careful survey of the book industry in 1930 asserts: "the life of a good seller ranges from two months to ten months, and only in extremely rare cases does the life go beyond eighteen months." [41] Undoubtedly, he would wish to exempt many educational and reference books from this generality.

Although books undoubtedly had a longer life in the late nineteenth and early twentieth centuries, it is questionable that the difference was appreciable. As early as 1877, *Publishers' Weekly* intimated that nine out of ten inquiries at the bookstores concerned books of the current year. While the report has the tone of a guess, it must be taken to indicate the essential truth of the matter.[42] "There is no doubt in my mind," Scribner wrote to his partner, Charles Welford, "that the most unsatisfactory feature of the business is the accumulation of stock which goes on from year to year." [43] *Publishers' Weekly,* perhaps forgetful of its early pronouncement and nostalgic for days which had not existed, looked back sorrowfully from 1900 to the years when "a popular book seemed to enjoy a lingering death, and a bookseller might hope by clever manipulation to get rid of his remainders." [44] In any event, the situation got worse rather than better, for four years later the journal concluded that "the best of books is almost sure to be crushed to death by the new books piled on top of it." [45] Cheney expressed the thought succinctly when he said, "Books are cannibals." [46] Dead inventory and difficulty in building up a satisfactory "back-list" could be attributed in part to cannibalism made easier by suffocation.

Although the Olympian view of a trade journal enabled it occasionally, though not consistently, to question the wisdom of multiplying endlessly the number of titles competing for the limited book market, the individual publishers whose policies determined the actual decision continued to think their salvation lay in larger lists. Basic to this attitude was the judgment that the business was speculative; the more chances one took on the wheel, the better the odds of winning the big prize of a runaway best seller. "Keep publishing novels," pontificated a publisher in 1901, "and you will be sure to strike some big successes. The book you bank on may fail, and the one you think the least of will go." [47] Henry Holt was not so confident of the certainty of the outcome: [48]

> I have lately awakened with a bang to the realization that all the time I have spent over American fiction during over forty years, has brought us just two books that paid a decent profit. I feel about it, however, a good deal as the Cuban must feel about continuing to pay for lottery numbers—that the time when they will win a prize must be nearer at hand than it was when he began. . . . Of course, I hope to win in each case, particularly in yours. . . .

It would seem that even when the ailment was diagnosed, the publisher considered it incurable. The dictum of the trade that of five books published, three fail, one covers its cost, and the fifth provides the profit,[49] was taken as an inescapable fact which a higher degree of selectivity could not modify.

The persistent complaints of the trade from 1865 to about 1905 concern not the hordes of titles, but irregular discounts by publishers, price-cutting among retailers, and the confusion caused by the piracy of uncopyrighted works. If these conditions could be remedied, the industry thought that it would become at least normally prosperous. But in 1910, when these problems were, to a varying extent, solved and the trade still remained in the doldrums, astute publishers such as George Brett pointed to the basic trouble of an inadequate machinery of distribution being constantly inundated by a flood of books.[50] Discussion continues even today with the fundamental question concerning the reduction of the speculative element in publishing still substantially unanswered.

The economics of the industry indicated that a publisher would be best off if he produced each year one title which sold a million copies. That this ideal was not considered attainable is understandable. But that the opposite principle—associating business expansion almost solely with list expansion—was so commonly held seems a curiosity of the business which is only partly explained by the unpredictability of public tastes. For the rest of the answer, one must consult a variety of factors. If it was true that the capacity of a printing plant subsidiary often led to the publication of books which would otherwise have gone unpublished, the same inducement to overproduction was present in the large staffs of readers, clerks, secretaries, and editors which the most prominent firms assembled. A house geared to publish a book every three days consumed a lot of manuscripts—more than warranted publication. An expensive overhead of salaries and rent continued regardless of how many works were in progress. "I am going more extensively into publishing," wrote Charles Scribner, "as it is necessary in order to make use of the 'machinery' we have, or the expenses will be too great for the business." [51] The "machinery" did not include a printing plant. What is equally revealing is that less than five months before, Scribner advised the same correspondent he was satisfied that "the best business policy is to deal in fewer books in larger quantities." [52]

Under these circumstances, the temptation to put out books with no better hope than to have them pay their proportionate share of fixed expenses becomes easily understandable. Beyond this lay the attitude which the average publisher took towards his business. Its attractiveness did not ordinarily come from the tedious details of marketing and manufacture, but from the exhilaration of making a critical judgment and gambling that it was a correct one. The stimulation which came from the discovery of an unknown talent produced an optimism which all too often bore little relation to commercial facts.

If this attitude led to too many books, it also was associated with the limited and often negative view which many of the prominent publishers took of the merchandising of books. An editor of one of today's prominent houses recently said, "Publishers are the only business men I know who spend thousands of dollars producing a product, then take it to a warehouse and sit on their hands hoping that someone will find out about it and buy it." [53] No complaint was more common at the turn of the century than that publishing had become infested with "commercialism." It is a little difficult to know what was meant. The disruption of traditional relations between publishers and authors, and the higher royalties, had something to do with the phrase. But a more important part derived from what was, to the older publishers, the unseemly spectacle of "high-pressure" bookselling, which included a large ingredient of advertising. Up to the 1890's, a gentlemanly restraint had been the rule in the regular trade, and even the "Gilded Age" found the rule occasionally absurd. *The New York Times* attacked this stodginess in 1885: [54]

When a man desires to sell a new hair dye, does he content himself with announcing the fact once, or even twice, by a few lines inserted in a newspaper? He knows better than that. . . . But publishers know nothing about the art of advertising, and consequently few books sell. They do not seem to understand that anything that is advertised will sell, and they are content to let books sell "on their merits", as they express it.

Five years later *Publishers' Weekly* took up the defense of the traditional attitude in language which the Dodds, the Scribners, the Holts, and the Putnams often echoed: [55]

This is an age of ambition. The countersign in commercial circles is push, energy, snap. . . . While this spirit of unsatisfied ambition has brought compensation and developed an activity not to be ignored, it has nevertheless been at the expense of certain elements of character which should not be abused or uncultivated. Dignity is very often forgotten. . . . If literature and art are to be treated as common merchandise . . . it will make commonplace the manners of our people and their intelligence restricted to the counting-room.

What had given rise to this editorial was the news that a book was being used as a premium for the purchase of soap. While this device undoubtedly meant a profit for its publisher which the trade journal did not deign to consider, the episode was sufficiently unusual at the time to provoke a protest. But *Publishers' Weekly*, speaking for the trade, went further. Books should not be contaminated even by being in the same store with miscellaneous merchandise.[56]

It is quite as incongruous for an art dealer to run a meat-shop in conjunction with his business as a linen-draper and haberdasher to run a bookstore. You cannot sell books together with a line of corsets and gloves and do justice to your patrons. It is this "bazaar-spirit" which has placed an undeserved indignity upon literature. Lower the tone of the individual and you lessen the dignity of the national character.

There is something slightly precious about this statement, but at the same time something quite true that Walter Page had in mind when he wrote, "A book is a commodity. Yet the moment it is treated as a mere commodity it takes severe revenge on its author and on its publisher." [57] The halfway house in which publishers saw themselves, partly a repository for a civilization's highest expression and partly a market place, was enough of a reality to pose commercial problems which the manufacturer of a hair dye never had to meet. That a compromise with a faster-paced world had to be made by the book trade ultimately become evident even to the most dignified and Victorian of publishers. But the form that it should take was not clear on the eve of the First World War. In 1913 George Brett was able to touch on a vital weakness when he blamed the industry's ills on its distributive machinery, but he was unable to suggest how it could be fundamentally improved to meet the modern competition.[58]

However, it must be remembered that the sales lethargy of the publishers was matched by the apathy of the book-buying public. A recent commentator, R. L. Duffus, has noted that the industry has been traditionally unimaginative and unsystematic in exploiting the existing market, but he was quick to acknowledge that the market itself has been generally unresponsive to any efforts: [59]

> There are many cultural bases for the present chaotic condition of the book trade in the United States, among them the book illiteracy of the American middle class, which may be ascribed to a faulty educational system and in part to the commercial preoccupation of that class; the stress and strain of industrial life . . . ; and the increasing appeal and availability of competing diversions, such as radio and the cinema.

Whatever the glories of the American home, a large and well-used library has not been among them.

One of the circumstances which made the multiplicity of titles even more burdensome for the individual publisher was the relative unimportance of his imprint to the general public. The books of houses which zealously guarded a reputation for high editorial standards and fair business practices had no particular head-start except among academics, librarians, critics, and a commercially unimportant group of discerning readers. The value of the firm's standing was not, however, a negligible factor within the trade itself. Booksellers, for example, might be disposed to favor books issued by a firm known to be reputable.

Equally beneficial was the attraction to authors of a list containing best-selling titles or the works of prominent writers. But these gains were more than offset by the inability to establish a "brand-name" which would offer an important inducement to the ordinary purchaser of books. Binding, paper, the quality of printing might be uniform, but the essence of the product changed with each title. Even the name of an established writer on the cover was no guarantee that the pages between would hold the same skill or knowledge or entertainment that a reader had found in previous works.[60]

The unimportance of a publisher's imprint is one of several reasons, some of them already indicated, why limits were placed on the degree of centralization which could be effected in the industry. When it is recalled that the era was one of increasing monopoly in other fields, the continued diffuseness of control in publishing becomes the more conspicuous. Since a publisher did not face an insurmountable handicap by having his books printed by an outside firm, the cost of entering the business was relatively little. At the close of the Civil War, advertising and distributive expenses were low, and large advances to American authors were practically unknown. The most expensive branch of the business was the reprinting of uncopyrighted English books. Honorariums of several thousand dollars in advance of publication were relatively common, and the arrangements with the foreign publishers and authors usually involved frequent trips to London or the establishment of a branch office overseas. Yet these expenses were entirely circumvented by the simple device of ignoring the British interests; "piracy" made the most expensive publishing operation the least susceptible to monopoly and effectively limited the advantage of large financial resources.

As the end of the century approached the cost of doing business increased. Reprinting popular English novelists was restricted by the passage of an international copyright law by Congress in 1891. Commercial travellers became more important, and it required a reasonably large volume to keep an adequate staff of them busy. Although manufacturing costs did not greatly increase, the "break-even" point for a single title was advanced by the greater use of advertising. Authors demanded and received as much as $5,000 advance against future royalties on the delivery of manuscripts, a practice which strained the resources of the smaller firms.

Even so, the necessary capital investment remained small, and it was relatively easy for new firms to compete. The beginnings of Doubleday, Page and Company dated from the reorganization of Harper and Brothers in 1900; but neither Harpers' eighty years of business experience nor the interest of J. P. Morgan and Company prevented the neophyte from placing five times as many titles as its competitor on Mott's list of outstanding commercial successes in the decade before the First World War.[61] Robert Sterling Yard, one of the partners in Moffat and Yard, a latecomer to the business, suggested from his own experience the minimum volume of sales required in 1913: [62]

> Speaking generally, it may be said to require about one hundred and fifty thousand dollars gross receipts yearly to support the simplest general publishing business, unaided by special de-

partments in other publishing fields; at two hundred thousand dollars there will be a profit; and at four hundred thousand, prosperity.

These figures have some usefulness as a generality, but may not be taken as evidence that every firm with gross profits of a half-million showed a surplus. Harper and Brothers lost over $100,000 in 1908, when its book sales exceeded $900,000.[63]

As important to the dispersion of the business as the small cost of entering it, was the inability of any houses or group of houses to control the supply of manuscripts. The reservoir greatly exceeded the capacity of the publishers to consume, although it was believed that there was a frequent dearth of desirable manuscripts. But beyond the quantitative obstacle to monopoly was the independence of the popular writers. The reluctance of authors to change publishers, characteristic of the immediate post-Civil War years, was never the universal rule nor was it formalized in contractual relations. By 1900, many writers shopped for the best terms and their independence was thereby increased. That they found the terms of a contract more important than the facilities or the experience of the house that gave the terms is further evidence of the absence of a "trust" situation. While publishing spokesmen deplored the habit of "publisher-jumping," they at the same time insisted that the personal relations between author and editor were sufficiently necessary to the business not only to cause this practice to disappear, but also to prevent an industrial combination from developing. Walter Page wrote: [64]

This is why a great publishing trust, or "merger", is impossible. The successful publisher sustains a relation to a successful author that is not easily transferable. . . . A great corporation cannot take a real publisher's place in his attitude to the author he serves.

The span of fifty years brought about two developments which threatened temporarily to place a large premium on capital resources and to reconcile publishing with the centralizing trends of the times. The first of these was the appearance of a textbook trust; the second was the growth of magazine affiliates endangering the publishing houses whose resources did not permit them to compete in the periodical field.

The association of magazines with book publishing was a form of horizontal integration not unusual even before the Civil War. Harper and Brothers had two periodicals in the field, a monthly started in 1850 and *Harper's Weekly,* begun in 1857 for a slightly more popular audience. Ticknor and Fields had entered the competition in 1859 by purchasing the *Atlantic Monthly,* which had been established two years before under other auspices. *Putnam's Monthly Magazine* was as ill-fated as the publishing house which gave rise to it, and had its brief life of four years snuffed out by the Panic of 1857.

Being chiefly literary, these magazines were designed for much the same audience as the books of the day and formed a logical extension of, and complement to, the publishing business. Their success generated a rash of imitators once the war had been concluded. By 1870 *Scribner's*

Monthly, Lippincott's Magazine, Harper's Bazaar, Appleton's Journal, and *Putnam's Monthly* appeared on the newsstands, their titles revealing the houses which were financing them. Significantly enough, the largest publishers were all represented in the periodical field, and several had more than one entry. The Harpers' three magazines, for example, were outnumbered by the four owned by James R. Osgood and Company, whose advertisements prominently displayed its interest in *The North American Review, Atlantic Monthly, Our Young Folks,* and *Every Saturday.*[65]

Although mass circulation was still in the future, magazines of even this rather staid variety excited considerable interest. Charles Scribner reported in 1883 to his London partner: [66]

The American book trade opens rather briskly but here, as with you, the magazines seem to be the principal feature and the yearly announcements of *Harpers* [magazines], the *Century* and the others together with the prospectus of *Macmillans* attract much more attention than the announcements of the publishers.

These periodicals became valuable properties in themselves; but at least two additional advantages accrued to their owners in connection with their book businesses. Serialization of a novel in a magazine publicized it in a way which was believed to attract more book buyers than it satisfied. Wrote Charles Scribner: [67]

It has always been our custom to print novels which have appeared in "Scribner's" as close as possible upon the last magazine installment; as in this way we secure the benefit of all the advertising done for the Magazine, and many readers wait for the book to read the last few chapters.

A second benefit arose from the attraction popular writers found in an organization which could offer two mediums for their work. A single contract was often used to cover both outlets. For example, an agreement drawn by Harper and Brothers in 1885 gave William Dean Howells $10,000 for the serial and periodical rights to his annual output, while a royalty of 12½ per cent was to be paid on book sales.[68] Occasionally, authors would return unsigned book contracts which did not specify concurrent serialization.[69]

We infer from your letter that unless arrangements can be made for its appearance in the *Scribner,* and your remuneration for your literary work thus be increased, you would be unwilling to accept our offer for publication in book form.

The connection between the two forms of publication was common enough to lead to a custom of the trade which awarded to a firm contracting for book publication a first option on magazine use, even in the absence of a contractual arrangement. Maurice Thompson, the author of *The Witchery of Archery,* received this note from Charles Scribner's Sons calling attention to the courtesy of the trade:[70]

There is one precaution which we desire to take at once. We want to feel assured that the Harpers will not consider the publication in book form of matter which formerly appeared in their magazine any infringement on their rights. If you have not already done so, will you kindly write to them on the subject and communicate their reply to us?

By the turn of the twentieth century, publishers' fancies still turned to thoughts of magazines. A speaker representing the "young publisher" at the annual banquet of the Booksellers' League in 1897, defined the publisher's ambition as a wish "to grow large enough that he may undertake the launching of a magazine, the chief aim of which will be to further the fortunes of his own publications." [71]

Yet the time was approaching, probably it had already arrived, when the tail was to wag the dog. Advertising, popular prices, and mass circulation methods were to make magazines too profitable and too complex to be handled as subsidiaries to the book business. Popular novelists could receive higher fees from such periodicals as *Cosmopolitan* and the *Ladies' Home Journal* than a literary monthly could afford to pay, and they were encouraged by the authors' agents, who appeared with the 1890's, to retain serial rights for separate disposal. When Rudyard Kipling suddenly decided to change the ending of *The Light that Failed,* he had to cable the new text to three different firms who were to publish it simultaneously in book, magazine, and newspaper form. [72] The diversions with which books had to compete—Henry Holt listed trolley cars, baseball, and telephones among them [73]—were present also to contract the market for serious periodicals. Even the writers were distracted. The rewards of writing for magazines, especially of the popular variety, were larger and more certain than the returns from books; and many authors were tempted away from the longer works which were suitable for serial and book publication.[74]

Before the First World War ended, *Harper's Weekly* was absorbed, and *Harper's Bazaar* purchased by William Randolph Hearst. *Putnam's* appeared for a brief interval only to merge with the *Atlantic Monthly*. *Lippincott's Magazine* surrendered fifty years of independence to combine with *Scribner's*, which, in turn, survived the 1920's to lose its identity in the depression. Taken as a whole, the excursion of bookmakers into magazine publication was hardly a commercial triumph, although the quality of the work was distinguished, and, for several decades, profits had been considerable. Periodicals were desirable enough to inspire envy among the publishers who did not own them, but not of such crucial importance as to drive these underprivileged firms out of business. When magazines assumed their full dimensions, they removed themselves from the world of books and attracted independent publishers with different horizons and fatter pocketbooks.

The publishing of textbooks was a specialty in which many of the general trade houses participated, but which they seldom led. Several factors set this branch of the business apart and made it susceptible to monopolistic devices. Of these the most important were the differences in the system of distribution and the nature of the market. While trade books were normally sold in single copies through retail bookstores to private individuals, the purchaser of texts was usually a government body operating through a school board or a politically appointed agent. Because each sale was a quantity purchase to known individuals—state-wide contracts involving many thousands of dollars—the competition became bitterly intense even before the Civil War, and necessitated methods which were unknown in other literary marts. In 1859, S. A. Rollo, a patriarch of the trade, purchased an advertisement to describe the reasons for his alienation from the textbook field: [75]

In retiring from my old School Book publishing firm, . . . I wish to be understood by the public. One reason for the change is, that my friends and customers who purchased their bills in good faith for home markets have been impoverished by the antagonistic system of rivalry in the publication and introduction of school books. Agents were to be found in almost every city, town and village in the continent, forcing into notoriety the works of their different publishers, all of which were represented as the *model school books.* I am heartily sick of all this humbug and nonsense, and I cannot be true to myself and associated with it any longer. It is too much of a patent medicine business for educational publishers.

The atmosphere of the "Gilded Age" was hardly designed to lessen the evils of excessive competition, or to keep it from becoming more sordid. Bribery of school-board officials was an acknowledged practice, although its extent cannot even be estimated.[76] Various attempts to secure some measure of self-restraint were made in the 1870's and 1880's; [77] but these were no more successful than the railroad pools of the day. In 1879, *Publishers' Weekly* lamented: [78]

We regret that we cannot this year report the desired improvement in the educational book business. It is very questionable whether, balancing all the publishing trade together, any money has been made beyond expenses in the school-book business. . . . It is the willingness to spend every cent of margin in agent's expenses, to the exclusion of any at all for legitimate handling; to permit anything that will get somebody else's books out and yours in, even if the books must be given away; to supply specimen copies and books at "introduction" rates when books have been in use for years—it is this which is unsound from any and every point of view.

Although the trade as a whole proved unmanageable, several leading companies found it profitable to form a combination which effectively restricted competition among its members. The only prominent general trade publisher in this group was D. Appleton and Company, which joined with Ivison, Phinney, Blakeman, Taylor and Company, A. S. Barnes and Company, and Bragg and Company of Cincinnati to form the dominant interest in the field. "These houses," explained Scribner in 1883, "have formed a syndicate . . . , at least they have made a formal agreement not to displace one another's books without repaying an equivalent in money. They also have begun to publish certain books in common." [79] In this same year, Scribner sold his text business to Ivison, receiving $45,000 for the plates and the cost of his inventory. He wrote: [80]

> I would have disposed of the business if necessary at a considerable sacrifice. The methods employed in the school book business are even more objectionable than ever before and the whole business has grown apart from the other departments of the publishing business and is carried on by Educational houses which confine their attention to it.

Following a trend discernible in other industries, the loose coalition ultimately gave way to a single corporation. Incorporated in New Jersey in 1890, the American Book Company combined the assets of the five largest textbook publishers in the country. The most important independent had been Harper and Brothers, which decided the new company was too formidable and sold out to it for an estimated $750,000.[81] It is difficult to determine the extent of monopoly which it enjoyed. *Publishers' Weekly* thought it exceeded 50 per cent, and urged caution in the use of its unprecedented power.[82] A year after its formation, the head of a competing house, Ginn and Company, asserted that the new syndicate controlled about 90 per cent of the grammar-school book business of the country. Such concentration, Edwin Ginn insisted, could not fail to affect adversely the whole trade.[83] Many legislators agreed with him. In 1909, the state of Texas brought suit against the American Book Company under its antitrust laws, and a decree for $15,000 was entered against the original New Jersey corporation. Its successor, chartered the year before in New York, was thoroughly investigated but found to be free from taint.[84]

The limited evidence available seems to show that the company enjoyed its most complete control at the time of its formation, and thereafter slowly declined until it became merely one of several large companies in the field. Perhaps this may be attributed to the greater probity of school boards, but probably it came about because the text business had too much in common with general trade publishing to be easily controlled. Two years after the "textbook trust" was formed, the annual "Educational Catalogue" compiled by *Publishers' Weekly* listed 188 text publishers. Of these, the eighty-five devoted exclusively to school books were distributed in all parts of the country, New York's total of twenty-seven comprising the largest group.[85] By 1913 this number had been reduced to 162; but the return of Charles Scribner's Sons to the list was a fact of more significance to the American Book Company.[86] After the war, the re-establishment of Harper and Brothers educational department would testify to the further deterioration of whatever monopoly had existed.

Textbooks ultimately proved to be somewhat more compatible than magazines to a general trade business, although the experience of the "Gilded Age" tended to establish the opposite view. Both textbook and magazine publishing put a premium upon size and financial strength which trade publishing does not seem to have required, and which for a time threatened to introduce into publishing a degree of concentration it had not known since the 1850's. However, the movement was defeated in each case. The attempt to secure an advantage through affiliated magazines succumbed to forces external to the trade, but an attempted textbook monopoly was defeated from within.

The Antagonisms and Friendships of Publishing

chapter 3

The peculiarities of the publishing business are nowhere better exhibited than in its essential reliance upon the uncertain efforts of authors. Instead of dealing with a relatively uniform substance like iron ore, cotton, or wheat, the publisher must work with words—a raw material whose value is largely a matter of speculation. The trade's frank confession that it did not know what made a book sell suggests that neither the intrinsic merit of the words nor the previous business experience of the publishers offered dependable criteria for judging the commercial worth of a manuscript. If such tests existed, the history of the business would not be dotted with episodes such as that of Edward Wescott, whose *David Harum* was rejected by a half dozen houses before it became the best-selling novel of 1898.[1]

With the producers of these words of speculative value, the publisher must join in temporary partnerships—as Henry Holt put it—for the purpose of determining how the losses will be shared.[2] The views taken by publishers of their creative associates have ranged from admiration to rage. Characteristically, they seemed to regard writers in their commercial capacity as suspicious and equally avaricious children who should learn to have faith in their publishers' integrity and superior wisdom. "Why will an occasional one of you lambs," wrote Holt to an author, "struggle when he gets into the hands of a benevolent wolf. . . . Hadn't you better resign yourself to your fate, and let me shape it?" [3] George Haven Putnam attributed the differences between authors and publishers to "authors' ignorance of costs and distribution." [4]

But the writers were at least equally unwilling to proclaim their business associates free from fault. Indignant complaints ranged from charges of neglect to accusations of deliberate dishonesty. Perhaps fundamental to their dissatisfaction, as Putnam himself acknowledged, is the fact that "compensation for literary production can never be made proportionate to the amount of labor, skilled and unskilled, that has been put into it." [5] Often the publisher has borne the brunt of criticism which more properly could be directed against an unenthusiastic public. For example, one of the authors' traditional irritations arose from their visits to bookstores which did not stock their works, a deficiency which they customarily attributed to their publishers' lack of initiative rather than to the booksellers' judgment of the market.[6] Writers, of course, felt that the obstacle posed by the retailers' indifference could easily be overcome by blanketing the country with copies sent out on consignment. "To meet your views," wrote Henry Holt in answer to such a proposal, "we would have to have had to manufacture and send out 'on sale' several thousand copies of this book, when we were unwilling to take the risk for 1250. On almost any book, a dollar's worth of effort will produce ten cents' worth of return." [7]

As new developments occurred in marketing and book promotion, the authors followed them with uncritical interest, and tended to be suspicious of publishers who did not exploit them fully. The growth of a system of commercial travellers brought a writers' demand for more commercial travellers; even those publishers who questioned the value of salesmen felt obliged to hire them to satisfy their authors.[8] After the turn of the century inadequate advertising became the whipping-boy for many book failures, and authors tended increasingly to judge the worth of publishers in direct proportion to their advertising appropriations.[9]

Probably the most serious accusation, heard more often in England than in America, charged that publishers' accounts were deliberately falsified to show fewer than actual sales—hence, less than the actual royalty due to authors. This feeling was sufficiently widespread in the 1880's to be a primary cause for the organization in England of a Society of Authors designed to forewarn and otherwise advise writers on contractual matters and to form a united front against alleged exploitative practices.[10] When news of this organization reached America, Joseph Henry Harper, Jr., Henry Holt, Anson Randolph, and other trade leaders, were quick to question figures used by the English novelist, Walter Besant, to substantiate these abuses. With some justifiable satisfaction, they pointed out that such accusations were rare in America and that author-publisher relations were not characterized by the acrimony which had been displayed abroad.[11] However, at least three authors' societies devoted to increasing the rewards of authorship arose here in the 1890's.[12] With this momentum achieved, it was not surprising that a cooperative publishing scheme should be attempted. A venture sponsored by the American Authors' Guild appeared in 1896 under the name of the Associated Authors' Publishing Company. The corporation, capitalized at $50,000, offered to publish books at the expense of the members, but with all the profits accruing to the authors rather than the firm.[13] Several years later, *Publishers' Weekly* reported that the "silly season" had produced a similar plan in England.[14] The ephemeral nature of these publishing schemes, as well as of merely advisory organizations, was indicated when the Authors' League of America was formed on the eve of the First World War precisely because no effective authors' society existed after some twenty years of continuous effort.[15]

The trade publishers ordinarily met these authors' complaints with vigorous denials of their validity. Particularly annoying was the charge of falsified accounts. Some publishers, among them Joseph Harper, argued that the juggling of figures and inventory was a conspiracy too involved to be feasible; [16] others like Walter Page acknowledged ample opportunity for it, but asserted that business morality precluded these thefts.[17] Probably most of the important publishers echoed the sentiments of the second Charles Scribner when he pointed out to Robert Louis Stevenson's agent that these practices would do injury to a firm greatly surpassing any possible advantage.[18] The smallest rumor of such action could quickly alienate the authors on whom the publishers depended. Walter Page remarked that a more natural tendency—though certainly a repressible one—would be to give writers an exaggerated report of sales figures in order to make them more amenable to future dealings.[19] Most publishers were sympathetic to the desire of writers to have proof of an accurate accounting.[20] When the Appellate Division of the New York Supreme Court decided in the case of *Savage v. Neely* (1896) that writers could demand access to the sales records of their books, few questioned the wisdom of the decision or anticipated that reputable publishers would be troubled by it.[21]

The authors' attempts at cooperative publication aroused no great concern in the trade. The nature of the publishing business, which dictated a small percentage of successful books, made the characteristic individual financing of each title a discouraging experience for all except writers so popular as to be able to exact the best terms from commercial houses. It was also true that authors customarily underestimated, as the publishers maintained, the expense of publication. George Haven Putnam was so confident of the failure of such enterprises that he was inclined to welcome them because of the business education which they offered to authors unappreciative of publishers' problems.[22] More typical, however, was a resentment against these self-publication efforts. Not only did they seem to impugn the integrity of the trade; it was also true that the self-portrait drawn by the typical publisher of himself as a patron of literature as well as a business man, became somewhat less satisfying when the authors showed suspicion rather than gratitude.

Publishers whose careers stretched back to the days of Grant's presidency professed, by the turn of the century, to have observed a steady and deplorable growth of the commercial spirit among the writing profession. Writing to E. A. Dithmar of the *New York Times* in 1903, Henry Holt asserted: [23]

> The number of people making literature a business, and the tendency of those with whom it is a natural mission, to turn it into a business, are both greatly on the increase. A well-known author, who has done work in some respects very good indeed, lately said to me, in all seriousness: "All I care for is to turn out the greatest amount of work in the shortest time, and get the most pay that I can." Upon my laughing I was assured that it was really so, and upon my having suggested some revisions, which the author approved, was informed that there was so much else to do, and so many other publishers ready to take the mss., if I didn't, that making the revisions was not worth while. This same spirt I find nearly everywhere, and on the increase.

Less choleric and probably more accurate a characteristic is one offered by Walter H. Page, whose diplomatic efforts were prefaced by a successful career in the publishing trade: "Commercial as this generation of writers may be, almost every writer of books has an ambition to win literary esteem. They want dignity. They seek reputation on as high a level as possible." [24]

However generally publishers tended to deprecate the business ability and to abhor the avarice of their authors, they continued to feel that a fundamental respect for the works which they published and for the writers who produced them was an essential ingredient of the business. Few would take exception to Walter Page's assertion that "every great publishing house has been built on the strong friendships between writers and publishers. There is, in fact, no other sound basis to build on." [25] In the files of any of the great houses there is ample evidence of this personal regard, expressed in terms whose sincerity cannot be questioned. Charles Scribner took as much delight in his friendships with Thomas Nelson Page and Richard Harding Davis [26] as James Fields had experienced in converting Boston's Corner Book Store into a clubhouse for Longfellow, Oliver Wendell Holmes, and James Lowell in the years before the Civil War. "It is with pleasure," wrote the novelist Winston Churchill, ". . . that I undertake . . . an appreciation of my friend and publisher, George P. Brett, the president of The Macmillan Company. I would repeat the words—friend and publisher. Mr. Brett has an undoubted genius for publishing, but he possesses likewise the higher genius for friendship." [27]

One of the most disturbing results of the growth of "commercialism" among authors at the turn of the century was the decline of this personal ingredient in author-publisher relations. When strong ties of friendship existed, it was more or less assumed that all of an author's books would be produced by the same house—an expectation which the publisher found personally gratifying and commercially desirable for the most part. Indeed, a group of loyal authors was considered to be an indispensable asset for a regular trade publisher. To insure a maximum of continuity of relationship between individual authors and publishers, the trade depended not only on friendship with writers, but on a code of ethics which attempted to place limits on the overtures which a publisher could make to an author already identified with another house.

These unwritten but widely accepted rules of conduct constituted one of the trade's most important attempts at self-regulation. Before the Civil War, the principle had been established that no offer should be made to an established American author until he himself had indicated a desire to change publishers. Frank Dodd somewhat overstated the case, but described the common practice, in a nostalgic speech delivered in 1905 to the Booksellers' Association: "No publisher would have dreamed of approaching an author who had been discovered and published by another, with an offer of better terms." [28]

It should not be surprising that in the decades following the Civil War the effectiveness of this "trade courtesy" gradually diminished. What seems more remarkable in this ruthlessly competitive era is that it continued to be as influential as it was among the leading publishers. Reflecting a sentiment still common in the 1880's is a letter written by Henry Holt, not for public consumption, but for the guidance of one of his assistants: [29]

> I ought to have written you before that in the interest of what little "trade courtesy" can still be preserved, I ought to offer Mrs. Hunt's book to the Harpers. If they don't take it, I can properly go on with it. The reason is that a publisher introducing an author is conceded to be entitled to a first consideration of the next book.

An equal scrupulousness was shown by Charles Scribner in reporting to a rival house the loss of one of its authors to his own: [30]

Very unexpectedly to us Mr. Lathrop has offered to us for publication his novel, *Newport,* and upon his assurance that he had previously declined your offer for its publication and that if we did not take it he would seek another publisher, we have agreed to publish the book. I write this to you directly and immediately in order that there may be no doubt about our course in this matter for I do not wish the least suspicion of anything unfair to mar our friendly relations, and independently of this, I have myself the strongest views on the question of interference between publishers. . . . Mr. Lathrop came to us entirely unsolicited and we refused to make any proposition until he assured us that his book would not be published by you in any case; we do not know what your proposal for the book was and our offer was not made with a view to competition but was a conservative one.

The reading of several thousand letters from Scribner's business correspondence suggests no possibility that he did not mean what he wrote. Even more remarkable was Frank H. Dodd's behavior towards William Dean Howells. When Howells' regular publisher, Harper and Brothers, faced bankruptcy and was reorganized in 1900, the author was upset over the change in management and offered a manuscript to Dodd, Mead and Company. Although Dodd was delighted to accept it for publication, he coupled his acceptance with his assurances that Harper's new staff would be as accommodating as the old and urged Howells to consider the matter further. Ultimately, the prediction proved to be correct and the manuscript was published by Harper and Brothers with Dodd's willing consent.[31]

To what extent this reluctance to compete depressed authors' incomes is difficult to say. It seems not to have been designed for that purpose, but for the mutual benefit of both publisher and author. On the other hand, at least some publishers realized that competition for a manuscript produced a better contract for its author. "When two publishers are seeking an author," wrote George Haven Putnam, "the proportion of the proceeds offered to the author, goes up." [32] Yet such a conclusion does not necessarily imply that authors as a whole would benefit from constantly changing their publishers. The unsuccessful books of many young writers, for example, were published chiefly for the sake of the promise they offered of their author's future achievements; such manuscripts would not receive the same consideration were there no expectation of continuity in author-publisher relationships. "Do you mind telling me," wrote Henry Holt, "how old the author appears to be and what you know of her experience? This I would like to get at for the sake of the future. For the sake of the future I should feel disposed to take some risks." [33] In any event, "trade courtesy" was considered by the publishers as a restraint upon themselves, rather than upon the writers. Its most ardent exponents, among them Charles Scribner, vigorously asserted the right of a dissatisfied author to seek a new connection, maintaining that anything smacking of a boycott of such a writer was clearly wrong: [34]

We know of no recognized courtesy rights among publishers which restrict an author from changing his publishers if he desires to do so or from receiving a proposal from another publisher if he is not satisfied with the terms on which his books are published. . . . Any arrangement among publishers which would interfere with such a procedure on our part would be most unfair to both authors and publishers. . . . In this case we have done what is done every year among the best publishers.

The fact that "trade courtesy" left ample room for the independence of authors became increasingly apparent as the twentieth century advanced. Whatever self-restraint publishers exercised among themselves was relatively unimportant if the writers chose to ignore the importance of remaining with a single house. Frank H. Dodd observed sadly that "many of the authors of the day do not hesitate to seek offers from various publishers for each one of their forthcoming books, almost putting them up at auction. . . . The old relation between author and publisher has disappeared."[35] A partial cause could be found in the gradual separation of the literary profession from its genteel associations. Both personal friendships between authors and publishers and ethical niceties within the trade itself were easier to maintain when writers had independent incomes which relieved them of the necessity of shopping for the best contracts. James Russell Lowell could accept his publisher's friendship in partial payment for his work, but Jack London viewed each contract as a business arrangement. The genteel tradition seems to have lingered longer among the leading trade publishers than in the writing profession, possibly because it was less demanding.

However, the deterioration of "trade courtesy" and personal relations can be attributed to changes within the trade as well as outside of it. Publishers became increasingly competitive, and not above soliciting manuscripts from authors under contract with their rivals. Walter Page described the extreme to which these activities were carried: [36]

> There are others—others who keep "literary drummers", men who go to see popular writers and solicit books. . . . There are two men in the United States who have gone about making commercial calls on practically every man and woman who has ever written a successful book. . . . Every other publisher hears of their journeyings and of their "drumming".

Only a few firms clung to the ethics—Henry Holt named "Scribner, and Doubleday . . . very likely Dodd-Mead and Putnam, and perhaps a few others who don't crowd themselves on my imagination at present." [37]

Long before the Civil War, a somewhat more complicated version of this same "trade courtesy" had been attempted as a substitute for an international copyright. American publishers who wished to bring out their own editions of the work of foreign—principally English—writers, often paid substantial honorariums for early sheets of the foreign editions. Two advantages could be secured by this procedure. Since production could be started before the text became generally available, a head-start of several days could be gained over rival publishers—known as "pirates"—who reproduced this uncopyrighted material without paying anyone. In addition to securing a time advantage over the pirated editions, the payment of an honorarium carried with it the assurance that the other publishers adhering to the principle of "trade courtesy" would treat the material as if it were copyrighted and voluntarily surrender the right to publish it. It is difficult to know exactly when this practice arose. Henry C. Lea recalled that the Philadelphia firm of Carey, Lea and Blanchard customarily paid Sir Walter Scott £75 for advance sheets of each of the Waverley novels, and in 1826 had paid £300 for his *Life of Napoleon Bonaparte.*[38] However, it was not until the 1840's that piracy subjected the honorarium system to its first serious test. In 1842 Park Benjamin began issuing the most popular of the English novels in paper covers at prices ranging from seven to twenty-five cents. The sales of these literary "extras," which were marketed like newspapers rather than books, reached such proportions that they upset the book market and led the regular publishers to retaliatory measures. Book prices lowered, and the first wide-scale effort of the trade to reach a mass buying public ensued.[39]

This fiercely competitive struggle with a new type of book publisher caused the older members of the trade to make more explicit their own understanding concerning honorariums. On the eve of the Civil War "trade courtesy" was a clearly defined, even if occasionally ignored, principle of self-regulation. However, those firms which had entered the low-price field found it difficult to resist the temptation to disregard the rights of British authors to remuneration. Harper's Library of Select Novels, which by 1850 numbered over six hundred titles, was built largely upon pirated works.[40] But there is indisputable evidence that the same company on other occasions paid large honorariums to foreign authors. Dickens, for example, received £1,250 from it for *Great Expectations*, and similar amounts for other works in the 1850's and 1860's.[41]

But despite the opportunistic course pursued by the country's largest house, "trade courtesy" was an effective force in the business and most of the regular publishers supported it with some consistency. A dispute which occurred in 1860 over the right to publish the correspondence of Alexander Von Humboldt illustrates some of the details of its operation. The firm of Carleton and Rudd obtained an early copy of the German edition, had it translated, and prepared it for production only to discover that the Appletons had purchased advance sheets of the English edition and were also about to issue the work. Upon a payment of £40—the amount they had already invested—the Appletons agreed to withdraw in favor of Carleton and Rudd. But before the issue was settled, additional negotiations had to be conducted with Harper and Brothers, which by this time had its own edition ready to go to press. Ultimately, the field was clear for Carleton and Rudd, although "trade courtesy" had required that competing investments made in good faith be compensated.[42] Apparently there was more than patriotic bluster, although less than complete truth, in the assertion of the *American Publishers' Circular and Literary Gazette* in 1862 that it was "an undeniable fact that there is no living English author of established reputation, whose books are extensively republished in this country, who is not freely and properly compensated by the American publisher." [43]

During the interval between Appomattox and the passage in 1891 of American legislation protecting foreign authors, "trade courtesy" declined in its effectiveness, but remained the working principle of a substantial proportion of the larger publishers. Government hearings held in connection with copyright legislation brought to light the accusation that the agreement was little more than a trust method by which a few established firms respected one another's rights while trampling on those of the smaller houses. This was vigorously denied by Henry Holt, who cited his own experience when he began a company in the 1860's. The extant records seem to confirm Holt's view that "trade courtesy" was open to anyone who would practice it. The threat to the established houses came from a number of individually unimportant reprint houses whose failure to participate in this self-regulatory scheme was precisely the reason why they were collectively important.[44]

One of the significant additions to the operation of "trade courtesy" after the Civil War was the adoption of a single medium in which official announcements were made of intention to publish foreign authors. Upon completion of an arrangement with a British author, the American house purchased an advertisement in the *Commercial Advertiser* to disseminate the news of the forthcoming publication. This performance established a claim to the work which was cited if another publisher subsequently announced the same book. The following letter to Messrs. Roberts Brothers, typical of many in the correspondence of Scribner, Armstrong and Co., indicates the common practice: [45]

We notice in last evening's *Commercial Advertiser* your "in press" announcement of the "Life of Marie Antoinette" by

C. D. Yonge. We beg to call your attention to our previous announcement (March 29th) and to an early copy of the work in hand. We hope therefore that you will not interfere with us in the matter.

The effectiveness of such requests is revealed by another group of letters in the files of the same firm showing that a prior announcement was at least sometimes as effective as a copyright: [46]

In reply to your favor regarding our "in press" announcement of M. Tissot's "Land of the Milliards" and referring to your previous announcement of the same book in the *Commercial Advertiser,* we hasten to say that we cheerfully retire in your favor.

Only the roughest estimate can be made of the number of firms which were willing to abide by these self-imposed rules. The outgoing correspondence of Charles Scribner's Sons for the decade of the 1870's reveals forty such letters, written to nine firms. Since many of these letters refer amicably to satisfactory adjustments, and since all the recipients were leaders in the trade, it may safely be concluded that these nine companies were addressed because they generally respected "trade courtesy" rather than because they ignored it. The names mentioned are: J. B. Lippincott and Co., J. R. Osgood and Co., D. Appleton and Co., Roberts Brothers, G. P. Putnam's Sons, Harper and Brothers, Macmillan and Co., E. P. Dutton and Co., and Henry Holt and Co. This list is confirmed in an acrimonious exchange between Henry Holt and one of the pirate publishers, Henry Altemus: [47]

We are perfectly aware . . . that our "views of trade courtesy are recognized only in theory" by a certain class of publishers. They are, and have been, recognized practically however, by, among others, Harper, Appleton, Scribner, Roberts, Putnam, and Lippincott.

If to these were added a few more such as Houghton, Mifflin and Co., Little, Brown and Co., and Dodd, Mead and Co., the total would probably include a large percentage of those who participated in the attempts of the business to regulate itself in the absence of an international copyright.

Of course, the acceptance of the principle of "trade courtesy" did not guarantee, and should not be taken to imply, its perfect operation even among this limited group. Yet it is interesting that when disputes arose, each side strove to base its case upon the principle rather than to ignore it. One of the most spectacular disagreements pitted Charles Scribner's Sons against Harper and Brothers in a controversy over the right to publish Thomas Carlyle's *Reminiscences*. On a theoretical level, the fight concerned conflicting interpretations of the prevailing trade ethics. The *Reminiscences* had been edited by James Anthony Froude, who was also Carlyle's literary executor. Scribner, having published previous works of Froude, concluded an arrangement with him for this one, offering £100 for the advance sheets, and a 10 per cent royalty on all copies sold. The proceeds were to go to Carlyle's niece. This contract was challenged in the name of "trade courtesy" by Harper and Brothers, which considered itself Carlyle's regular American publisher, and which claimed to have made an arrangement through an agent with Carlyle himself before his death in 1881. The dispute fast became a *cause célèbre* in the trade. An extended correspondence was followed by paid advertisements and circulars which each company issued to publicize and justify its position. *Publishers' Weekly* announced its "painful duty to take cognizance of a controversy between two of our most prominent houses . . . which cannot but have a depressing effect at home and abroad." [48]

Efforts to resolve the dispute ended in complete failure, and both houses produced editions of the work. Then Harper's, which often played the bully in the trade, proceeded to issue in inexpensive format a number of Scribner's best English titles, about which there had previously been no question. Charles Scribner, with fewer resources and more scruples, declined to retaliate. There was little profit in such a course, and he hoped that by not descending to blatant piracy he could establish the ethical superiority of his own firm in the minds of British writers. Although Harper ceased, after a short time, to raid the Scribner list, a residue of ill-will and mutual suspicion continued to mar the relations of the two firms for a decade.[49]

However unsuccessfully "trade courtesy" operated in this dispute, the incident demonstrates that it was not lightly regarded. Such bitter warfare among houses which claimed to be guided by the principle was infrequent enough to cause wide comment when it did occur. More common, of course, were arguments in which one side gave way before news of the differences became public property. Since there was no appeal to law in cases involving uncopyrighted material, the offended party had no recourse except to retaliation of the kind in which Harper's had indulged, or to threats of retaliation in future dealings. Yet reprisals necessarily involved piracy, and houses which considered themselves respectable hesitated to employ a weapon which they genuinely deplored. Henry Holt conveyed much of this reluctance, couched in the peculiar delicacy which often characterized publishers' correspondence, in a letter addressed to George Haven Putnam in 1880: [50]

> I was very far from intending to intimate that your publishing Tell would "be a grievance calling for reprisals." . . . The most that I did intend to intimate was that the degree of consideration that I should show for any interests of yours not protected by copyright, would naturally bear some relation to the consideration that you show for similar interests of mine—that if I wanted, for its own sake, to do anything that might be prejudicial to you, the fact that it would be prejudicial to you, would not be as apt to prevent me from doing it, if you make Tell, as it would now.
>
> I don't believe, under any ordinary circumstances, in the reprisal policy, and there's no form of stupidity that I so thoroughly detest (whether I am exempt from it or not) as that which attempts to make its own success out of successes legitimately belonging to other people. Nowhere that I know of does intelligent selfishness so much consist in altruism as in American publishing.

Occasionally, a satisfactory compromise could be arranged when two publishers appeared to have equal claim to the same book. For example, a standard device was to arrange for one house to issue a regular edition in cloth, while the other claimant confined himself to bringing out the same book in an inexpensive paper-bound format.[51] When a disputed work was one of a series, the right to the title in question could be balanced against the right to succeeding volumes.[52]

The treatment meted out to foreign authors under "trade courtesy" varied considerably, the ethic accommodating itself to the commercial value of the work in question. For the most popular titles, the custom of paying large lump sums for advance sheets, common at the time of the Civil War, gradually gave way in the 1870's to a system of smaller initial payments and a royalty on copies sold. However, if the sales of the American edition were not sufficiently large to pay for its cost, then it was considered ethical to pay no royalty.[53] While this practice was not especially generous to the British authors, it was not unlike many of the contracts negotiated both here and in England for original editions. Books in less demand might bring either a single payment for advance sheets or a royalty, the practice varying with the publisher. When it was questionable that the cost of manufacturing an edition here would be met by subsequent sales, a publisher could import a quantity of unbound sheets from the English house, and market the book in America with its own imprint,[54] or jointly with that of the originating company.[55] If no firm in this country made inquiry concerning a forthcoming foreign publication, then advance sheets were often shipped from abroad and circulated among the American houses in hopes of finding a buyer. The original publisher was willing to accept whatever any user thought they were worth.[56] Many individual American and British publishers paired off and made arrangements under which each gave the other the first option on the export market. Under this plan advance sheets on minor publications would be exchanged automatically.[57] When options were not exercised, the participating houses acted as agents in attempting to place the unwanted titles.[58]

If a foreign publication had merit but seemed to be designed for a too small audience to justify even the importation of unbound sheets, a quantity of the original edition would be imported. Such an operation converted the publisher into a mere distributor, although an unexpectedly large demand might ultimately lead to a separate American edition. A number of the American houses dealt indirectly with such operations through affiliated companies. Scribner and Welford, for example, was the importing division of Charles Scribner's Sons.

The purchase of copies of the English edition did not, under the rules of trade courtesy, carry with it the exclusive right to the American market. Occasionally the original and the natively produced editions, each sponsored by a different publisher, would be offered concurrently on the market. At least one publisher, Charles Scribner, believed that under these circumstances good business practice precluded any competition in price. In 1881, he wrote to Charles Welford: [59]

We shall be very glad to use all we can of Murray's edition of Rawlinson and the greater advantage he can offer us the more copies we can sell. We do not want to push it particularly as against Dodd and Mead; but we shall reduce the price so that the English edition can compete on about even terms.

But while Scribner was willing to concede equality to a competing edition, he tried to obtain assurances from the English publisher that he alone would be given the privilege of importing the original edition. This was an unreasonable request, which became even more difficult to grant as the years advanced. By the 1880's the regular jobbers began to purchase books abroad, and leading retailers, such as Brentano, found it easier to meet their needs by direct negotiation with the English producers.[60]

All these arrangements contemplated some degree of remuneration for British interests. However "trade courtesy" permitted another practice, one used quite frequently, which made no immediate provision for the authors. The works of new and unknown foreign writers were reprinted without consideration, but at the same time were protected in America by the institution of "prior announcement." In this case the ethic was designed to permit an experiment at minimum cost, and to allow the experimenter to enjoy the profits of his speculation without interference. Such a venture had the further advantage of securing for the publisher a right to the author's future books. It is worth observing that precisely the opposite treatment came to be accorded an established foreign author. One of the refinements added to the institution of "trade courtesy" in the twenty years after the Civil War was the custom of denying a publisher a priority in his claim to the later books of a prominent author if he had not paid for the previous ones.[61]

Precisely how the distinction was made between an "established" and an "unknown" writer is not indicated.

The confusion which underlay the operation of "trade courtesy" resulted not only from such ambiguities of definition in America, but also from the erratic behavior of authors and publishers abroad. Not infrequently the purchaser of an edition which carried with it the exclusive rights to the market would discover that the English author had sold the same book to another American publisher. Other times the author and the publisher would conduct negotiations independently of one another, with the end result of selling exclusive publication rights to two different houses.[62] Considerable controversy arose in 1884 when the English house of Field and Tuer sold the American rights to Max O'Rell's *John Bull and his Island* without ever having owned them. After having paid Field and Tuer $250 for the advance sheets, the American buyer, Charles Scribner's Sons, was naturally surprised, and somewhat indignant, upon receiving from the author a letter castigating it for its piracy. An inquiry directed by Scribner's to the English house brought forth the lame excuse that the advance sheets were not intended to bestow the right of publication—an explanation which the *London Bookseller* thought ridiculous.[63] Although convinced that he had acted honorably, Charles Scribner wrote O'Rell that he was agreeable to paying him an additional sum, the amount of which he was willing to leave to the judgment of an arbitrator.[64]

Further problems and ill-feeling arose because of the failure of the British authors and publishers to make explicit how their American spoils were to be divided. An American house contracting with an author might discover later that additional compensation was expected for the publisher. "We agreed to pay *you* 10% royalty," wrote Scribner to Robert Louis Stevenson. "If you think that you should share with Longmans 50-50, O.K.—not our business; but we won't pay them any more." [65] Although it was commonly assumed that the publisher received the payment for advance sheets while the author took the proceeds from royalties, the American houses did not have access to the British contracts and had no way of knowing how the payments would be divided. While they preferred to deal with writers rather than publishers, they could not be certain that the authors were authorized to negotiate with them.[66] By the turn of the century, contracts with authors on both sides of the Atlantic had come to include explicit references to such subsidiary points as the profits from foreign markets. English interests had particular cause to regulate their affairs more carefully after 1891, when the passage of an international copyright law by Congress made the returns from the sale of American rights larger and more certain.

It was unquestionably true that less protection was furnished to foreign authors by the institution of "trade courtesy" than they received under a law which gave them access to the courts in the defense of their rights. After 1891, payment for advance sheets substantially disappeared, and pirates vanished with them. Although royalties had been paid by a few houses before, they now became the rule rather than the exception. Extant records of contracts drawn between 1892 and 1914 indicate that foreign writers received about the same terms given to American writers. The royalties on ten contracts signed by Charles Scribner's Sons between 1901 and 1906 varied from 10 per cent to 20 per cent, which was also the range of this firm for its domestic writers.[67] In competing for the work of the most popular British writers, Harper and Brothers reached what was considered to be the outside limit for remuneration to authors. Thomas Hardy received a 20 per cent royalty on *Jude the Obscure,* and H. G. Wells' *The War of the Worlds* brought a contract which rose from 15 per cent on the first 3,000 copies sold to 25 per cent for sales over the 20,000 mark.[68]

At about the same time that foreign writers obtained legal protection for their books in America, literary agents began to become important in the publishing world, adding another arrow to the authors' quiver. American publishers were fond of observing that agents first arose in Great Britain, a fact which they were eager to attribute to the superior amicability and business wisdom of authors and publishers in this country.[69] Originating in their modern form in the 1880's, literary agents were first identified with the efforts of younger writers to place manuscripts which were in no particular demand. But they soon supplemented this not especially lucrative business by negotiating contracts for the well-established authors. The English firm of A. P. Watt was the most successful of the early agents, representing such important writers as Walter Besant, Rudyard Kipling, and Conan Doyle before the turn of the century.[70]

The activities of the literary agent were extremely exasperating to the publishers. William Heinemann, the President of the Publishers' Association of Great Britain and Ireland, called him "a parasite living on our vital forces." [71] Nor was he merely unproductive, receiving a commission without performing a useful service; rather, his contribution was a negative one, which threatened the personal relations between author and publisher on which the business was presumed to be built. It is difficult to draw the line in this resentment between the self-interest which balked at larger royalties and a more general concern for an essential of the trade. No one can question that the agents attached little importance to the continuity of relations between a client and the publisher of his last book. Instead, their basic mode of operation seems to have been to offer each manuscript at auction, and to award it to the highest bidder. This procedure was at direct odds with "trade courtesy," and the older houses attempted to resist it. "If the matter is to be made in any sense one of competition among publishers," wrote Henry Holt to A. P. Watt, "pray spare yourself the trouble of communicating with us any farther as we do not enter into competitions." [72] Since Watt was demanding a 33⅓ per cent royalty for an author, one cannot be certain whether it was the futility of the competition or the principle of it which made Holt so dogmatic.

Actually, the publishers had no choice but to compete if they wished to maintain their relations with the popular British authors. And playing the game according to rules they had newly learned, many of them passed through a period when they not only bid against one another, but frequently overbid.

Although the publishers were aware that there was something suicidal engulfing them, they were temporarily at a loss to do more than protest. Charles Scribner wrote in 1899: [73]

> Some of the new firms without reputation or organization have made large bids for popular authors but many of them such as Stone and Kimball, Lamsen, Wolfe and Company, Copeland and Day, and Way and Williams have already failed or gone out of business and I know several authors who have lost a large part of their royalties. I do not think that you are right in supposing that publication by one firm is worth no more than by another. There may easily be a difference equal to 5% or more in the royalty.
>
> I think 25% of the retail price more than can be paid and leave the publishers a suitable margin to manufacture, advertise, and sell the book but I am unwilling to lose an author so identified with our house. . . . We will therefore pay the 25% royalty.

Testifying to the fact that old firms were as susceptible as the new ones is the bankruptcy of Harper and Brothers in 1899, a failure in which ten years of this new competition for authors undoubtedly played a part.

So little did the publishers realize what was happening that they clung to the hope that literary agents would prove to be a fad rather than an institution. Writing to his London representative in 1893, Charles Scribner said: [74]

> There certainly is a great strike among authors and the open bidding which is sometimes insisted upon favors prices too high in most cases but perhaps it is a temporary phase of business which will disappear—as many others have. You will remem-

ber the ten cent Franklin Square and Seaside Library which promised to revolutionize the business. Then the authors all expected to become rich on the newspaper syndicates which have collapsed. I think authors' agents will go the same way; prices will come down again, and the reliable publishers will be in better esteem after a few more failures like the A. S. Book Co. and Cassell.

Twenty years later, many publishers had accepted the agents as a permanent—even if troublesome—part of the structure of their business. What had insured against their disappearance was the increasing complexity of marketing literary property. The perfection of the copyright made international markets a more serious and detailed consideration. Further, novelists especially had need of expert guidance in arranging for the first and second serial rights to their works, which might be sought by the magazines. Syndicates supplying newspapers with fiction began to make their appearance, and the dramatization of books became more common.[75] Just ahead lay the rewards to be gained from motion pictures, radio, and the book clubs. These new outlets created a maze of problems which the author was happy to leave to the more experienced hands of a specialist. Even the publishers acknowledged the assistance which the agents were able to offer in negotiating the complicated contracts necessitated by these conditions.[76]

Yet the fact that the agent had a legitimate function in disposing of secondary rights did not make more palatable the higher royalties and temporary relationships which he continued to induce by the auctioning of manuscripts. "It is only when slack business and excessive zeal drives him into forcing royalties or luring authors from their natural publishers in order to win a commission by placing them with others that he becomes the devil," wrote Robert Sterling Yard.[77] Others gloomily concluded that the "devil" quality was basal rather than tangential, since friendship between authors and publishers became impossible when agents were present.[78] The future was to show that at least some of this pessimism was unwarranted. Not only did agents come to realize the value of more stable relations; the publishers were to discover that the agency system did not preclude the personal ties with authors upon which they placed such value. If the drawing of contracts became a contest between business men, the relation between editor and author remained relatively undisturbed. There was even a place in this twentieth century world for "trade courtesy," especially among those older houses which remembered the days of Jay Gould and Commodore Vanderbilt as an era of gentlemanly ethics.

Contracts Between Authors and Publishers

chapter 4

The records of the "Gilded Age" contain very little to reveal what division of the profits on a book was contemplated by the usual contract between author and publisher. "Royalties exceeding ten per cent are immoral," Henry Holt is reputed to have said,[1] a statement which indicates less a principle than a desire to avoid formulating one. Few questioned that authors' returns were grossly inadequate. The novelist Julian Hawthorne described the plight of the writers in 1888: [2]

> I will engage to entertain at dinner, at a round table five feet in diameter, all the American novelists who make more than a thousand dollars a year out of the royalty on any one of their novels, and to give them all they want to eat and drink, and three of the best cigars apiece afterward, and a hack to take them home in; and I will agree to forfeit a thousand dollars . . . if $25 does not liquidate the bill and leave enough over to buy a cloth copy of each of the works in question, with the author's autograph on the fly-leaf.

Thirty years later, despite an increase in royalty rates, writers were not appreciably better off. Yet, if the publishers may be believed, the lion's portion of the profit on the average book was received by its author. Writing in 1913, publisher Robert Yard asserted: [3]

If I should tell you that your favorite novelist has to write short stories, and sell at least one a month to the magazines in order to average $3,500 a year, you would be surprised. There are not many who do so well as that. . . . And yet your novelist will make 2 or 3 times out of a book what his publisher does; and many, many times his publisher actually loses money.

The best example of a clear-cut principle of profit-sharing is shown in the "half-profit arrangement." No return was made to either party until the cost of production was met, but subsequent returns above the cost of doing business were divided equally. While the "half-profit" contract was standard in Great Britain, its unpopularity in the United States makes it poor evidence of the theory behind the contract-making of American publishers. One must conclude that instead of a formula, there was merely a test of strength in which each contestant attempted to secure a maximum advantage. However, the lack of a guiding principle did not prevent contract forms from becoming standardized during the fifty years following the Civil War. This trend towards uniformity paralleled the gradual clarification of the publishing function. When booksellers like Daniel Appleton and Moses Dodd were making their first tentative efforts in the 1840's, there were few precedents to guide publishers and authors in reaching an agreement. A generation behind lay the days when authors had to depend on the subscriptions of friends and patrons to pay the printer's bill.[4]

The earliest original contracts made available for this

study date from the decade of the 1850's. They concern nineteen books published by Moses Dodd. No two of the agreements were identical, although all fall into one of three general categories. Five manuscripts were purchased outright. The least remunerative to its author was *The Gospel Harmony,* for which Walter King received $1 and "a small number of copies." If the book proved successful, the author was to be reimbursed for the expenses of his journey from Utica to New York to sign the contract. Dodd's outstanding writer, the clergyman Gardiner Spring, was paid $1,200 for *The Contract,* the largest sum mentioned. Nine contracts provided for royalties, each of them on different terms. The poorest rate gave Reverend Thomas Lope "8% in copies of the work bound on every eighth copy published and sold," while the most generous was the 20 per cent awarded to Theodore Spencer for his *Conversion and Its Theory and Process Practically Delineated.* Usually the return was figured on the retail price, but two contracts called for a percentage of the wholesale proceeds. The agreement for James Boyd's *Westminster Catechism* was the only one which specified a sliding scale of returns, and this provided for a payment of 10 per cent on the first 4,000 copies sold, 8 per cent on the second 4,000, and 6 per cent for all subsequent sales. A third group of contracts insured against the publisher's loss by requiring the author to pay for a substantial part of the costs of publication. After supervising the manufacture, Dodd received a royalty of 10 per cent on the copies he sold.

Ten additional agreements from the same period concern previously published books for which Dodd undertook to perform a variety of services. Provision was made in four of these for the rental of stereotype plates, the publisher paying royalties ranging up to 20 per cent of the retail price for their use. One cast Dodd in the role of distributing agent of books already produced, while another required him to manufacture and deliver copies of a work for a specified price.[5]

During the "Gilded Age" the place of the publisher was more clearly defined by a framework of accepted practices and responsibilities. However, the reluctance of the trade to view its association with writers as a simple matter of commerce continued to lend a distinctively informal note to contractual relationships. One evidence of this was an apparent lack of interest in reducing an agreement to writing. Henry Holt wrote in 1880: [6]

> About the time that I started the American Science Series, I learned (on what I now believe to have been false authority) that one of the oldest and wisest houses makes no written contracts and (partly, perhaps, because my firm name had changed about that time and rendered the old forms unusable) I gave up the habit of having written contracts.

For the self-sufficient Mr. Holt to take his example from a rumor or to base his practice on the difficulty of securing correct forms during twelve years of business does not seem plausible. In any event, his expressed reasons for relying upon a loose verbal understanding in 1880 do not explain why in 1910 one of his authors had to request a written contract for a book already in press.[7] It is plain that one publisher, at least, occasionally thought the customs of the business sufficiently clear to reasonable men to obviate the need for an explicit agreement.

It is possible that the same habits of thought explain the enthusiasm of the trade for arbitration devices. Holt himself used such a clause, although even this seemed to him an unnecessary concession to unreason: [8]

> You seem to have overlooked the protection given to both sides by a reference to arbitration in case of difference. I earnestly hope that my business will never be owned by people foolish enough to go to arbitration in such questions as you indicate; and if they should go, surely the question could not be decided as you fear they might be unless the arbitrators were all knaves or fools.

In this instance, the question at issue which Holt found so simple concerned the rather subtle problem of the author's right to contract with other publishers for books similar to one which Holt was about to bring out.

The typical form of arbitration provided for each party to the contract to name a representative. If these two could not agree on a settlement, they were permitted to select a third man whose decision would be final.[9]

Apparently, this machinery sometimes served to compound the dilemma, since the arbitrators originally appointed might have difficulty agreeing even on a person to resolve their deadlocks.[10] In 1897, George Haven Putnam unsuccessfully suggested a permanent board representing both publishers and authors which would serve for the whole industry, the object being to dispense entirely with court litigation.[11] For reasons which seemed inexplicable to the publishers, many writers individually, and collectively through the Author's League, vigorously opposed the use of arbitration. What must have been the inspiration for this hostility was the feeling, justified or not, that a settlement obtained outside the formal processes of law would be more subject to the extra-legal influences of a publishing corporation. The trade took some pains to popularize arbitration, and ultimately the writers came to agree that it was an effective and inexpensive substitute well suited to their purposes.[12]

However, the differences which arose between publishers and their authors after contracts had been signed seldom concerned the subject of greatest interest to them both—the manner and the amount of the writer's return for preparing the manuscript. This compensation was carefully set forth in each of several types of contracts upon which the trade came to rely. From the publisher's viewpoint, the least ambitious and least speculative were the agreements under which books were published entirely or primarily at the author's expense. This was one of the oldest types of agreements, and one which reflected a rather primitive stage of trade book publishing. Its use constantly declined among the better houses. That it persisted at all can be attributed to the presence of works of a special literary or scientific character with which the reputable publishers liked to associate themselves but which they could not undertake independently as commercial ventures.[13] Ultimately, these firms decided against placing their imprint on any book, whatever its intrinsic merits, unless they were willing also to pay for its publication.

However, at the turn of the century there came into being a number of companies, more printers than publishers, which took advantage of the frustrated authors of worthless manuscripts and made considerable profits by offering their questionable imprints in return for publication expenses. The bill, paid in advance, was usually twice the actual cost, and to this amount could be added the sum received when the author was later compelled to purchase the plates of his unsuccessful book. Speaking of this group in 1905, Walter Page said: [14]

> It is only by accident that they ever get a book that sells; and they hardly pretend to put books on the market, for of course the booksellers will not buy them. . . . A writer who asks a publisher to bring out a book that has no commercial reason for its existence is asking him to imitate the "fake" publisher. . . . These pseudo-publishers sometimes solicit manuscripts from ignorant writers. They have veiled advertisements in the literary journals. Ignorance and ambition is a susceptible combination. Several years ago one of these plausible swindlers bribed a reader in one of the larger publishing houses to report to him the names of all the writers whose novels were declined there. The fakir then plied them with circulars and letters.

Such a letter could not have been written in 1850. The assumption that a publisher would finance the average book on his list had taken a half-century to establish itself. But despite the trade's contempt for job printers posing as publishers, the custom of requiring authors to pay for the cost of plates remained respectable and widespread up to the 1890's and even to the First World War. "We are not sufficiently sure of its commercial success to justify us in running the entire risk of the manufacture of the book," wrote Charles Scribner to an author in 1894. "Our proposal therefore is that you bear the expense of making the plates. . . ." [15] Henry Holt's exacting concern for trade ethics did not prevent him from writing: "We have concluded that if you will have the plates made and deliver them to us, we shall be willing to publish the book. . . ." [16] Actually, the difference between houses requiring full payment by the author and those which asked him to provide plates went beyond money. While the services of the former were available to anyone with a manuscript and money to pay for its publication, men like Scribner and Holt would not put their names to a book which failed to meet fixed editorial standards. They desired to reduce costs on a commercially questionable manuscript, but not to make a profit as the manufacturers of an intrinsically worthless one. However, the trend was clearly away from requiring an investment from the author, even for reasons which the trade considered legitimate. A transition attempt to compensate the author's purchase of plates by paying an additional royalty for their use does not appear to have been satisfactory, since the publisher thereby penalized himself heavily on successful books and the writers were no less burdened with an initial cost of publication.

The outright purchase of manuscripts was another form of agreement which became less common as the years advanced. From the publishers' viewpoint, the outlay of a considerable sum in advance of publication merely increased the speculative nature of the business and employed additional capital. On the other hand, it protected the author against a failure. However, most writers had sufficient faith in their works to prefer a percentage arrangement which enabled them to share in the proceeds of a successful book. Because of the uncertainty of sales, the single payments paid to all but the most prominent novelists were usually less than sufficient to cover the writers' living costs during composition. Louisa May Alcott, for example, was offered $1,000 for *Little Women*, but ultimately received over a hundred times as much by accepting her publisher's advice to sign for a royalty.[17] As the twentieth century approached, the need for ready cash which had been the chief inducement to writers to sell their manuscripts outright came to be supplied by the more customary use of advances. These increased in size until they equalled the amounts formerly offered for outright purchases.

The twenty years between 1880 and 1900 were the transition period for these, as well as for basic changes in contracts. A series of letters exchanged in 1888 between Charles Scribner and the popular novelist, Frances Hodgson Burnett, reveals a useful comparison between royalty and single payment rates. For the book rights to *Sara Crewe* the publisher was willing to give either $3,000 cash, or a 15 per cent royalty. Since the book was a short one which would have to be sold for $1, the sum was the equivalent of a royalty on 20,000 copies.[18] A more standard offer was one made by Scribner to Helen Hunt in 1879 for $1,000 on a novel to be sold for $1.50, the usual price for fiction. Alternatively, the firm was willing to pay a 12½ per cent royalty, which would match the single payment at about 5,000 copies.[19] There is something suspiciously unscientific about the frequency with which $1,000 is mentioned in these negotiations. If complete sales figures were available for the manuscripts for which this amount was paid, they would undoubtedly show an average distribution of many fewer than 5,000; and, translated in terms of a royalty, the returns to authors would be at a rate more than double what the publishers customarily paid. When one considers the financial risk to publishers of outright purchases, and the defeatism which they implied to authors, there can be little wonder that such contracts were ordinarily confined to editors and translators.

A large majority of the contracts signed after the Civil War did not call for a single payment, but for a certain percentage of the proceeds from sales. The practice of paying royalties, or "copyrights"—as they were often called—had begun much earlier in the nineteenth century, and, indeed, had become standard by the 1840's. However, the years ahead were to witness important changes in the rate at which the author's share was computed and in the terms under which it was paid.

One of the points which had to be settled was whether royalties would begin with the first copy, or whether the author would be compelled to forego returns until some portion of the expenses had been met. Unquestionably, the publishers wished to establish a rule and to apply it as generally as possible, exempting as many copies as were necessary to cover the nonrecurring costs of publication. Henry Holt wrote in 1880: [20]

> . . . It is our custom to offer authors ten percent of the retail price of each copy sold after enough (probably 1000 to 1200)

have been sold to return our outlay for plates and advertising. If this meets your views, we will submit a contract embracing all details.

Holt's company used this principle often enough to incorporate it in a printed form which read: [21]

Our contract for the publication of ______________ provides that the publisher shall begin to pay royalty, except in certain specified cases, after ______________ copies are sold.

We regret the necessity of saying that the total sales up to ______________ were but ______________ copies, those for the six months preceding that date being ____________ copies.

The regular contract form used by Harper and Brothers in 1899 contained the phrase, "they agree to pay the author ten percent. on their trade-list (retail) price for each copy thereof by them sold over and above one thousand copies." [22]

Despite the strong support of the publishers, the principle of exemption was never accepted by a majority of the writers. Even when it was successfully incorporated into contracts, the compromise of a higher royalty on subsequent sales was often coupled with it. A letter written by Henry Holt in 1903 shows a significant development from his typical practice twenty years before: [23]

Our ordinary contract for a first novel is to exempt enough copies to enable us to get our money back before beginning paying royalty, then to pay twice the usual initial royalty . . . until the exemption is made good.

By the turn of the century, most publishers did not attempt to withhold royalties on more than a thousand copies. This in itself was a surrender of principle, since the savings were scarcely adequate to pay the cost of composition and plates. But even this half-loaf was denied more often than it was given. The exemption clause continued to appear in the printed contracts of Harper and Brothers, but it was ordinarily crossed out during negotiations with the writers. Only 6 per cent of 776 agreements signed by the firm between 1900 and 1914 retained this provision.[24]

This losing battle was paralleled by the publishers' rather sudden retreat before the authors' demands for higher royalties. The most complete record of contract terms used between 1870 and 1914 is offered in the "Royalty Ledgers" of Harper and Brothers. These reveal the rates for approximately 1,629 agreements, distributed as follows: 1870-80, 56 titles; 1880–90, 217 titles; 1890–1900, 580 titles; 1900–1914, 776 titles. Although it is common knowledge that the customary royalty rate of the period immediately following the Civil War was 10 per cent, no statistical survey had been made to confirm the fact, or to show the extent of the transition to higher rates in later years. The following table summarizes the information now made available by the Harper ledgers:

HARPER ROYALTY RATES, 1870–1914

Contract Terms	10%	12½%	15%	20%
1870–80	75%	5%	5%	——
1880–90	85%	3%	3%	.4%
1890–1900	53%	4%	22%	4%
1900–14	28%	.6%	18%	14%

After 1890, there were a number of contracts which specified a royalty of 25 per cent; a few reached 30 per cent. But most of these involved books for which the authors supplied the plates, inducing the publisher to concede an extra 5 per cent. The most prominent writers—Gertrude Atherton, Rex Beach, Irving Bacheller, and Finley Peter Dunne among them—received 20 per cent.

However, these figures should be corrected to take some account of the contracts which specified a sliding scale of royalty rates, increasing proportionately to sales. Almost unknown in the 1880's, this clause appeared in 13 per cent of the Harper contracts of the next decade and in 32 per cent of those negotiated between 1900 and 1914. It may be considered as another evidence of the improved position of authors, although it harmonized also with the publishers' desire to minimize the writers' returns until the original costs of publication were met. That it met the logical wishes of both is perhaps revealed by the fact that the sliding scale contract continued to increase in popularity until it became a common feature of most agreements.

On the other hand, the use of such a scale was often merely a theoretical rather than a practical advantage to the writers, since the sales were seldom large enough to make the higher royalty rates operative. Although the trade was considered speculative enough to prevent accurate prognostications of sales, Harper and Brothers appeared to have an uncanny ability to draw these contracts so that the minimum rate was usually the only one employed. That this may be attributed solely to accurate predictions is doubtful; but there can be little question that publishers found the sliding scale an inexpensive device with which to meet their authors' unwarranted optimism.

Up to 1914, very few contracts called for the same scale of increases. All except a few specified a minimum rate of either 10 per cent or 15 per cent, the former accounting for 21 per cent of the Harper contracts, while one in ten commenced at the latter percentage. But both the amount of the increase and the number of sales after which a higher rate would apply varied immensely. Among those agreements which started at 10 per cent, there were as many providing for a 12½ per cent or 15 per cent rate of return after the sale of 10,000 copies as after 1,500. The contracts with a minimum of 15 per cent called for an average sale of 5,000 copies before an increase; but several employed a higher rate after half as many sales and in two agreements 50,000 copies had to be sold before the royalty was advanced.

Although differences in initial advertising appropriations and the costs of manufacture help explain these gyrations, the evidence favors an interpretation giving more credit to the skill of Harper and Brothers in anticipating the probable sales of each book. The firm's ledgers contain the sales records of ninety-five books published between 1900 and 1914 whose contracts contained a sliding-scale clause. Only two of these passed the mark at which other than the minimum royalty applied. What is even more remarkable is the large number of titles whose sales fell just short of the required number. For example, the contract with Gilbert Parker for *A Ladder of Swords* gave him a 15 per cent royalty up to 50,000 copies, but 20 per cent over that amount; after the book had been in print eight years, the total sales were 47,368. William N. Harben's *Nobody's* sold 3,801 copies under a contract specifying an advanced royalty after 5,000 copies. His next book, *Jane Dawson,* sold 9,676 copies, but the agreement under which it was published required a sale of 10,000 before his 15 per cent royalty was raised to 20 per cent. Less popular books had a similarly frustrating time in reaching their lower minimums. A sale of 1,000 would have increased Rudolf Eickemeyer's royalty on *Winter* from 10 per cent to 15 per cent, but in nine years the book found only 789 buyers. Philip Mighels' *Dunny* was to bring 15 per cent after 2,500 copies had been disposed of, but the sales of six years amounted to but 2,458.

After the First World War, the bargaining element which appears to have been present in the early use of the sliding scale gradually disappeared, leaving merely a principle that the higher rates of authors' returns would await the partial reimbursement to the publisher of his initial fixed costs. In place of a multiplicity of scales there would be a more or less standard contract providing for 10 per cent on the first 2,500 copies, 12½ per cent on the subsequent 2,500, and 15 per cent on all sales above 5,000.

Since writers commonly received no more than the minimum rate, the contracts specifying a sliding scale can be added to those used in the preceding table without causing a sizeable distortion. The combined totals show the following:

HARPER ROYALTY RATES

Contract Terms	10%*	12½%	15%**	20%
1870–80	75%	5%	5%	——
1880–90	87%	3%	3%	.4%
1890–1900	62%	4%	26%	4%
1900–14	49%	.6%	29%	14%

* Includes sliding scale contracts providing for a minimum of 10%.

* * Includes sliding scale contracts providing for a minimum of 15%.

While the decline in the use of a 10 per cent royalty is thus revealed to be less precipitous, the number of contracts calling for a royalty of 15 per cent or more is increased to 43 per cent for the years after 1900, as opposed to the less than 4 per cent of the decade of the 1880's.[25]

Even these figures do not adequately represent the more favored position which the writers came to assume after 1890. Previous mention has been made of the use of advances to authors, which became significant at about the same date. "This matter of big advances," wrote Robert Yard in 1905, "is another English institution as unwelcome as the English sparrow, and it is his insistence upon it that has chiefly caused the literary agent's American unpopularity." [26] Not only did these advance payments against as yet unearned royalties put a severe strain on working capital; they also heightened the speculative element of the business by obliging the publisher to gamble that the sales of a book would be sufficient for the royalties to equal the sum advanced. Indeed, an advance resembled a one-sided bet between author and publisher in which the latter had much to lose but nothing, except the writer's good will, to win. Charles Scribner described the common practice when he wrote: [27]

I think there is no misunderstanding about the $2500. We regard it as an advance payment of royalties, the sum to be made good to us from the royalties derived from the book, but we do not hold you in any way responsible for its payment if by any chance the royalties do not equal that sum. It is usual to pay the advance on the date of publication.

Put in general terms, an advance constituted a liability for the author only to the extent that he was able to discharge it from the earnings of his book. If the accrued royalties were inadequate to repay the debt, then the publisher had no recourse except to charge off the deficit in his accounts. It was the practice of Harper and Brothers to make an adjustment each year, posting a loss on books which had not sold sufficiently to meet the advances on them and for which there was little or no prospect of future earnings. In 1900, a total loss of over $17,000 was taken on the advances for thirty-six books, the average being $488 and the greatest single amount being the $4,588 sacrificed on John Motley's *Correspondence*.[28] The historian was in respectable company, for the delinquent titles include books by H. G. Wells, Henry James, and Stephen Crane. If the average royalty is assumed to be 12½ per cent and the average selling price of these volumes is figured at $2, it can be estimated that each author received royalties on about 1,900 more copies than were sold. Stated differently, the royalties paid on the copies actually sold were at a rate substantially in excess of that provided in the contracts.

Unfortunately, the records do not reveal the total royalties paid in 1900 by Harper and Brothers. But if the $17,000 loss on advances in 1900 is compared with the royalty disbursements for 1894—the latest year for which a total can be computed—its significance becomes clear. In that year, the writers received $45,332. Even if this sum is tripled to account for the lapse in time, the amount paid out in excessive advances adds some 13 per cent to the collective income of the Harper authors.[29]

Another practice which grew was the custom of signing contracts for unwritten manuscripts. Since the offers were generally confined to established writers, it is difficult to say whether publishing was thereby made more speculative or less. In either case, one of the peculiarities of the industry is clearly exhibited by this willingness or necessity to make commitments involving many thousands of dollars for unexamined merchandise. Charles Scribner wrote to Richard T. Ely in 1898: [30]

> We do not think it necessary for us to see the notes for your *Distribution of Wealth* if you are reluctant to part with them. If you can tell us more definitely about the size of the work and when the volume will be ready, and how much advance you would require for the stenographer, we are sure a contract for that book could be quickly made. . . . The ten percent royalty is a very reasonable demand and we think we might pay a little larger royalty.

The earliest important use of these agreements in advance of creation was connected with uncopyrighted British works. However dubious the commercial advantage of receiving advance sheets, the certain popularity of any work by the great Victorian novelists made the contracts more plausible than many signed in the 1890's with lesser writers whose works were fully protected by law. The value of a story in the mind of Dickens was scarcely a matter of speculation. But it was questionable that there were many others whose talent was so sure and whose public was so devoted that their books were assured successes before they were written. Harper and Brothers, for example, were committed to large sums for whatever William Dean Howells cared to write, but some of his books sold less than 3,000 copies.[31]

To understand the relation of these higher royalties to cost, one must remember that the rates came to be universally reckoned on the basis of retail price. Consequently, an increase of 5 per cent in the author's return added more than that percentage to the publisher's expenses. For example, a book priced at $1.50 brought the publisher, under the prevailing 40 per cent wholesale discount, only 90¢. If the writer's royalty was 10 per cent, then the 15¢ which he received equalled 17 per cent of the publisher's gross profit. But if the royalty was increased to 15 per cent, it amounted to 25 per cent of the publisher's proceeds. In a business where the net profit on a successful book averaged 10¢, and might be as little as 2½¢,[32] royalties could not continue to rise except at the peril of the industry.

The years between 1900 and 1910 witnessed the climax of the authors' drive for a greater share of the profits of publishing. On the eve of the World War, it was apparent that the peak had been passed. Some few writers continued to receive 20 per cent royalties, but 15 per cent was considered the maximum for all but the most popular novelists, and the hopes of the average were restricted to the dubious promise contained in the sliding-scale clause.[33] Nevertheless, authors did not as a whole lose all that they had gained, and the general improvement from which they benefited after 1890 is significant enough to deserve further comment. A partial explanation has been offered in the preceding chapter. At the root of the matter lay a more intense competition among publishers for the desirable manuscripts. Literary agents who solicited bids and took the best offer, popular magazines which raised the rates for literary production, undoubtedly had a part in increasing the rivalry. Among the causative factors, the passage in 1891 of a Congressional act protecting foreign authors from exploitation is the most difficult to judge. For many years before this time, American authors had urged such a law, asserting that they could not compete with pirated works which cost the publishers nothing. Publishers who paid honorariums to English authors under "trade courtesy," and those who excluded themselves from the market rather than to stoop to theft, were equally vociferous in advocating an international copyright agreement for the protection of writers both here and abroad.

As early as 1840, the famous Philadelphia house of Carey wrote William Gilmore Simms: [34]

> We do not see much hope in the future for the American writer of light literature—as a matter of profit it might be abandoned. The channel seems to be glutted with periodical literature, par-

ticularly the mammoth weeklies—besides which we go into market for $1.50 a copy against English reprints at 90¢.

Forty years later, Charles Scribner was writing: [35]

We regret very much that the sales are not larger. As we wrote in regard to "Louisiana", the sales of all *copyrighted* novels have very materially fallen off, owing to the unfair competition which makes it possible to sell any of George Eliot's novels for 10 cts.

One of the first best-seller polls, conducted by *Publishers' Weekly* in 1876 as a contest among booksellers, contained this instruction to the participants: "It should be noted that from these lists, works of Bulwer, Dickens, George Eliot, Scott and Thackeray were excluded since they, of course, stood at the head of standard novelists. . . ." [36] Even to the fondest admirers of English prose, it was evident that cheap availability was as important to this popularity as was intrinsic worth. On the eve of copyright, the British continued to dominate the market.

In 1900, Charles Scribner was requested by the U. S. Department of Commerce and Labor to answer a series of questions about the International Copyright law, then in its eighth year of operation. Part of his reply reads: [37]

The American author has been benefited . . . in that there is more encouragement for the publisher to pay the American author when he cannot take for nothing the works of English authors. It is an interesting fact that since the law was passed, books which have the greatest sale in America are by native authors, such as Churchill's "Richard Carvel", Wescott's "David Harum", Major's "When Knighthood was in Flower", Ford's "Janice Meredith", Page's "Red Rock", etc., whereas a few years ago such a list would be made up almost entirely of books of foreign authorship.

Unfortunately, it is impossible to support this generalization with statistical proof; but since it was confirmed by other leading publishers and meets any test imposed by the logic of the situation, it may not be seriously questioned.

It should be remembered also that for long years, much of the bitter competition in the publishing industry was generated by these pirated works. A situation was created in which most of the prominent trade houses presented a common front against the reprint firms, limiting their own rivalry by such devices as honorariums. Once the copyright act was passed, a major change took place in the book market. With the departure of the "pirates," the regular publishers were left facing each other in a scramble not only for writers, but also for what seemed to be a more attractive market. It is not too much to suppose that apart from the improved bargaining position of both English and American authors, the better business prospects encouraged higher royalties generally. Further, it was at about this time that the publishers appear to have "discovered" advertising, and for a time flirted with the idea that they had found a panacea for the trade which it was beyond the power of large royalties to destroy. It is no coincidence that the partial return to earlier rates accompanied the first wave of disillusion with expensive publicity.[38]

Private Publishing and Public Speech

chapter 5

The social function of the publishing industry was to supply the nation with its books, a grave duty of which the trade was steadily aware. Upon the manner in which this responsibility was discharged depended the extent to which the principle of free speech was made an actuality in the world of books, which gives thought its most permanent and probably its most important expression.

In the files of Scribner, Armstrong and Company for 1877 there is a letter from a translator proposing an American edition of Karl Marx's *Das Kapital.* Appended is a note with the initials of Blair Scribner: "Please send an answer—of course we don't want the book." [1] In 1887 there appeared in the trade journal called *The Book Buyer* a large advertisement for the firm of Scribner and Welford offering for sale the same book which had been so curtly and contemptuously dismissed ten years before.[2] Perhaps no problem is more serious for the student of American publishing than to determine which of the two incidents characterized the trade as a whole. Yet there are large difficulties in the way of discovering why some books were chosen for publication and others were rejected. More often than not, publishers did not reveal to authors why manuscripts were declined. If the memoranda from readers to editors had been retained, they would undoubtedly be more informative than the extant outgoing correspondence. But such matters of policy as whether to publish a good exposition of an heretical view were usually settled at a conference table from which no records emerged. The devotion and assiduity which Morris Ernst has lavished on documenting the progress of free opinion in America has produced splendid historical studies, but none of them contains more than a word in passing about the publisher as censor. What little evidence is available for this present study is somewhat contradictory, but worthy of careful analysis.

Alfred Harcourt, who commenced his successful career near the turn of the century, thought that the publications of a given house necessarily took their character from the tastes and opinions of its members.[3]

> Essentially, the standards of the imprint are the standards of the publisher and his editorial colleagues. The fields covered by the books of a particular house cannot significantly, except by accident, go much beyond the intellectual interests and standards of the publishing personnel. . . . A publisher who doesn't follow his personal interests and those of his colleagues, who sees that certain sorts of books sell and so tries to get books in realms in which no one on his staff is particularly interested, is apt to come a cropper on these ventures and to find he is publishing "just another book" or promoting some sensational title which in the long run does harm to his reputation.

Once the specialties of a firm were established, there was a natural tendency for them to be continued. Not only was there a continuity to editorial policy; it was also true that travel books on a list attracted other travel books to it. Even though the public was oblivious to the significance of an imprint, writers and booksellers learned to associate certain kinds of books with particular houses. Beyond the matter of taste and tradition, there was the fact of experience. A company which customarily published books dealing with public questions gained a facility in handling them. Henry Holt wrote: [4]

> Not a little experience in the particular direction in question convinces us that the more books of the same general character and appealing to the same general class there are on one list, the better for each of them. . . . The closer any publisher associates with a given market, the better he is able to serve his clients.

At about the same time Charles Scribner was advising a successful author: "We are not the best ones to publish the book, which should be pushed in directions where our machinery is not especially effective." [5]

However, the independence of a publisher was subject to important limitations. While his list could acquire its own personality, it could not ever divorce itself from the interests of the buying public. If the public was addicted to historical novels, it was going to be supplied with them, even by publishers who much preferred poetry. Popular reading tastes influenced the trade as much as the trade influenced popular reading tastes. A book which caught the public fancy was likely to institute a search by other publishers for similar books. To Frederick Crofts this imitativeness seemed a major determinant in publishing practice: [6]

The tendency to follow the leader is one which all publishers seem unable to resist. An innovation in format, an unusual locale, or an original approach which results in a best seller is promptly duplicated. This is partially due to the fact that a publishing house is not an eleemosynary institution, and is entitled to profit from any definite indication of the public's immediate interest.

Far from being a deterrent to free expression, the profit motive appears to have been its greatest ally. "Publishers have a duty to publish stuff containing ideas they don't like—besides there's money in it," said Crofts.[7] A half-century before, Charles Scribner wrote his London partner, "You write that you do not know what I want in books to reprint. I can only say I want anything that *will sell*. . . ."[8] But this statement fails to reveal a number of assumptions in Scribner's mind which set up tests any book had to pass before its commercial desirability could become operative. The leading publishers of the "Gilded Age" were a reasonably homogeneous group which took pride in its conservatism. As pillars of the church and guardians of the family, they were as steadfastly traditional in their personal ideals as in their public convictions. The contest for the unhampered expression of ideas pitted these standards against the gleam of gold. Hovering in the background, and emerging from time to time to tilt a favorable balance, was the democratic principle which intelligent Americans of all beliefs shared, that the country's welfare was best served by the free exchange of opinion.

The most formidable censorship in the publishing world was directed against religious heresy, "We have been and are loth to publish much of the current scientific literature because it is mostly atheistic in its tendency," wrote Blair Scribner in 1877.[9] A half-century later, another Scribner was similarly inclined to put faith before profits: [10]

On the 5th I cabled "Decline reprint Carpenter's Creeds". . . . It is very radical—anti-Christian. We have done very well with the author's other books and would be willing to buy an edition of this one and supply it to customers, but we could not give it our moral support.

An excerpt from Henry Holt's correspondence reveals the typical mood, couched in an acidity which betrays the depth of feeling an heretical writer had to overcome: [11]

You are, permit me to say, in some little danger of confusing your book with some inferior ones by frequent use of their characteristic terms. "Free-thought" . . . has more implications of freedom from thought than of free range of thought, while a "free-thinker" is generally an unshorn and unwashed person, loud with misrepresentations of other people's thoughts and innocent from birth to death of any thought of his own.

However, this repulsion was seldom absolute. If means existed to disassociate the name of the house from a good book advocating repugnant religious views, most publishers were not loath to assist in its distribution. Sometimes, the line at which acquiescence turned to sanction was so thin that one wonders why it was drawn at all. Charles Scribner wrote to his London representative in 1886: [12]

I send to you enclosed . . . a letter from Edgar Saltus about a new book of his. He is a well-known literary fellow here and has published two good books with *Houghton.* He offered this book to me but I did not care to publish it, mainly on account of its atheism. It would be a capital book for S[cribner] & W[elford] and I write to him today that we should be glad to arrange with Williams and Norgate. I think we could sell 250 at a fair price. The book should bear the imprint of S[cribner] & W[elford] and the copyright notice 1886 by Edgar Saltus.

Since the firm of Scribner and Welford was owned by Scribner and carried his name, one wonders why the distinction between it and Charles Scribner's Sons was important enough to satisfy his moral objections. But whether the move was inspired by commercial opportunism or an adherence to some principle of free expression seems less important than that the industry was flexible enough to give circulation to unpopular thoughts.

Probably the most effective sponsor of unorthodox viewpoints among the prominent houses was D. Appleton and Company, the American publisher of Charles Darwin, John Tyndall, and Thomas Huxley. When the distinguished William H. Appleton died in 1899, *Publishers' Weekly* considered it laudatory to say of him: [13]

Throughout his career Mr. Appleton, himself a strong clergyman, took the position that while a publisher should decline immoral or absolutely irreligious books, he was at liberty to issue books representing radically different phases of belief without the presumption that his imprint meant endorsement.

A perusal of the company's lists over a long span of years testifies to the correctness of this appraisal. For example, ten years before his death, a front cover advertisement in *Publishers' Weekly* announced: "*Christianity and Agnosticism—a Controversy;* Consisting of Papers by Henry Wace, Prof. Thomas H. Huxley, The Bishop of Peterborough, W. H. Mallock, Mrs. Humphry Ward." [14] The proof of the system was in the eating, and America had a diet of exotic as well as of familiar foods.

Concern over the protection of the orthodox faiths blended naturally into an apprehensiveness about the effect of "bad" books on morals. The confusion of literature with Victorian pretense produced more saccharinity than artistic achievement. A sample bit is reflected in Scribner's announcement in 1872 of a new series of books called "A Library of Choice Fiction," the leading characteristics of which were proclaimed to be "purity and elevation of tone." The prospectus promised that "no place shall be found in this 'library' for works in the remotest degree demoralizing or purely sensation." [15] One of the important differences between the 1859 and 1872 catalogues of Harper and Brothers was the large increase in the number of third-rate novels designed primarily for their moral effect. Miss Bremer's *The Home* was recommended for "the moral beauty and womanly purity which steadily illuminate her narrative," while Mrs. Dana's *Forecastle Tom* was described as "a delightful little domestic story, inculcating morality, religion, and temperance in a most attractive manner." [16] The prominent trade houses shared in the same impulse which led in 1873 to the formation of the New York Society for the Suppression of Vice under the fanatic leadership of Anthony Comstock.[17]

Publishers were especially on guard against any manuscript which seemed to condone a sin against the marriage vows. One of Scribner's editorial assistants reported in 1887: [18]

> I have no hesitation in advising you to decline Mrs. Gertrude Atherton's novel, "The Randolphs",—principally for the reason that it is an apology for adultery. . . . The defense of the intended adulterous connection is delivered from the mouth of St. John, who uses the customary free-love sophistries, treating marriage as a "conventionality" and the "union of souls" as the only bond, etc., but the writer leaves us in little doubt that the sentiments of her hero are her own. . . .

Three days before, Charles Scribner had more diplomatically informed the author, "Your stories are entirely unsuitable for our list of publications both in motive and treatment." [19] When the publishers retreated before a public demand for franker expression, they took their next stand in an insistence not only that sexual irregularities be condemned—even though described—but also that a pretense of an artistic intent higher than vulgar titillation be employed wherever possible. Henry Holt explained this point to an author in 1903: [20]

> Your erotics are a little more outspoken than they need to be. An allusion is generally enough, and in your inevitable character of twentieth century author, the freedom at Karl's feast should be "explained" as the fashion of the time. . . . A word of incidental "explanation" in such places will change, for many readers, an impression of bad taste on your part, into one of scholarship, and into gratitude for instruction.

One suspects that Holt may be credited for having set down, at a single stroke, the formula for many modern historical novels.

The trend of naturalistic fiction after 1890 caused considerable confusion in the ranks of publishers who were at the same time conscientiously moral and sincerely devoted to good literature. *Publishers' Weekly,* which had long crusaded against "sensational" fiction, was frank to observe that Shakespeare and the Bible had passages calculated to bring on a maiden's blush; and unlike the morbid Mr. Comstock, it was willing to acknowledge Zola's greatness as a writer.[21] After careful consideration, the influential trade organ concluded: [22]

> Books that are obviously literature—marked, that is to say, by a certain intelligence and culture and intended to be read by cultivated people—whose prime intent is evidently not to incite to vice, though in the hands of the unwary they may have that effect, are not fit subjects for the voluntary censor's action.

This was a formula which many respectable publishers ultimately followed. But before it could be established, the trade went through a period of soul-searching which persisted to the eve of the First World War. Charles Scribner expressed the dilemma in 1911: [23]

> That is one of the great difficulties now; so many of the well-known English authors—like Wells, Arnold Bennett, George Moore, and others—are too free and coarse in their handling of delicate questions, to suit us. I enjoy their books personally but our imprint would sometimes be injured by association with such books. It is very hard to tell where the dividing line comes and we sometimes make mistakes, for the public is becoming more and more calloused.

At least one mistake had been made five years before when the firm rejected Arnold Bennett's great novel, *The Old Wives' Tale,* because of its "unpleasant and sordid details." [24]

A new group of American novelists presented a similar

problem. George H. Doran recently expressed his satisfaction at having rejected in the beginning of his career, "everything by that ruffian Dreiser." [25] Harper and Brothers similarly turned its back on *Sister Carrie,* which was finally accepted by Doubleday, Page. The latter firm soon questioned its decision, and when the author refused to release it from a contract, brought out the novel in a small edition to minimize circulation. However, Harper and Brothers gathered sufficient strength to publish *Jennie Gerhardt* a few years later as the era ended.[26]

The ultimate stand of the trade gave wide latitude to an author's choice of materials and expression when they were joined to an artistic purpose. However reluctantly their decision was taken, the best publishers did not insist upon imposing their morality or upon limiting writers to the vocabulary they used in their homes. Although the literary *avant-garde* continued to protest, the average book-buyer had small cause to feel that literature was being stifled by Victorian prudes masquerading as publishers. Rather, those who knew the exacting personal codes by which men like Frank Dodd and Charles Scribner lived, had more reason to be amazed that the accommodation had been so quick and complete. Looking back over fifty years of experience, the patriarch Frederick Stokes expressed the youthful outlook of the trade when he said: [27]

Publishers have the courage of their convictions when certain phases of human life are treated with high artistic purpose. They are constantly seeking new technique in literary work and perhaps have found some rather extreme examples of this. However, just as modernism in music and painting have affected those arts favorably, . . . so has literature generally received benefits from the tendencies of the time. However, it seems true that certain writers, to quote Victor Hugo's words, "confuse the stars of heaven with the tracks made by a duck's feet in the mud."

As a test of freedom of thought, the extent to which conflicting political and economic doctrines could be urged in the publications of the leading houses was far more significant than the latitude allowed to advocates of radical moralities and unconventional literary devices. There can be little question that the social Darwinism of Herbert Spencer had no less appeal for publishers than for other men of business. Indeed, Spencer owed much of his initial popularity to the enthusiasm of Edward Youmans and his employer, William Appleton, who first issued *Social Statics* in America.[28] The complaints of the trade that government was interfering unduly in business were almost as constant as the requests for an international copyright law. As early as 1877, *Publishers' Weekly* felt obliged to remind the Post Office Department: "It is one of the cardinal American principles that our government is not to run other people's business."[29] If voting habits are a test of receptivity to new ideas, unorthodox political writers had reason to be dismayed at the steadfast Republicanism of the publishing fraternity. Charles Scribner placed himself with the most unenlightened faction of the party when he said in 1880 that Grant's re-election was "far preferable to that of any Democrat."[30]

That the trade's spokesmen would be more responsive to political and economic works which reflected their own viewpoints should not be surprising. Many radical writers, even of the stature of Henry George, had to become their own publishers in order to reach the reading public.[31] So eminently worthy a nineteenth century target as Tammany Hall acquired the protection of the publishers' sensitivities when it was subjected to the radical attack of Gustavus Myers. Henry Holt confessed that an exposure couched in terms with which he himself agreed would not be accepted for publication because of the "unpleasantries its publishers would have to endure." [32] Myers' comprehensive assault on American capitalists, the *History of the Great American Fortunes*, encountered an even more hostile reception, some details of which the author recounted in the preface to a recent edition. The excerpts quoted from his correspondence with established publishers give the impression —undoubtedly because Myers chose them for that purpose —that it was the truth rather than any distortion of it which was the obstacle to publication.[33]

> It seems to me . . . that if the narratives were presented with accuracy, they must, of necessity, contain certain statements or data which would be considered objectionable by the present representatives of the families concerned. . . . As a practical example, it would not be possible to present the career of Jay Gould without describing in pretty plain English certain noteworthy undertakings in which he was concerned. On the other hand we should be entirely unwilling to print anything that could possibly cause offense to his daughter, Helen Gould, who is one of the best citizens in this country. . . . It is possible that some more enterprising or less scrupulous house might be ready to give favorable consideration to the plan.

When naturalistic novelists like Theodore Dreiser turned from the degradation of the slums to the moral delinquencies of business leaders, they found the regular publishers loath to follow them. *The Titan,* based on the unsavory career of C. T. Yerkes, was purchased in 1914 by Harper and Brothers only to be repressed.[34] Upton Sinclair's *The Jungle,* with his plea for socialism scattered through its pages, was rejected by five houses before it became a best-selling novel of 1906.[35]

Were this the whole story, it would not be an encouraging one for those who expect a system of publishing to produce outstanding books of every shade of opinion. But balancing these evidences of censorship is a more impressive record of a willingness among conservative houses to place their imprints upon works highly critical of the American system. The reasons for this display of accommodation are less important than the results of it, but supply a useful framework for exposition. Among them, a desire for profits must take a first rank. Today's generation, taught to be aware of the limitations placed on free expression by the power of advertisers and the extension of monopolistic control over media of communication, has special reason to remember that neither monopoly nor advertisers characterize the world of books. Because of this, the capitalistic compulsion for more sales and wider markets operated with a freedom which produced works of a great variety of viewpoints, many of them not remotely resembling those of the publishers.

An instructive example of the alliance between commercial values and free thought is contained in a letter written by Charles Scribner to his London agent in 1910: [36]

> By this mail I send you sheets of a new book by Frederic C. Howe entitled "Privilege and Democracy in America." . . . Of course its title stamps it as more American but it is socialistic in its tendency and almost sensational in its attack upon the trusts and privilege and it might appeal to British interest.

The significance of such a book being published by a man who loathed the tenets of socialism pales before the spectacle of the work being urged on a buyer precisely because it was socialistic.

Supporting this commercial motivation was an intelligent recognition that however admirable the American system, it had produced mistakes and injustices better corrected than ignored. Jacob Riis' books on the slums of New York and the exploitation of working people were not calculated to inspire national pride, but Charles Scribner did not hesitate to place his imprint upon them, and to admire their author for his constructive investigations. A respect for the American form of government and its achievements did not prevent the members of the old Boston firm of Roberts Brothers from publishing Helen Hunt's *A Century of Dishonor,* which indicted the country for its shabby treatment of the Indian population.

Incomplete records make it impossible to determine the exact motivation for the publication under conservative auspices of many books attacking the capitalist system as a whole, or giving special prominence to its weaknesses. But at least it can be said negatively that such titles show that the censorship of publishers in the field of government and economics was of a restrained variety. Examples of this kind are numerous enough to support a generalization. Within a few months of its publication, Scribner and Welford imported an edition of the first English translation of Karl Marx's *Das Kapital,* which was sold for $12 a set. Less than a year later, D. Appleton and Company announced the same book at one-fourth the price, an enterprise which can scarcely be credited to William Appleton's deep antipathy to radical thought.[37] The scholarly assaults of Thorstein Veblen similarly bore the imprints of publishers who disagreed violently with much that they sought to prove; *The Theory of the Leisure Class* was brought out in 1899 by The Macmillan Company and *The Theory of Business Enterprise* by another staunch defender of capitalism, Charles Scribner.[38] Henry Demarest Lloyd's *Wealth Against Commonwealth,* denouncing John D. Rockefeller and the Standard Oil Company, received the backing of Harper and Brothers in 1894. Even an association with J. P. Morgan did not restrain that firm from publishing *The Financier,* Theodore Dreiser's fictionalized attack on banking in high places. When The Macmillan Company put its name in 1904 on the title page of John Spargo's *The Bitter Cry of the Children,* it gave circulation not only to a denunciation of child labor, but also to the work of a writer who believed that socialism was the only remedy for the future. The Marxist coloring of Jack London's *War of the Classes* and the mechanistic economic determinism of Charles Beard's *An Economic Interpretation of the Constitution of the United States* proved to be no insurmountable barriers to publication by The Macmillan Company.

This survey subjects the system of private publishing to a severe test, since it accounts only for the assistance given to the dissemination of radical thought by the oldest and most conservative houses. Whatever opportunity was withheld by the occasional reluctance of these firms was more often than not supplied by new firms with fewer traditions and perhaps more need for spectacular books. Doubleday, Page and Company was hardly inspired by a radical philosophy, but in the decade following its organization in 1899 it published, among others, Henry Demarest Lloyd's *Men, the Workers,* Upton Sinclair's *The Jungle,* Frank Norris' *The Octopus* and *The Pit,* and Ray Stannard Baker's *Following the Color Line.*

But even these firms, devoted to commerce rather than ideology, did not define the outside limit of the outlets available to unorthodox social and economic thinkers. There was no legal obstacle to prevent the crusaders of the left from forming their own publishing houses. Neither was the business such that their costs of publication would be appreciably greater than those of the most efficient traditional firms. *Frenzied Finance,* containing Thomas Lawson's exposure of methods in the copper industry, and *The Greatest Trust in the World,* in which Charles Edward Russell revealed the iniquities of the beef trust, both bore the imprint of The Ridgway-Thayer Company. Many socialist works, including John Spargo's *The Common Sense of Socialism,* came out under the auspices of an otherwise inconspicuous Chicago firm, C. H. Kerr and Company. The same hospitality shown to the muckrakers by *McClure's Magazine, Everybody's Magazine,* and *Cosmopolitan* was identified with the book publishing house of McClure, Phillips and Company, which printed Lincoln Steffens' *The Shame of the Cities* and Burton J. Hendrick's exposure of corruption in the life insurance business.[39]

There is one notable area of publishing to which this freedom did not extend. Educational publishers were not only compelled to conform to the desires of a multitude of official judgments, but also desired themselves to have textbooks reflect the more orthodox economic and social ideas. Unfortunately, the number of concrete instances which could be cited of the censorship of publishers in this period are too few and too petty to permit an extended discussion. For this reason, educational books are not included in the present analysis.

Comparing the various kinds of censorship in which publishers indulged, one must consider the possibility that it was more severe in matters of religion and morals than in the fields of economics and politics. George H. Doran took pride in having rejected Dreiser and Hemingway and in censoring Dos Passos' naturalistic vocabulary,[40] but he was willing to publish Charles Edward Russell's *Why I Am a Socialist*. Charles Scribner was repelled by the coarseness of Arnold Bennett's *The Old Wives' Tale*, but brought out the work of Thorstein Veblen. The difference between Herbert Spencer and a Marxist or a muckraker was essentially greater than that between *Huckleberry Finn* and *The American Tragedy*. Yet Dreiser's difficulties in getting published were no less than John Spargo's or Henry Demarest Lloyd's, and there is reason to think they were more considerable.

The greater strength of moral objections among publishers seems less remarkable when it is recalled that the same emphasis was shown in law and in the work of the numerous semiofficial censoring bodies which trailed after Anthony Comstock. Morris Ernst and William Seagle defined the Victorian attitude when they wrote: [41]

If the Age of Faith adopted the index of heresy, the Age of Divine Right the index of treason, it was inevitable for the Age of Democracy to adopt the index of sex.

Although it was not until 1917 that the United States found it necessary to curb the tradition of "unfettered political criticism," [42] the years immediately after the Civil War saw the passage of many laws concerning immoral books. In 1873, "with less than ten minutes of debate, the Congress of the United States enacted the Comstock Law, under which there was placed in a separate banned area all material which would excite sexually impure thoughts." Every state except New Mexico followed the lead of the federal government.[43] New York was among the few states which, even before the national postal law was enacted, made illegal the sale and distribution of "obscene, lewd, lascivious, filthy, indecent, or disgusting" books.[44]

The vagueness of the obscenity laws was both their strength and weakness. As they were interpreted by such groups as the New York Society for the Prevention of Vice and Boston's Watch and Ward Society, they outlawed poetical masterpieces like Walt Whitman's *Leaves of Grass,* naturalistic fiction from Boccaccio to Dreiser, and scientific works designed for sex education. Tolstoi's *Kreut-*

zer Sonata was one of Comstock's successful targets. When the book was excluded from the mails, Theodore Roosevelt felt called upon as an official of New York's police department to denounce the author as a "sexual and moral pervert." [45] The height of absurdity was reached when in 1911 the post office forbade John D. Rockefeller to use the mails to send copies of the Report of the Chicago Vice Commission to a group of trained sociologists.[46]

In such an atmosphere, publishers were justified in feeling apprehensive. Although persecution sometimes aided a book's sales, the notoriety of a trial was hardly welcomed. While the vice societies ordinarily attacked small booksellers or defenseless clerks rather than corporations,[47] conscientious publishers shared some measure of the blame when a verdict of guilty was reached. The Watch and Ward Society ultimately became powerful enough to induce the Boston booksellers voluntarily to forego circulating any book which the Society labeled undesirable.[48] Morris Ernst has revealed that some of the reputable publishers were equally cooperative, submitting manuscripts to Comstock for his approval before their publication.[49] Although no indication is given when the practice arose, it is Ernst's further contention that the forms used by editorial assistants in reporting on manuscripts often required an answer to the question: "Is there anything in the book that would make it liable to prosecution by the Society for the Suppression of Vice? If so, please designate such pages." [50]

If such a formula was used during the half-century between the Civil and the World Wars, the archives of at least four New York houses do not reveal it. Perhaps this was partly because reputable publishers were as antagonistic to pornography as Comstock was, although they defined it differently; and they were similarly convinced of their moral responsibility to the public. But there are other reasons for questioning the completeness and willingness of the publishers' subservience to vice societies, from which Ernst feels they did not emerge between 1870 and 1915.[51] One of these was the strong stand which the leading trade organ occasionally took against the excesses of book prosecution. When, in 1902, the Chicago courts declared works of Edmond Rostand and Balzac to be "obscene," *Publishers' Weekly* came out with an editorial saying: [52]

> For the sake of the literary leadership so insisted upon for Chicago, it is to be hoped that she will not again for some time feel called upon to make or mar any literary reputation, or to decide upon the literary or moral character of the works of French authors.

Ten years before, the same journal had given unusual prominence to a report of a trial under the headline "Anthony Comstock Rebuked," and with an excerpt from the judge's decision which stated: "There are some things in this world that are much worse than sending obscene matter through the mail. One of them is the practice of fraud of which Mr. Comstock has apparently been guilty." [53] In 1910, there came from the same source a caustic attack upon some misguided zealots who had seen fit to exclude H. G. Wells' *Mr. Polly* and the works of Robert W. Chambers from a Midwestern library. "One is surprised," said the industry's spokesman, "only to notice the omission of 'Uncle Remus,' 'Uncle Tom's Cabin,' and Dickens' 'Christmas Carol.' " [54]

Neither should it be forgotten that many reputable publishers lent the sanction of their names to prosecuted books, a situation which would probably not have existed had the prior approval of vice societies and attorney generals been solicited and obtained. The name of the future Ambassador to Great Britain, Walter H. Page, appeared as publisher on the title page of both Dreiser's *Sister Carrie,* officially repressed in 1900,[55] and Sinclair's *The Jungle,* against whose mailing privileges an attack was made unsuccessfully a few years later.[56] Since Comstock's intended victims ranged over such classics as Henry Fielding's *Tom Jones,* Ovid's *Art of Love,* and Jean Jacques Rousseau's *Confessions,*[57] it would be difficult to imagine how any large publisher could cooperate fully with him and not sacrifice more than was gained.

Apart from the independence of publishers from such professional guardians of the public morality, there is the larger question of whether the censorship of publishers, added to the official strictures and the broad semiofficial interpretation of them, were, taken together, powerful enough to constitute a serious repression of thought. Without being able to make a very accurate quantitative estimate, one can safely conclude that in matters of faith and morals the combined censorship was material. However, the most serious test of free expression was posed by revolutionary political and economic doctrines; and in this field the joint efforts of publishers, Comstocks, and legislative bodies were the least repressive. In two books, Ernst has commented on the availability of laws of sex censorship for the purposes of limiting written political discussion.[58] Yet this opportunity was not exploited to any extent during the "Gilded Age," which produced more than its share of radical books under conservative auspices.

The words of Frederick Crofts approximate what seems to have been the working principle of the best part of the trade: [59]

> Regardless of the publisher's personal reactions to the "New Education", the "New History", or even the "New Deal", he must base his decision whether or not to publish a manuscript in any of these fields on the quality of the work and its adaptability to the market at which it is aimed. Should it happen that the phrase "Progressive Education" is the red flag to his particular bull, he should, nevertheless, publish an outstanding book in that field when the opportunity offers itself. This is more than good business discrimination. It is a duty which cannot be escaped.

The Creativeness of Publishing

chapter 6

While a few manuscripts were rejected for their questionable viewpoints, a large majority were declined simply because they held out so little hope of commercial success. As production facilities and markets multiplied and the annual total of new publications steadily rose, the maladjustment between the good writings produced and those which the trade could accommodate increased rather than declined. Such a situation was advantageous to well-executed works of an unorthodox variety, provided that they were not esoteric. By the turn of the century, trade leaders were inclined to apply the single test of marketability, and to stress the opportunities provided by the scarcity of manuscripts which satisfied this requirement. George Haven Putnam wrote in 1897: [1]

> It is certainly true that authors who can produce wares possessing commercial value find little difficulty in securing for them such value. Publishers are always on the lookout for real material.

Walter Page was equally persuaded of the opportunity for writers of talent: "There is not much danger (I do not believe there is any danger) that a manuscript of any value whatever will under present conditions fail to find a legitimate purchaser." [2]

One practical evidence that the publishers were never surfeited was their general unwillingness to let unsolicited manuscripts pass through their hands without being read. To accommodate the hundreds of works submitted each month to the leading houses required an outlay of many thousand dollars annually for editorial assistants.[3] The rewards of this diligence were meagre, since only a small fraction were selected for publication. But the wisdom of reading all the writing submitted was never seriously questioned by the trade publishers. Indeed, the practice appears to have been confirmed and regularized during the years when unsolicited books were gradually declining in importance on the publishers' lists.

As long as the trade stood ready to accept sizeable financial contributions from authors, the initiative for many books did not come from the publishers. Writers who guaranteed the expenses of publication were more like customers than partners, and there was good reason for welcoming their efforts. However, at the close of the era, the average house refused to enter such arrangements. The emphasis in publication gradually shifted from completed manuscripts which sought publishers to manuscripts which publishers sought and in which they were interested from their conception. Yet at the same time, unsolicited work received no less attention, and its volume necessitated an increasingly large editorial staff. Henry Holt explained this in part by saying: [4]

In our earlier and great age of authorship, most of the manuscripts offered to publishers could be safely rejected in five minutes, while in this slack water period of literature nearly every manuscript is so well written as to justify considerable attention.

In the dawn of publishing, a large percentage of all the manuscripts received were examined by the publishers themselves. For example, before Harper and Brothers grew to gigantic proportions in the 1850's, Fletcher Harper personally assumed the burden for the four partners.[5] However, the initial sifting was gradually turned over to editorial assistants. Although the publishers concentrated their attention on solicited materials already under contract, the system generally used at the turn of the century insured that every manuscript "above the level of illiteracy" received careful consideration. Most trade publishers submitted each work to at least two different "readers," who independently reported their opinions of its commercial value. A difference of opinion ordinarily led to a third reading, either by a member of the firm or a special consultant. Among the successful and better organized houses, the reports concerning books of any promise were referred to an editorial conference at which it was decided whether they merited further efforts.

The most valuable "first readers" were men and women who combined literary judgment with a common sense view of what kinds of manuscripts made commercially successful books. An ability to pronounce a writing definitely unfit was more cherished by employers than the capacity to find some cause for encouragement in a glimmer of talent shining through a mass of muddled prose.[6] Most "readers" did not work for a salary, but received a fee for each evaluation. Those who could be trusted to recognize a bad book in a minimum of pages were often paid on an hourly basis. Henry Holt outlined the scale of pay in the 1880's: [7]

Females—unaided light of nature ... 50¢
Males—general knowledge ... $1.00
Ditto—special knowledge—don't have any regular tariff and, in fact, are unknown in the business, but I think they are entitled to more than the general knowledge fellows.

A more common practice was to pay $5 for each report.[8] This fee, standard at the close of the nineteenth century, was still being offered a half-century later, a fact which may be attributed either to the declining importance of the "outside reader," or to the increase in the number of English "majors" graduated from Smith College.[9]

The group of "readers" who were consulted because of their special knowledge seldom received the regular fee, but could not be certain whether they would get more or less for their work. Often these experts were academic acquaintances whose relations with the publishers fell into a twilight zone between friendship and business. Henry Holt often avoided the necessity of placing a monetary value on their services by inviting them to select some books from his list.[10] Charles Scribner customarily paid them about three times as much as ordinary "first readers." [11]

Whether or not mistakes were made because books could

be rejected by relatively inexperienced editorial assistants is not revealed by the record. Holt's correspondence contains so many references to his custom of not reading incoming manuscripts that he appears almost to have assumed that it was not a publisher's responsibility.[12] On the other hand, Walter Page believed that the weakness of most American publishing houses lay in the fact that "the publisher himself does not read many manuscripts." [13] It is easier to explain why it happened than to estimate its effect. The editorial heads of the larger houses simply did not have time to read all the manuscripts submitted and fulfill their other responsibilities. But equally decisive was the decreasing dependence on works which came unheralded through the mails.

The failure of the authors to anticipate fully the manuscript needs of the trade is only one of several reasons why the publishing function came to include a large participation in the planning of books. The previously mentioned "commercializing" of the industry implied a closer attention to market demands which did not necessarily coincide with the independent interests of writers. To insure that his list would reflect public tastes, the publisher depended more and more on his own initiative. The mere hope that an author would submit a particular kind of book gave way to a deliberate effort to persuade someone to write it.

In its most extreme form, this editorial aggressiveness led to the founding of "literary factories." Edward Bok described their operation in the 1890's. A dozen or more employees were kept busy reading newspapers and periodicals, with instructions to mark any articles having unusual human interest. The best of these stories were then given to specialists to transform into outlines for the plots of novels. Each company had on file hundreds of writers to whom these skeletons of books would be sent with a blank form reading: [14]

To ________________

Please make of the inclosed material a _____ part story, not to exceed ________ words for each part.

Delivery of copy must be by ________ at the latest.

A check for $______ will be sent on receipt of the manuscript.

Notify us at once whether you can carry out this commission for us.

What was most surprising to Bok was the participation in this scheme of writers of considerable prominence, although their eagerness became more understandable when he learned the high prices paid for the completed material.

While this manufacture to order did not represent the standard practice of the trade, it suggests an important development. A suit of Estes and Lauriat against General Benjamin Butler for breach of contract brought forth from a representative of the Methodist Book Concern the testimony that the sale of large quantities of topical books by unknown authors was quite frequent. He added "We keep a book carpenter whose business it is to get up books on subjects we select." [15] Even this statement rather overstates the case by implying a degree of mechanization to the trade which did not exist among reputable firms. William Ellsworth told a story which reveals the more typical pattern: [16]

I remember long ago reading in a Sunday Tribune a paragraph which seemed to me just made for a story by Miss Mary E. Wilkins [later, Freeman]. I sent it to her. . . . Miss Wilkins was very grateful; she made a story out of it—and sent it, by the way, to another magazine.

The ingenuity of the reputable publishers was most often displayed in arranging for the writing of nonfiction rather than novels. Among the devices used to encourage desired books, none was more successful, and more representative of the creative thinking of the trade, than the planning of a series of titles grouped around some common theme. As early as 1869, J. B. Lippincott and Company produced "The Reason Why Series," which owed its existence not to the chance availability of a number of similar manuscripts, but to the decision of the house to produce it. George Putnam cited among the more successful projects instituted by the publishers "the *English Men of Letters* series, the *International Science* series, the *Stories of the Nation,* the *Heroes of the Nation.*" [17] Such a list could be extended almost endlessly. Charles Scribner, for example, conceived of a number of books dealing with *American Epochs,* and could count among his most successful publications the ten volumes collectively entitled *Campaigns of the Civil War.*[18] The correspondence of Henry Holt contains constant references to projected series on poets, the classics, and the various branches of natural and physical science. Among the many, the *American Scientific Series* and the *American Nature Series* were the most conspicuous.

Usually the planning of the publisher included the selection not only of a central theme, but also of the general level of the studies and the audience at which they would be directed. In 1879 Henry Holt wrote to Dr. S. Weir Mitchell: [19]

The book I ought to have suggested, would be best described by some such general title as "The Human Body" and should contain only the general knowledge required by the average educated man. Special and controverted questions should be merely steered away from.

However, such decisions were ordinarily not reached until specialists had been consulted, and a general editor appointed to assist in the selection of authors and the criticism of manuscripts. Occasionally these editors were themselves responsible for initiating the projects. Appleton's *International Scientific Series* owed more to Edward Youmans than to any member of the house. More often, they were brought in to lend their knowledge and the prestige of their names after the planning was well underway.

The publishers of series having some pretense to learning relied heavily upon the advice of academic experts. Henry Holt had a wide circle of acquaintances in the universities and few of his nonfiction titles were settled upon until after he had drawn on it for confirmation of his ideas. Such men as Daniel Coit Gilman of Johns Hopkins and T. R. Lounsbury of Yale often served as editors without portfolio, or pay, in helping to clarify the concept of a book and verify the ability of a particular man to write it.[20] This informal collaboration became especially common in the field of textbooks, where there was a steady decline in the number of unsolicited manuscripts. Travellers' visits to campuses increased in regularity and came to be as important for the editorial conferences in which they resulted as for sales.[21] The more publishers arranged for their books, whether educational or trade, the greater was their need for expert help.

Although the numerous series of books with which most lists came to abound is the best testimony to the creative planning of the trade, many individual nonfiction titles arose from the original initiative of publishers. There was a special incentive to suggest writing projects which would be equally useful for book and magazine publication. Charles Scribner had both outlets in mind when he attempted in 1893 to induce General A. W. Greely to prepare a series on "American Travellers": [22]

> Our idea for the book is a popular one. . . . Of course it should be accurate and comprehensive so far as it went, but biographical, and first of all, entertaining and popular. The selection of travellers would be left to you, though we should like to know your selections, and have some voice in it. They should all be American travellers.

Sometimes it required a considerable sum of money to bring these ideas to fruition. Richard Watson Gilder succeeded in getting the explorer and engineer George Kennan to prepare a series of articles on the "Russian Exile System." But before it was completed, the Century Company had invested nearly $15,000 in getting Kennan to Siberia and maintaining him during a long period of research and writing.[23]

Wide-awake publishers were constantly on the lookout for appropriate shorter writings which could be grouped for book publication. Magazine material was often well adapted to the purpose. While the authors themselves could be counted on to arrange for the joint publication of novels, collections of short stories and of articles usually revealed the planning of the publishers. Charles Scribner wrote to John Muir in 1878: [24]

We have read with much interest your paper in the November number of Scribner's. . . . We understand that is the 1st of a series of articles that have been accepted for publication in the magazine. We write particularly to say that should you intend hereafter bringing these papers together in a volume together with other articles that have appeared elsewhere (in "Harper's Magazine", etc.) we hope that you will without fail confer with us on the subject.

The lecture platform also produced grist for the publisher's mill. If the speaker was a prominent one, there was considerable competition for his notes, and he could secure a contract even before he had been heard.[25]

Dr. Fisher of Yale University informs us that you are to deliver the Lyman Beecher Lectures on Preaching at New Haven this year. If you have not already arranged for their American publication, it would give us great pleasure to act as their publishers.

Similar encouragement was often given to college teachers, who were urged to wave a literary wand over their classroom preparations and effortlessly produce a text.[26]

One of the lowest forms of literary life, the anthology, gave the publisher another opportunity to display his ingenuity and to produce a book where none had existed before. The result might be a perfunctory collection of excerpts out of context, but occasionally could reflect a creative idea. Henry Holt, for example, was lured by profits into proposing a rather ingenious compilation from the classics, designed to provide a basis for comparing the ancient and the modern mind.[27]

Looked at from the viewpoint of the individual publisher rather than of the trade as a whole, an important source of books came from the transfer of publications from one house to another. Although bankruptcy was usually the cause of such sales, the desire of a company to prune and consolidate its list might have the same result. Probably the most notable liquidation of the "Gilded Age" took place in 1876 when the James R. Osgood Company sold at auction the stereotype plates of some 500 volumes costing $300,000 and a stock whose retail value was approximately $125,000. *Publishers' Weekly* thought that the sale was chiefly of service to three classes of buyers: [28]

> . . . publishers just starting business, or who had but small lists which they wished to extend; the owners of printing establishments which they wished to keep busy, who would naturally seek the plates; and the jobbers and large retailers who had the capital and custom to handle the stock.

While the special interest of the younger and smaller firms is not unexpected, it would be incorrect to assume that Osgood's more substantial rivals did not avail themselves of the opportunity to acquire standard sets at bargain prices. Among others, H. O. Houghton and Co. purchased plates for the works of DeQuincy and Sir Walter Scott, and Lee and Shepard bought stereotypes of Dickens' and Thackeray's novels.[29] When the transfers were made, the new owners were obliged to fulfill whatever obligations to authors were still outstanding. Although many of the titles were by English writers, and hence not protected by law from the "pirates," the trade journal observed, "It is rather curious that the presence or absence of a copyright seems to make very little difference on the price." [30]

A practice more common among the large publishers was to purchase the rights to the earlier works of their outstanding authors. "We are very anxious," wrote Charles Scribner to Thomas Nelson Page, "to bring all your books together on our list and shall not mind if the cash account goes against us for a short time." [31] Such a step was gratifying to a writer, and served to confirm his identification with the house performing it. Further, if the purchase was made early enough, it might result in considerable saving when the time came for the publishing of collected works. Gebbie and Company was obliged to pay Charles Scribner $2,500 for the right to include *The Rough Riders* and *Cromwell* in a subscription edition of Theodore Roosevelt's writings limited to 1,250 copies, a royalty of a dollar a volume.[32]

Another solicited portion of the list of many publishers came from abroad. The desire to secure the American market of popular British works has already been mentioned. But an additional impulse to import arose from the fact that unbound sheets presented an inexpensive opportunity for adding new publications to a list. Without having any of the expense of composition and plates, an American publisher could bind these sheets with his imprint and present them as his own books—an attractive procedure when the industry was depressed or the house short of funds.

Charles Scribner was pleased to find that "padding" the list rather than serious importation was the motive of H. O. Houghton and Company when it entered the English market in 1881: [33]

I spoke to Mifflin, of Houghton's firm, about their recent purchases of sheets in 250. He confesses that they do it to "freshen up" their list. They have decided to publish very little with the market in its present state, but to make the most of their old plates with new editions, etc.; but as they must be able to show *something* new they have taken the small editions of English books which, of course, they have little difficulty in getting rid of.

Although the passage of the international copyright law in 1891 put a stop to piracy, the centuries before had produced a tremendous storehouse of literature on which publishers could draw freely. There were at least two large advantages to specializing in the publication of "classics." The expense of remunerating authors was avoided, and the life of the individual titles was much longer than that of a best seller—presumably it was endless. However, like the "pirates," the publisher of a well-known "classic" could never be secure from rival editions. There was also the disagreeable fact that a permanent demand did not necessarily imply a turnover quick enough to insure a profitable investment. Consequently publishers found themselves caught between a fear of competition and a dread of slowly moving inventory. The most common solution was to choose the best works, and hope that an attractive format and a minimum price would bring success. Such publications sometimes involved another set of advisers. When

Henry Holt undertook in 1903 to bring out a series of historical novels, he based his selections upon a poll which he conducted among librarians.[34]

While the editorial services performed for these staple books were limited, the work connected with original manuscripts had scarcely begun once the contracts were signed. Even before a publisher saw a manuscript, he might offer advice which would induce the author to change its entire concept. A letter written by Holt to George Waring in 1880 may be taken as a fair sample of editorial assistance at its earliest stage: [35]

> If that book of yours is as good a book as you can write, I'll take it p.d.q. If it's as bad a book as many a good author occasionally produces, I'll take it q. enough to spare your feelings, but I'll make the terms more Egyptian than in the other case. . . . I suspect that a real *practical* book, teaching everything that words can teach of what one should do on horseback, might find a paying public. It would, of course, need to be systematic, but if a little of the ———— were thrown into the system, it might help. . . . I don't believe a book that you would scratch off in a hurry, without some previous half-involuntary collection of material would do much. I think it ought to be pretty substantial.

Stripped of the Holt charm, the advice was designed to convert a hurried "pot-boiler" into a carefully constructed summary.

Between the class of manuscripts which could be definitely declined and those worthy of prompt acceptance, there were the tantalizing writings which seemed to the publisher to require large revisions before they could become suitable for publication. Whether the changes could be made successfully often depended upon such intangibles as the author's willingness and ability to use the editorial advice given him. Two alternatives were available to the publisher. Either he could put the book under contract and hope for the best, or he could reject it with an invitation to the writer to submit it again once the indicated corrections had been made. Although the latter plan left the door open for another house, it had the merit of postponing a definite financial commitment on a manuscript of uncertain value. In either case, considerable effort might have to be expended by the editors. The decision to defer a judgment could be made only at the price of offering detailed criticism which might be wasted; and consequently most manuscripts either were given a contract or rejected without comment. But a large number of Henry Holt's letters merely pay lip service to this common practice. They begin with a statement that it was the policy of the house never to explain why a manuscript was declined, and end with an extended discussion of what the author could do to make his work acceptable. In several cases, the report of the "readers" was forwarded in its entirety, while Holt himself occasionally summarized the criticism or offered his own. One of Holt's letters declining a manuscript called *The Philosophy of Horatio*, which he never published, reveals the effort which at least one publisher was willing to expend on free advice: [36]

I am satisfied that there is no public for the gruesome story despite its merits. I am also satisfied that if the author sees fit to avail herself of the opportunity she has thrown away that she can write a story (whether she will or not is another question) for which there is a public.

Making the beautiful Princess Rediviva a mere carnivorous beast of the most repulsive form will simply repel readers. If Miss Taylor sees fit to make her fatality lie in her charms, to use perfume, music, and dreams of luxury, she has a chance not only to make an interesting and attractive story, but to apply a pretty good sort of a moral, whereas the present story applies none at all.

If she decides to do what I venture to recommend, she had better make each victim go once and come back enraptured, but let the second going mean death. It might be a good scheme though, when she comes to the American element, to have the princess relent, perhaps even to get in love with the victim. It might be a good scheme to have her begin with the American boy, and at last tire of him and tackle Dean, and then even Merritt himself, but have Merritt strong enough to clear out when he finds they are too much for him.

Perhaps the length of time which Holt took to say "no" can be attributed to his ego rather than to his profession.

The increasingly common practice of signing a contract before a manuscript existed gave to the later publishers an editorial opportunity which rarely was present for their pre-Civil War predecessors. Frequently a synopsis sufficed to induce an agreement, and an outline was much more malleable than a polished text upon which an author had lavished such care that every word was precious to him. If Charles Scribners' correspondence is good indication of his editorial attitude, he was quite reluctant to offer extended criticism of a completed manuscript. Yet he often made suggestions concerning a projected work, even to an experienced contributor like Donald Mitchell, to whom he wrote in 1893: [37]

I do not think the possible repetition of some ideas which you have elsewhere given to print would matter in the Irving Chapter. As to the final chapter, I see no reason for limiting it to the four mentioned—the broader it could be made the better—without of course degenerating into a mere catalogue. I hardly see how the Presidents could be introduced; they seem in some cases such incidental landmarks. Some of them do represent and suggest changing phases of National Life but others have little significance. However, you are the better judge and I do not like to venture an opinion. Some method of keeping the literary history in touch with National Progress is certainly desirable but at first thought the Presidents strike me as a slender thread on which to hang our literature.

The earlier a publisher became identified with a manuscript, the more he could share in the creative process. The over-all design of a work was usually beyond the ability of both writer and editor to alter once it was originally composed; but it could be changed with comparatively little effort in its initial stages.

However, the fact that a manuscript was completed hardly precluded the possibility of change; indeed, most of the editors' work was probably devoted to the details of revision. Often the criticism led merely to a few deletions of phrases of questionable taste, placing the editor in the role of censor. Textbook houses were obliged to take special care and greater liberties with manuscripts to insure their innocuousness. Henry Holt issued these instructions to his editor in 1883: [38]

A Frenchman has written a lot of anecdotes for school use, among which his French standard has permitted the introduction of some that the extra squeamishness prevalent in American schools make it impracticable to introduce. The three specimens enclosed will show what I mean. Will you be kind enough to run through all of them, and take out any that may be open to similar objection.

In the exchange of books across the seas, American publishers felt obliged to bowdlerize naturalistic writers like George Moore,[39] and were willing to remove from their own books any native slang or references offensive in the export market.[40] An excessive display of erotics in a novel was almost certain to be deleted.[41]

But censorship was but a small part of the editor's work. His main concern was with literary not moral delinquency. It is impossible to reduce the editorial process to a formula. Not only were there as many methods as editors; it was also true that no two books presented the same problem or admitted the same solution. Criticism could be as brief as that offered to William E. Bailey by the editors of Henry Holt and Company: "If you will take out of your MSS every word that can possibly be spared, we will be happy to look at it again." [42] Other manuscripts required long editorial conferences and extended correspondence. Sometimes the weakness of a novel lay in a badly conceived character: [43]

The hero is not the sort of a man who would ever have given up his love without finding out the reason of her letter to him, and finding it out from her own lips. Possibly you can get him to sail by the influence of his old mentor, but you cannot get him to land on the other side without turning around and coming back, much less to stay there months and make arrangements to marry another woman. To straighten out this difficulty may involve a very considerable shift in your story. The other difficulties are all trifling.

Bad endings were equally common among editors' complaints: [44]

I generally find that books, and, for some strange reason, especially women's books, slump at the end. Yours ends with a nice little homily on divorce. That's no ending for a novel. There's a great deal to be said in favor of the theory that the last clause of the last sentence ought to be the most thrilling clause of the most thrilling sentence in the book.

When the relations between authors and publishers were as close as publishers often claimed they should be, the editorial function went beyond the criticism of words into suggestions for personality adjustment. A half-century of editorial conferences gave Henry Holt enough experience with authors' problems to make some of his letters read like a psychoanalyst's rather than a publisher's. Witness this letter written to an author in 1907: [45]

Do hold yourself in and let yourself trot, and not gallop so much—not to say cavort. In other words, to put it more rationally, I was disappointed to find that your release from some of your great cares and anxieties has not permitted your spirit to settle down to more calm; for I believe your art absolutely requires it—the first element of art, some people think, is temperance, and I guess they are two-thirds right—two-thirds? Yes, ninety-nine hundredths right. Of course, it was not in a work of art (except as your letters are so) that you show the tempestuousness of which I am speaking. I am only speaking of the habit of keeping storms down.

The success of an editor was highly dependent upon his ability to present his recommendations forcibly without antagonizing creative artists who were apt to be easily offended. The more important an author considered himself to be or was considered to be, the more delicate became the task of informing him of his errors. Sometimes the desire not to offend resulted in a brand of sycophancy which seems almost repulsive to the outsider. A letter addressed to Robert Louis Stevenson by Edward Burlingame with suggestions for *The Wrecker* contains much of this seemingly excessive flattery. The tone is one of self-accusation for disturbing a great man with cantankerous trivialities, an attitude which could not have been sincere unless the publisher thought that petty annoyances were the key to a writer's loyalty. Further, the content of the letter, describing the book's strongly anti-American bias, indicated a need for considerable revision.[46] However, the incident can scarcely be considered a reflection on the character or ability of Burlingame, who was one of Scribner's most talented editors; its significance consists rather in the lengths to which publishers might be pushed to make criticism palatable to temperamental authors. The personality of Stevenson was the one revealed.

One of Henry Holt's letters shows equal consideration conveyed without any loss of dignity. Addressing General Adam Badeau, he wrote: [47]

> I enclose several comments and suggestions from my reader, and send your MSS herewith. On it you will find pencilled many more suggestions.
>
> It is inevitable to human nature, no matter how sound the critic, that some of these suggestions should tax your equanimity, and that some (even among those which do not tax your equanimity) should be mistaken. This is true to an extent which only a publisher's or editor's experience can realize, no matter, as I said, how good the critic.

I hope I have succeeded in putting you well on your guard. Another thing that I beg you to realize is that few works even from hands practiced in the departments to which they belong, ever see the light without much modification from their original shape in response to such criticism.

Such a message shows at the same time the problem of editorial diplomacy and the grace and sensitivity which a distinguished publisher could bring to its solution.

Unfortunately, there is no statistical method for measuring the value of the editor to literature. But despite the frequent errors which publishers were usually willing to admit, at least in retrospect, there can be little question that most manuscripts were made better rather than worse by being revised. Were the records of publishing more nearly complete, they would undoubtedly reveal numerous Thomas Wolfes being ministered to by the editors who created the tradition in which Maxwell Perkins was to serve.

The Machinery of Wholesale Distribution

chapter 7

At the conclusion of the half-century span leading to the First World War, the publishing trade was obliged to acknowledge that its attempts to adapt the machinery of book distribution to a new industrial age had been a failure. "The world," said *Publishers' Weekly* in 1913, "is still looking for a publisher who will 'discover or invent' a new method which shall be both practical and effective for the distribution of books of general literature." [1]

A list of the methods of distribution current in 1864, provided by the leading trade organ of the day, reveals that the product of fifty years of effort had consisted primarily of the addition of commercial travellers. Summarizing the methods of the Civil War era, the journal explained: [2]

> Books are sold wholesale by written orders, trade-sales, auctions and otherwise. Country dealers are in the habit of visiting the great book-depots of Boston, New York and Philadelphia, and there personally making their selections.

This emphasis upon the retailers coming to the publishers instead of the publishers going to them was not solely a product of the trade's lack of initiative. A predominantly rural America, its population scattered over a large area, could not sustain enough local bookstores to supply its reading matter. Consequently, in the wake of the circuit-rider and the village schoolmaster came a third advance agent of civilization, the itinerant book peddler, whose business address a publisher was hard put to discover. The ubiquitous Parson Weems was only the most conspicuous in a profession which appears to have had a unique attraction for men later to become famous in other fields of endeavor. George Washington's early career included an experience canvassing for a book called *The American Savage; How He May be Tamed by the Weapons of Civilization,* of which he disposed of two hundred copies. Daniel Webster paid part of his tuition at Dartmouth College by acting as a local book agent; and James G. Blaine, appropriately enough, began his career in Pennsylvania selling a *Life of Henry Clay; the Mill Boy of the Slashes.* Even Jay Gould and Phineas T. Barnum paused briefly in the world of books before moving on to more lucrative pursuits.[3]

Book peddlers who dealt in a variety of books instead of a single title had particular need for periodic visits to the publishing centers where they could gather their stock easily. For much the same reasons, the owners of book stores distant from New York and Philadelphia relied upon semi-annual visits to furnish them with their supplies. Not only was transportation difficult, but the life of the average book was sufficiently long, especially in outlying areas, to obviate the necessity for a quick turnover.

Reflecting these conditions and, indeed, contributing to them, were the now almost forgotten trade sales, which capped the system of wholesale selling for almost fifty years. These book auctions, in which all of the large publishers ultimately participated, had their modest beginnings in 1824 as a promotion device of the Philadelphia firm of Carey and Lea. By the end of the decade, the trade sale had become a cooperative venture of many houses, and had inspired similar enterprises in Boston and New York.[4] The growth of the sales thus coincided with the organization and early development of America's most important publishing houses. By 1836, four years after William Ticknor purchased the Old Corner Book Store, the proceeds of one of Boston's semi-annual sales exceeded $85,000. Up to the eve of the Civil War, the development of the trade sales reflected the shifting centers of the industry. Cincinnati symbolized its importance as the distribution center for Western business by commencing its own trade sale in 1841. The demise of Boston as America's literary capital was portended in the virtual extinction of its sale during the 1850's and the concentration of buyers in New York and, to a lesser extent, Philadelphia.[5]

The operations of the trade sales can best be studied during the five-year periods immediately preceding and following the Civil War when they were at the peak of their importance. The books of as many as 175 houses from all the publishing centers in the country were offered at a typical New York sale. Each sale received the official sanction of the industry through the appointment of a committee of reputable publishers chosen to supervise arrangements. In 1864, for example, the committee in whose name the sale was announced included William H. Appleton,

John Wiley, Birdsey Blakeman, Charles Scribner, A. S. Barnes, Lowell Mason, Jr., and Smith Sheldon. The auction ordinarily continued for eight full days, convening at eight o'clock in the morning and lasting until late at night; the auctioneer, George A. Leavitt, provided the meals which were the only interruptions in the day's schedule. The invoices of many firms included their entire list of publications. When selected titles were offered, they were more apt to be the current books than accumulated inventory; the trade sales of these years should in no way be identified with the remaindering of a later period.

Only an incomplete record is available of the actual mechanics of the auctioning system employed. Bids were by "lots" of books, but the size of the lots varied from five copies to several thousand. In the 1870's, and possibly before, it was the custom to offer first a limited quantity which would attract the interest of the smaller buyers. A second bidding on the same title would be for lots twice the size of the first, and each successive bidding would double the quantity until the entire invoice was sold. Since the price per copy became lower as the size of the lot increased, the procedure had the same effect as a scale of discounts which grew progressively greater as the amount of the purchase increased. The catalogue of the sale always indicated a definite number of copies for each book; but the publisher reserved the right to "duplicate," a privilege which was exercised if the bidding was brisk enough to bring high prices. This device also had the advantage of limiting his commitment if the sale was slow. Although the offering of a small lot tended to discourage the large buyers, most publishers were inclined to be cautious with the newer and the more valuable titles. In 1864, only twenty-seven copies of James Parton's *Life of Benjamin Butler* were listed in the catalogue, but 600 were sold; and Messrs. G. and C. Merriam found the prices sufficiently attractive to make available 576 more copies of *Webster's Dictionary* than they had originally specified.

The importance of the sales to the industry can easily be deduced from the incomplete reports which remain of the total number of copies of individual books disposed of at a single gathering. In 1859, the *American Publishers' Circular and Literary Gazette* observed: [6]

> Among the noticeable items of this sale are the following: . . . Little, Brown & Co. sold about 2,000 vols. of the British Poets, and 500 Bancroft's United States; Derby and Jackson, 1,500 Charlotte Bronte, 2,000 Library of Popular Tales and Biography, 2,500 Library of Travels and Adventure, 7,500 Library of Standard Fiction of which last Evans & Co., the "Gift-book" sellers, bought 5,000 vols. Peterson sold 2,600 vols of Dickens; Phillips, Sampson & Co., 4,000 vols. of Rollo books, 750 vols. of Prescott, 1,800 Gibbon and Macaulay, and 350 of Emerson's Works. . . .

Most of these totals resulted from the sale of a considerable number of small lots. The average buyer spent about $1,500 at the spring sale, spread among 100 different titles. At the fall sale, preceding the Christmas trade, his investment was apt to be twice as much.

There is very little to indicate the discount at which these books were sold. In 1867, the supervising auctioneer estimated that approximately 900,000 volumes had been disposed of for $300,000, an average of 33⅓¢ per book. But since the retail prices varied from 25¢ to $10, it is impossible to determine the spread between the auction price and the ordinary wholesale price. Harper and Brothers decided that year not to enter the general trade sale, but to have a competing sale of its own featuring fixed discounts from their regular wholesale prices. The fact that the maximum discount, reserved for orders over $2,000, was only 40 per cent suggests that when business was moderately good the auction device did not entail a large sacrifice. Some confirmation is given this conclusion by a report from the Philadelphia trade sale conducted under discouraging circumstances in 1860. Although many of the buyers had had their funds sorely depleted at the Boston and New York sales held a few weeks before, 5,000 copies of a geography text were sold at 62½¢, the regular trade price being 68¢.

Even more surprising was a notice of New York's spring trade sale in 1866 asserting that some books had brought prices "exceeding what would be charged on order from the publishing houses." [7] No explanation was offered for this extraordinary occurrence. The most likely possibility is that the titles were in short supply, although one would assume that a current work popular enough to bring a premium would ordinarily be reprinted. The tone of the report does not seem to indicate that the books were older titles about to go out of print. However, superior credit terms may have provided the extra attraction. Each buyer at the trade sales was billed for all his purchases together, and did not have to pay for six months if the total exceeded

$1,000. Less favorable terms, or even cash payment, might be required by an individual publisher in the regular course of trade.

After the books had been sold, each trade sale devoted at least one day to an auction of stereotype plates. This part of the proceedings introduced a different set of buyers, the publishers themselves. The flexibility offered to the industry by such transfers, presenting to some an opportunity to liquidate frozen assets and to others a chance to enlarge an anemic list, has been discussed previously. It remains to be observed that the trade sale was the normal market place for these exchanges, the one important exception being the separate sales which accompanied bankruptcies. In contrast to the book auctions, which at their height brought prices permitting a reasonable profit, the disposal of plates under almost any circumstances involved a considerable sacrifice. In 1862, for example, stereotypes valued at $360,000 were sold for 15 per cent of their cost.[8]

The impact of the industrial expansion following the Civil War is nowhere more apparent in publishing than in its effect upon the institution of the trade sale as a wholesaling mechanism. Even as early as the 1850's, it had been criticized for its clumsiness, and for the unfair advantage it offered to large buyers. A complainant in 1859 suggested that it be abolished in favor of a corps of travellers who would be hired collectively by the publishers in each city to visit the booksellers twice yearly and display the latest titles.[9] Four years after the war, the leading trade journal noted a slight decline in the volume of the fall trade sale in New York, attributing it to a falling off in the number of travelling booksellers "who at one time had been their chief support." The *Gazette* continued: [10]

The rapid growth of our cities in size and wealth, and the consequent extension of the regular book-selling business, have to a great extent done away with the necessity for these travelling booksellers and auctioneers, although there is still a wide field for their operations in the distant west, where many towns would be entirely without books were it not for their yearly visits.

While there was a kernel of truth in this analysis, it was much too oversimplified to be accurate. Urbanization was not born full-grown in America, but developed over many decades during which the travelling booksellers remained active and numerous. There was even a large place for them in a world of mail-order catalogues and suburban bookstores, as the publishers of the *Book of Knowledge* and many encyclopedias continue to prove. One authority describes the decades after the Civil War as the "heyday" of these independent canvassers, who benefited from the increased wealth and the fact that railroad tracks were being laid through territory too sparsely settled to support more than an occasional general store.[11] Mark Twain's first publisher, the American Publishing Company in the subscription center of Hartford, Connecticut, urged: [12]

The sale of our works is an honorable and praiseworthy employment, and is particularly adapted to disabled Soldiers, aged and other Clergymen having leisure hours, Teachers and students during vacation, etc., Invalids unable to endure hard physical labor, Young men who wish to travel, and gather knowledge and experience by contact with the world, and all who can bring industry, perseverance, and a determined will to work.

The assertion that "probably ninety percent of the book buyers of that time [the post Civil War decades] never entered a bookstore" [13] cannot be proven statistically; but even if the proportion is reduced by half it offers challenging evidence that the decline of the trade sales cannot be explained solely by the encroachment of cities on the book peddler's market.

More important was the increasing opposition of publishers and regular booksellers which arose because prices became disrupted by the auction system. As long as it was necessary to acquaint out-of-town buyers with the latest books and to give them a convenient opportunity to purchase them, the trade sale took its place within the regular machinery of wholesale distribution. However, as other means were perfected for reaching these buyers, the trade sales became associated with quantity purchases at lower prices. This came about partly because publishers used them to dispose of dead inventory which they were pleased to sell at any price, and partly because the very nature of the sales provided a unique opportunity for large purchasers, especially the book "jobbers," the wholesaling middlemen who became important after the Civil War.

During the 1870's, the trade sales occupied an ambiguous position. Avowedly fulfilling their traditional function of making available the current books at reasonably standard prices, they came more to resemble "remainder" sales of undesirable stock. However, the industry was sufficiently depressed during the decade to induce publishers to sell their best books at large discounts. *Publishers' Weekly* wrote in 1876: [14]

It is always a temptation to a business house to increase its capital at the opening of a season by throwing a considerable stock on the market, and there is also a supposition that the forced activity of an auction sale at the beginning of fall stimulates trade helpfully.

The desperateness of this device soon became apparent to the publishers, who found that private sales were as useful to stimulate buying and could be conducted with a calculated rather than an uncertain discount.

But even when the trade was willing to undermine its wholesale price structure, the objections of the ordinary retailers continued. "Publishers are finding out," scolded the trade journal, "that they cannot expect to sell the same goods at a regular price to the regular trade, and offer them at any price to whomsoever will buy." [15] The protests grew as the retailers discovered more evidence that the wholesale price they paid for books ordered through the commercial travellers was more than the retail price at which copies bought at the trade sales could be sold.

By 1876, the industry was sufficiently demoralized to experiment with a substitute suggested by Frederick Leypoldt, the editor of *Publishers' Weekly*. Leypoldt, who was constantly trying to remold the trade in a German image, was the leading figure in a "trade fair" held that year in imitation of the annual European exhibits at which all the houses exhibited their wares and took orders at the regular discounts. To satisfy the legitimate need for relief from surplus stock, the last day of the fair consisted of an auction frankly devoted to disposing of books of depreciated value. Care was taken that no current books would be mingled with the old as they had been at the trade sales.[16] That the fair was judged a conspicuous failure cannot be attributed to any lack of zeal on the part of the major publishers, all of whom supported it with an enthusiasm revealing their doubts about the older system.[17] Perhaps the wrong results were expected of it. Although the sales totalled but $40,000,[18] the register of buyers was impressive, and testified to the fact that retailers from Halifax, Nova Scotia to Vicksburg, Mississippi, and from Portland, Maine to San Francisco were acquainted with the publishers' latest offerings.[19]

But even *Publishers' Weekly* was unwilling to consider such indirect benefits, and took its sole consolation in the negative advantage which resulted from the absence of the trade sales. This fact alone seemed to justify the failure of the two trade fairs which were held in the Centennial Year. But the publishers were not convinced that the sacrifice had been worth while and turned again to the trade sales with renewed enthusiasm. Blair Scribner wrote to his London partner early in 1877: [20]

The Trade Sale is going to be revived this spring and much to our satisfaction, certainly, for the Book Fair was surely a great humbug at least as far as selling was concerned and that is the all essential thing. We had expected to welcome the old Trade Sale next Fall but not before. It seems however that Osgood started the ball rolling by contributing for the opening sale this spring a $50,000 (at retail prices) invoice of his own books and at once Leavitt [the auctioneer] issued his circular and it is now all arranged.

Publishers' Weekly immediately resumed its role of chief opponent to the return of the prodigal: [21]

We have soothing news in store for the fluttering book trade. The "Trade Sale" is back! It sounds as familiar and cheery to say Santa Claus is back, Barnum is back, Spring is back. Booksellers will smile all sorts of smiles at the tidings; and the fancy and dry-goods stores, the street-corner, sidewalk, and basement bibliopoles, the auction, gift, lottery, butcher, great combination, dollar and fifteen-cents-to-the-dollar concerns will chuckle, chuckle. How much per pound, yard, dozen, gross, and "what's off" to ministers, lawyers, doctors, school-teachers, students, soldiers, sailors, farmers, cobblers, tinkers, tailors, and other "friends in the trade"? After the wants of the bidder have been supplied, the lots will be doubled, "quadrupled", and so on, so on. "Going, going, going!" The committees are dead, the "Ring" is dead, the Book Fair is dead, but the Trade Sale is back! Le roi est mort; long live the king!

To attribute all of the ills of a business floundering in a depression to the trade sales was scarcely just. However, credit should be given to the trade journal for its perception and its constant opposition to an outmoded institution which was ultimately to disappear for precisely the reasons which it advanced cogently in less sarcastic moments. Even the initial success of the revival could not deter *Publishers' Weekly* from its crusade. It was happy to report in the fall of 1877 that prices on the new books were within ten per cent of the regular discounts, but concluded that such sales represented the kind of buying which did not need the stimulation of an auction.[22] The returning prosperity of the

1880's removed much of the despair of the trade which had made the 1876 experiment abortive. Further, the demands of the regular retailers became more insistent. The Northwestern Booksellers and Stationers' Association meeting in Chicago in 1882 singled out the trade sale for its special attack and passed a resolution reading: [23]

Resolved, That the trade sales as conducted by George A. Leavitt and Co., of New York, are detrimental to the book trade throughout the country, and we earnestly and respectfully request the publishers of books to discountenance the same by withdrawing their patronage therefrom.

Even the "jobbers" who had previously found in the trade sales their best opportunity became concerned about the lack of a price structure which could be relied upon. The increasing specialization of the industry elevated them from the role of "bargain hunters" to that of regular wholesalers dealing in standard books rather than "remainders." An open letter in 1882 to the leading publishers from a group of Western "jobbers" pronounced the trade sales "pernicious" in their influence.[24]

The 1880's saw the gradual withdrawal from the trade sales of the important houses. In 1884, the forty-six contributors did not include among them such previous supporters as D. Appleton and Company, G. P. Putnam's Sons, Harper and Brothers, Little, Brown, and Company, and Henry Holt and Company. *Publishers' Weekly* announced with some satisfaction that "with few exceptions" the invoices represent "clearance" stock,[25] although it was willing to acknowledge two weeks later that the sale was "more of a success than was anticipated" and that "the prices as a rule for the better class of books were fair." [26] For the next four years, almost every sale brought forth a similar confession from the trade journal. As late as 1887, the institution was sufficiently vital to attract a large number of out-of-town buyers and "New York City was represented by the principals or buyers of nearly all its bookstores." Full lists were offered by the contributors and the current books brought prices commensurate to their value.[27] The offering of Lee and Shepard alone comprised 60,000 volumes.[28]

Yet the end for which *Publishers' Weekly* had so long waited was now in sight, as one by one the publishers turned to more dependable means of distribution. In 1890, the spring sale seemed remarkable only "for its slim catalogue and the absence of all but three or four of the large houses." [29] The following year the institution expired after more than a half-century of service, held in such low esteem that the trade's official organ did not pause to pay respect to its memory.

The passing of the regular trade sale did not mean that book auctions were no longer held. Even before the Civil War auctions had been popular for the disposal of "remainders," and the publishers had no objection to participating in this kind of sale long after they were convinced that open bidding was not the proper method for disposing of new books. The most prominent of the auction houses, and the successor to that part of the trade sale which dealt with surplus stock, was Bangs and Company, founded in the 1850's as Bangs, Merwin and Company.[30] Almost as old an institution as the trade sales were the "parcel sales" sponsored by this company twice a year and at first distinguished by the emphasis given to imported titles. Although this company had sold "remainders" at auction for several decades, the demise of the trade sale gave it an opportunity to expand its activities. In January of 1895, Bangs announced his intention to hold an annual auction which would be limited to the sale of avowedly dead inventory.

Most of the large houses found it profitable to contribute their books to these sales until Bangs and Company went into bankruptcy in 1903. On the eve of the First World War the disposal of "remainders" had been taken over by the Syndicate Trading Company and other specialists in cheap books.[31]

A more important part of the function of the trade sale had been gradually usurped by another basic development in the industry's distributive machinery, the institution of commercial travelling. The memory of Frank H. Dodd, who entered his father's house in the 1850's, stretched back to the day when regular visits to even the more important out-of-town dealers was not considered a necessary part of the business. At the close of the Civil War, "few, if any, of the houses maintained a regular staff of travellers." However, a transition soon took place:[32]

> As the Trade Sales declined systematic travelling came in. We always used to go to Boston and Philadelphia to get the huge orders which were given out by Lippincott's and Lee and Shepard, but that was about all. In the more regular and persistent travelling the English branch houses, if I remember right, especially Nelsons and Routledges, took the lead.

If the British suggested the system, the Americans may take the credit for developing it to meet the needs of a domestic market which stretched across a continent three thousand miles wide. Actually, the example of a few importers was of little significance. Underlying both the deterioration of the trade sale and the rise of the travelling salesman was the much more substantial fact of the rapid expansion of railroads in all sections of the country. To this may be added some measure of the more aggressive exploitation of sales possibilities which characterized many businesses in the postwar era.

The trade contained within itself an old tradition which made the accommodation to new conditions easier. Travelling booksellers were scarcely a novelty, although they had previously confined their attention to the retail business. It is not too much to suppose that at least some of the first wholesale representatives of the publishers were recruited from the ranks of the independent canvassers. The first tentative step towards gathering a corps of salesmen often involved hiring a man already in the field who agreed to devote only a portion of his time to the works of a particular house. Dodd, Mead and Company, for example, engaged a salesman in 1877 for a salary of $1,500 and a commission on sales above $12,000 who retained the privilege "of doing any work he may see fit, or selling any stock he can," that did not conflict with the interests of his employer. The fact that he was already active in an area rather than assigned to one is attested to by a clause referring to "Baltimore, Washington and other places within his field." [33]

When publishers first ventured to secure the exclusive services of an agent, they sometimes met part of the salary by having him sell the publications of another house in return for a commission. Dodd, Mead and Company received 10 per cent of the proceeds for permitting its representative in Pennsylvania to handle the books of Houghton, Mifflin and Company.[34] This type of cooperation among publishers was already common within the cities. New York houses often acted as the special wholesale agents for Philadelphia and Boston firms, which performed a similar function within their own areas. For example, an 1862 advertisement of G. P. Putnam's Sons referred buyers in Philadelphia to J. B. Lippincott and Company; [35] Robert Clarke and Company of Cincinnati announced that the trade could be supplied in New York by C. T. Dillingham, Dodd, Mead and Company, and G. P. Putnam's Sons.[36] These sales activities belonged to the business of "jobbing" rather than publishing, but in the "Gilded Age" the two branches of the business were often joined in varying proportions. Charles T. Dillingham was a New York wholesaler who occasionally published; D. Appleton and Company was a publishing house which advertised its ability to supply the "country trade" with the "publications of all other publishers, and at their lowest jobbing prices." [37]

The growth of commercial travelling was only one of several reasons why these inter-publisher agreements tended gradually to disappear. The general wholesaling of books became a specialized business in its own right. Those houses which conducted it merely as an adjunct to publishing soon fell behind such firms as The Baker and Taylor

Company in New York and A. C. McClurg and Company in Chicago. The giant among wholesalers was the American News Company, formed in 1864 from a consolidation of a group of the largest news distributors of the day. Beginning with an extensive capital, the corporation grew steadily until it enjoyed the status of a monopoly in the distribution of magazines.[38] Although it made large inroads into the wholesale book trade, the diffuseness of the industry prevented it from becoming more than one of several prominent "jobbers." A report given by Charles Scribner to Edith Wharton in 1905 on the early sales of *The House of Mirth* gives a brief description and shows the relative importance of each of the largest purchasers of the era: [39]

American News Company This is the largest jobbing house in the country. Their principal quarters are in New York, with branches in all the larger cities.	7,500
Baker & Taylor Company The next largest jobbing house—a New York company.	5,000
A. C. McClurg & Company A Chicago company with both retail and wholesale business.	5,000
Wanamaker Divided between the New York and Philadelphia branches.	5,000
H. B. Claflin Company For use in department stores supplied by that company.	2,500

The largest number taken by any one house after those named would not be more than 500 copies.

Taken together, these five outlets accounted for about 30 per cent of the first two printings of 80,000 copies, a not exaggerated reflection of their importance in the industry. It should be noted that two of them, John A. Wanamaker and Company and H. B. Claflin Company, were essentially retailers whose demands were large enough to exceed the requirements of most "jobbers." Even greater quantities, occasionally approaching 100,000 copies,[40] were occasionally purchased by these wholesalers under individual arrangements which provided them either with a separate, inexpensive edition or a special price for purchasing all the inventory. In a letter in which he forwarded a check for $1,500 to Frances Hodgson Burnett, Charles Scribner explained: [41]

> This last is for 30,000 of the cheap edition of the "DeWilloughby Claim" already delivered to the News Company. The agreement with the News Company is to take the remaining 20,000 on or before the 1st of August. We do not receive the money until 90 days after delivery but our understanding with you is that we are to pay when the books are delivered and I will send the remaining $1,000 promptly.

The publishers conceded the "jobber" his place within the industry, but during the earlier days of the era found it difficult to accept fully their responsibility to him. Handling large numbers of books on a small unit margin of profit, the wholesaler had particular need for a stable price structure. Yet when the industry was depressed, many publishers in their anxiety for extra business destroyed whatever advantage they had given the "jobbers" by selling to ordinary retailers at the same price. In 1877, this practice had become sufficiently conspicuous to receive a scolding from *Publishers' Weekly*: [42]

> This is the dilemma of the jobber. He cannot, nor can any man, afford to buy goods for his customers if his customers are to be tempted away from him by the very parties from whom he has just bought goods for their supply. . . . The jobber does not ask that the publisher shall refuse to sell to anyone, but he does ask, as the retailer asks in turn, that the discounts, on the strength of which he projected business and bought goods shall be maintained.

But the blame can scarcely be put all on one side. During this same period, the "jobbers" were among the most assiduous attendants of the trade sales and the other auctions at which stock might be purchased below the regular discounts. When the wholesaler shared these savings with his customers, he disrupted the publishers' regular market; retailers were apt to be suspicious of houses who could not meet the best wholesale price for their own publications.[43] By the 1880's, both the publisher and the wholesale houses had agreed at least on the principle of coordinating their activities within a prescribed system of discounts. The practice took at least twenty years longer to establish.

Although the trade publishers gradually surrendered their general wholesale departments to better equipped specialists, they developed more extensive machinery for distributing their own titles. Many of the larger houses ultimately established a number of branches stretched across the country. In their most primitive form, these offices were little more than warehouse depots, staffed by manufacturers' agents who represented several houses, maintaining a stock on consignment and receiving a commission on sales.[44] But the branches also reflected the need of an expanding corps of commercial travellers for a local headquarters, particularly necessary if the publisher did an extensive business in texts or subscription books. The elaborate organization constructed by Dodd, Mead and Company in the 1890's for the sale of its *New International Encyclopedia* and the proliferous network of The Macmillan Company were typical of the trend at the close of the era.[45]

Two letters from the files of Henry Holt and Company reveal the large change in distributive machinery which took place within less than two decades. In 1884, Holt was obliged to inform an author: [46]

> We have not established general agencies in cities for the introduction of our publications, nor do we know of any New York publishers who have more than one or two such for school books.

Eighteen years later, the manager of the Chicago branch received this letter from the home office: [47]

> As compared with previous years, I should say that the Chicago territory has not been neglected. . . . Indiana has been gone over once, and the northern end of it two or three times. Similarly, all of the towns in your Illinois list, except some suburban, have been visited at least once. The same is true of Minnesota and Wisconsin. Michigan has been done two (yes, three) times, and done more extensively than ever before. Even Iowa has been more nearly covered than heretofore.

The end of the experimental period of travelling had been signalized by the formation in 1885 of a fraternal order called the "Brotherhood of Commercial Travellers," whose initial membership consisted of a hundred men "connected with the book, stationery, and kindred trades in New York City." The philosophy of the new organization can be judged by the mottoes it chose for the First Annual Banquet: "Competition is the Life of Trade"; "There is No Such Word as Fail"; and "Let Us All Pull Together." No more succinct expression of the changed conditions seems possible. The day had passed when the book trade took particular delight in its gentility; the newest part of it boldly proclaimed its identification with the world of commerce. Instead of toasting Dickens, it drank to "Hotels and Their Accommodations," and "Railroads and Extra Baggage." [48]

Most of the trade was willing to agree that the commercial travellers were as essential as they themselves believed they were. By the turn of the century, *Publishers' Weekly* conceded that "the most important . . . agent in the distribution of books is undoubtedly the salesman whose field of action is confined to the limits of the bookstore." [49] "Who will deny," wrote the editor Adolf Growoll, "that the commercial traveller is one of the greatest necessities of this growing country, and in the coming generations to grow in importance a hundred fold." [50] If the trade's official journal may be believed, the most respected members of the publishing profession on the eve of the World War were not its editors but its salesmen: [51]

In every publishing house the one employee who is the object of the most admiration, or envy it may be, is the salesman who goes "gunning" for business—and gets it. At heart every junior in the concern from the office boy up, envies the traveller for the opportunity he has, and the dream of all is someday, somehow, to win his chance.

Insofar as trade books were concerned, this extraordinary deference was built on a relatively slender foundation. In 1914, the number of salesmen assigned to visit bookstores was not large. A summary furnished by *Publishers' Weekly* revealed that most of the largest houses did not then employ more than four commercial travellers, and that they assigned to each territories so large as to make more than a running sales campaign impossible. For example, the roster of Harper and Brothers read as follows: [52]

George V. Price (all of the large cities of the country as far West as St. Louis); H. V. Patterson (the Pacific coast, some of the Middle West and New England); Adam Burger (the South, Middle West and some cities in Pennsylvania and New York State).

Dodd, Mead and Company listed: [53]

F. C. Dodd (Chicago, Boston, Philadelphia, Cleveland, Detroit); Harry M. Snyder (Texas, Pacific Coast, New York, New England, Baltimore, Washington, and the larger cities of the Middle West); Howard C. Lewis (South, and the smaller cities in New York, Pennsylvania, and the Middle West); G. G. Wyant (New York City).

It is difficult to reconcile the overwhelming importance assigned to salesmen with the number who were actually hired. No one appears to have publicly challenged the value of commercial travellers, but the suspicion is strong that at least a few agreed with the private estimate of Henry Holt: [54]

You know that I believe in travelling for the sake of information, of keeping in touch, but you appear to have forgotten that you believe that for the sake of selling books it is humbug. Scribner told me once that his man had been waiting in Chicago at a first class hotel six days to get a fall order. I told him I had received mine six days before without any man in Chicago. I cannot imagine why in the world Montgomery Ward's people or college professors should want emissaries bothering them regarding their choice of books. . . .

Notwithstanding this, Mr. Thompson, the manager of Scribner's sales department may quote a correct opinion that "the contact of the travellers with the dealers is the most important form of advertising." The percentage of buyers who take books on dealers' recommendations, according to Appleton's recent information, would seem to support that theory, but I think it is only seeming. . . . I want you to think over this aspect of the case very seriously, and to find out whether this notion of the salesman's influence is not, after all, a puffed-up humbug, tho' possibly honestly puffed-up, by men who naturally want to exalt the importance of their own trade.

At least indirect support for Holt's view may be drawn from the lamentations over the plight of the retail bookseller, which were as persistent in 1900 as they had been in the 1870's. There is something curiously inconsistent about hailing commercial travellers as the hope of the future and at the same time raising the question, "Shall the Retail Bookseller Survive?" [55] Precisely how a group of peripatetic wholesalers could survive the collapse of the retail structure was not even considered. Similarly, it was odd that the enthusiasm for commercial travellers was not perceptibly lessened in the face of the frank admission that the distributive machinery was the weakest part of the business.

When *Publishers' Weekly* confessed in 1913 that the industry was still looking for an effective method of distributing books,[56] it inadvertently cast doubt on the substantial worth of the commercial traveller, the trade's most conspicuous adjustment to the industrial era.

The Assault on the Consumer

chapter 8

As the nineteenth century came to a close, publishers turned to a more conscious consideration of the problem of what makes a book sell. The traditional answer, and the easiest one, paid scant tribute to the machinery of distribution which the trade was constructing. Henry Holt voiced it with a confident dogmatism when he said, "The fact is that the book and nothing but the book makes the sale." [1] Such an explanation placed the burden of commercial responsibility entirely upon authors and editors. Taken literally, it implied that the publisher had little to do after the process of manufacture was completed except to fill orders. This kind of resignation, one might almost say defeatism, was implicit in the attitude of most publishers, although they often found words to express it more reasonably. However many might question Holt's low opinion of the worth of salesmen, most agreed with Walter Page's analysis of the problem: [2]

To sell a novel that has the mysterious quality of popularity in it is not difficult. Properly launched, it sells itself. To sell a novel that lacks the inherent quality of popularity—that is almost impossible. . . . Every publisher has proved, over and over again, to his disgust, that he cannot make the people buy a novel that they do not want; and when a novel appears (no better novel) that they do want, the novel-readers find it out by some freemasonry and would buy it if the publisher himself tried to prevent it.

The experience of the trade offered ample support for the conclusion that the vital part of the business, sales to consumer, was an impenetrable mystery. "It is almost amusing," wrote Charles Scribner, "how one publisher takes up such a book . . . after so many others have declined and confirms what we all know, that publishing is very far from an exact science." [3] The head of the house of Lee and Shepard in Boston acknowledged that the largest single printing with which he had been associated was of a novel whose publication had been undertaken with great reluctance: [4]

> We had the manuscript in hand, for a long time, and had just about decided to throw it away, when one day we determined to let it go, just an experiment. The book went so fast—not a bit of advertising by us, either—that we had to run night and day for six days to supply the demand. Then we brought out . . . a companion piece, and it fell like lead on the market.

Occasionally the mystery of successful publishing, induced a mystically-phrased explanation. Robert Sterling Yard thought he had found the essential ingredient by referring to "the Will at the top" and the "success vibrations" emanated by a successful publisher which filtered down through his organization to the public.[5] But more frequently, as the atmosphere of publishing changed from that of a polite art to a business, an attempt was made to solve the riddle in a less metaphysical manner. In a survey conducted in 1901 retailers were unanimously agreed that the average customer did not know what he wanted to buy. The head salesman of a large New York department store was content to say simply that "a large majority" of his customers were undecided. Brentano's representative estimated the number at "two-thirds," while the head of the retail department of Dodd, Mead and Company asserted "perhaps one out of fifteen knows what book he will buy before he crosses the threshold." [6]

Such comments helped to define the problem, but not to answer it. If the purchase of general trade books was determined in most cases by impulse, it was necessary to discover what guided the quick decisions. The salesmen were less sure of these answers. Most agreed that their own recommendations carried considerable weight. But this, in turn, raised the question of why they advised some books and not others. Apparently, the major determinants were the personal tastes of individual salesmen, who confessed to recommending books they themselves liked, and the previous purchases of the customers whose likes and dislikes were thus revealed. It is significant that no one of the participants in the survey thought the urgings of the publishers' representatives important enough to mention even in passing.

Apart from the counsel of the retail seller, customers based their buying upon newspaper advertising, the opinions of personal acquaintances, and the display of a title in windows and within the store itself. The previous work of an author was judged to be important, and a price slightly higher than the one anticipated was not a deterrent. One salesman was at a loss to explain the appeal of the color of the cover: [7]

It is odd, but I find that the color of a cover has a great deal to do with a decision in favor of a book. . . . Red is the most catchy cover, if it is the right shade, and then a nice shade of green. The gilt and the cover designs show up well on either red or green. Let a red or a green be standing erect among a group of other colors, and most people will pick up the bright strong color first.

Increasing attention was to be paid to the appearance of a book and the appeal of its title as the years progressed. In today's market, the once lowly "dust jacket" has been so embellished with eye-compelling drawings and energized descriptions of the contents that it has become a major advertising medium.

Several years after the survey among salesmen was announced, its results were substantially confirmed by a poll conducted among the buyers of Chauncey C. Hotchkiss' novel, *For a Maiden Brave*. About 500 customers complied with the request of the publisher to indicate on a post card which of a number of specified reasons had led to their purchase. Given in order of their importance, the six chief inducements were: [8]

Because the bookseller recommended it	26%
Because you had read the author's previous work	16
Because a friend recommended it	14
Because you saw it reviewed	10
Because you were attracted by its outside appearance	9

One significant factor in retail buying was not mentioned in these investigations. The purpose for which a book was sought might have a decisive bearing on the title selected. Particularly important was the question of whether the purchase was made for the use of the buyer himself, or whether it was intended for someone else. The widespread opinion of modern booksellers that trade books may be considered part of the "gift" business is supported by current statistics which have their counterpart in the earlier era. O. H. Cheney's study of the trade in 1930 lists for both booksellers and publishers the percentage of the year's proceeds gathered in each month. These figures are reproduced below, and in an adjoining column is provided the monthly volume of Henry Holt and Company in 1912: [9]

Month	Per cent of publishers' sales	Per cent of booksellers' sales	Per cent of Holt's sales (1912)
January	8.2	8.1	9.3
February	8.3	7.8	6.8
March	8.9	7.9	4.8
April	6.7	7.4	4.4
May	5.7	6.9	3.2
June	5.9	7.1	3.0
July	7.1	5.6	4.4
August	9.0	5.5	2.0
September	10.9	6.4	20.8
October	11.1	7.8	14.5
November	8.9	8.1	6.3
December	9.3	21.4	7.3

Even if allowance is made for the larger anticipatory buying characteristic of an earlier age of poor transportation, it is apparent that the book trade was no less seasonal before the First World War. A heavy concentration of wholesale buying in the early fall seems to provide good evidence that books were commonly used as presents. Unfortunately, it does not indicate how many books and what kinds of titles were affected, and whether a customer in a retail store was guided by essentially different criteria in selecting a gift rather than a fireside companion.

Although the publisher was only indirectly connected with the sale of books in retail stores, his influence on those sales could be considerable. The personal tastes of the sales clerk were largely beyond his control, but many of the other reasons for book purchases depended upon circumstances which he himself helped to determine. The most obvious of these lay in his power to decide which manuscripts would be accepted for publication. It is not enough to say that the trade discharged its duty to itself when it adopted the single standard of judging any writing submitted in terms of its commercial worth. One must consider also whether the number of manuscripts individually found worthy of investment collectively fitted the requirements of the retail outlets for which they were ultimately intended. There is evidence that the adjustment was deplorable enough to merit constant criticism from *Publishers' Weekly.*[10] Indeed, it is evident that by publishing many times the number of titles that even the largest retailer could stock, the trade insured against a proper wholesale distribution of all but a fraction of the whole. As early as 1878, before the literary deluge had approached the height it was to assume thirty years later, Henry Holt wrote one of his authors: [11]

> You are entirely incorrect in supposing me to think "that Roscher should be in every bookstore, and that [I] have the facilities to place it there in the East." No house has or can have those facilities, and in the vast majority of bookstores, the book would remain on the shelves as long as the shelves should stand. . . . Since Dickens died, there is probably no person living whose work can be placed in "every bookstore."

The certain knowledge that only a small percentage of the total publications would reach the bookseller appears to have been completely ineffective as a deterrent to gradually expanding lists.

The concentration of retail sales around Christmas led to a practice which further assured that many titles would be neglected. Since it was apparent that books were being used "more and more as holiday souvenirs," [12] most houses scheduled the initial appearance of many of their new books to coincide with the peak in consumer demand. Although publication had been seasonal even before the Civil War, the opening of the new era was characterized by two focal points, the early spring and the fall.[13] On the eve of the First World War, *Publishers' Weekly* lamented that regardless of the character of a book, the trade seemed determined to bring it out for the holiday business. In 1910, 35 per cent of the total output came in the six weeks before Christmas, and another 30 per cent in the preceding month and a half. The effect of such a concentration was disastrous, the journal noted: [14]

The reviewer is swamped with good material which he cannot by any possibility adequately notice; the review magazines and departments are clogged with matter they cannot possibly use—material which at other times of the year they are eager for; the buying public is temporarily surfeited to the point of literary indigestion; and the dealer is forced in self defense to call a halt on publications of which at a more opportune time he would order freely.

The dilemma posed by this situation was a serious one to which an entirely satisfactory solution has not yet been found. It was logical for a publisher to meet the consumer demand with new and attractive products; but when all the houses acted together they not only destroyed the potential advantage but created an additional handicap to their business.

The most self-conscious effort to share in the shoppers' holiday budget were the "gift books," ordinarily consisting of a familiar classic or a piece of pretentious sentiment fully illustrated and encased in a highly ornamented binding. The vogue for these titles, which reached a peak in the 1840's and again in the 1880's, was started as early as 1825, when Carey and Lea published *The Atlantic Souvenir* with a declaration on the title page that it was intended as "A Gift for Christmas and the New Year." [15] A half-century later, publishers were no less deliberate in their attempt to capture this same market. Charles Scribner wrote in 1881: [16]

My great disappointment is that we have no Christmas book. The year is a good one and we must have something. I am looking about me and shall probably prepare some illustrated book, if it is only the conventional poem.

The "elegant eighties" had tastes of which the trade was later to disapprove. In 1910, *Publishers' Weekly* attacked the few remaining costly "illustrated gift books" as a bad investment for publisher and buyer alike, worth considerably less than their price and catering to a kind of low taste which was fortunately waning.[17] Since this criticism coincided with a new peak in fall publications, it hardly reflected a trend away from bidding for the Christmas market. But it did imply that the gift books of the future would tend to have solid merit rather than meretricious embellishments.

The publicizing of books gave the publisher another opportunity to affect the decision of the buyer in the retail store. The "commercialization" of publishing of which the older trade leaders complained at the turn of the twentieth century is nowhere more apparent than in the increased effort to impress forcibly upon the consumer the virtues of the current titles. At the close of the Civil War great wonder was expressed at the "stupendous advertising" characteristic of the British trade, in which the total budgets of the most ambitious houses reached the staggering total of £5,000.[18] The attitude taken in this country towards advertising was generally apathetic, one might almost say hostile. In 1875, Scribner, Armstrong and Company submitted "copy" to the *New York Daily Bulletin* with the instruction, "We should prefer that the ad. be not displayed too heavily in order that it may receive several insertions." [19] It may be doubted that the rest of the trade preferred their notices to be so inconspicuous that their novelty would not diminish with repeated use. But the advertisements of other firms do little to suggest the popularity of aggressive book promotion.

As the nineteenth century ended, the mood changed, and it was now the turn of the British to be amazed. Charles Scribner took some delight in reporting to Thomas Nelson Page in 1903 that "Mr. Hodder Williams of Hodder and Stoughton [the English publishers] was greatly impressed by the amount of advertising we were doing and almost fainted when I told him we expected to spend £2000 in that way on your book." [20] Undoubtedly the first Charles Scribner would have had a similar reaction.

The years between had seen a steady growth in the attention given to all the available forms of book publicity. Among the oldest and least spectacular of the devices was the custom of distributing copies of new titles for review in newspapers and magazines. The value of the editorial notices which resulted was the subject of considerable differences of opinion. Walter Page was certain that favorable notices meant very little: [21]

> I, for one, and I know no publisher who holds a different opinion, care nothing for the judgment of the professional literary class. Their judgment of a novel, for instance, is of little value or instruction. . . . Neither can it affect the sales of a new novel. . . . I look upon reviews as so much publicity—they have value, as they tell the public that a book is published and can be bought, and as they tell something about it which may prod the reader's curiosity. Further than this they are of no account. Not one of the three publishers whose personal habits I know as a rule takes the trouble to read the reviews of novels of his own publishing.

George Haven Putnam agreed: "It is, in fact, a constant cause of surprise to both authors and publishers that larger and more direct results in the matter of sales are not brought about by distinctive and favorable reviews." [22] Robert Sterling Yard pointed in 1913 to a survey made over a period of years which showed conclusively that the number and "quality" of the reviews bore little relation to sales, in contradiction to what nineteenth century publishers had long believed.[23] The reception given to the first newspaper literary supplements seemed to Frederick Stokes to suggest the popular opinion of critical reviews. So deplorable was the lack of interest that the sidewalks near the entrances of subways were littered with them. As a consequence, they were later distributed not with the Saturday paper, but on Sunday, "when presumably stay-at-home readers could deposit their unwanted literary pabulum in waste-paper baskets." [24] There was humor, but also an embarrassing amount of truth in Stokes' exaggerated description.

Doubt was cast also on the intrinsic worth of most reviews. *Publishers' Weekly* warned the uninitiated writer not to be surprised if the notices appearing in the newspapers bore a startling similarity not only to each other, but also to editorial matter appearing on the jacket of the book itself.[25] The suggestion that reviewing was ordinarily done with a pair of scissors and a paste-pot was confirmed somewhat by an investigation showing that copies sent out for review were ordinarily accompanied by a prepared notice which the critic was invited to paraphrase or use *verbatim*.[26] Even the literary monthlies came in for their share of criticism. In 1900, an article appeared tabulating the reviews of the four leading journals according to the severity of their judgments with the following results: [27]

	Total Reviews	High Praise	Some Praise	Says Nothing	Condemns
The Critic	75	40	15	17	3
The Book Buyer	60	31	20	4	5
The Bookman	54	39	9	5	1
The Nation	54	31	8	1	14

The author's conclusion that all except *The Nation* "lack the courage of condemnation" was hardly surprising, although deficiencies in critical acumen may have been as responsible as a lack of intellectual fortitude.

Neither would publishers have denied that there was a correlation between advertising and reviewing which was material to the results. George Haven Putnam put it bluntly when he wrote: [28]

With a certain class of periodicals, daily, weekly, and monthly, a pretty close connection is maintained between the editorial or literary department and the publishing or advertising control. If a book or a certain group of books has secured a fair measure of attention in the literary columns of such a periodical, the publisher is pretty sure to receive promptly thereafter a call from a representative of the advertising manager with the suggestion that a purchase of advertising space is now in order.

This was a principle which was understood by the book trade and the reviewing publications alike.

The effort which publishers made to get suitably impressive reviews belies the reports that they held them in contempt. Considerable correspondence was exchanged when books were inadequately mentioned. "It has seemed to me," Charles Scribner complained to the *Christian Union,* "that Grant's book would be a little overlooked if the enclosed is the only notice it received." [29] Henry Holt accused *The Literary World* of "an ingenious piece of injustice" for not mentioning his *Leisure Hour Series* of novels, and received from the editor rather excessive assurances that it would not be ignored in the future.[30]

Counterbalancing the investigations showing the unimportance of reviews to the trade were the results of canvasses made by *Publishers' Weekly* in 1902 and again in 1912. In the earlier poll, all of the participating houses acknowledged their commercial value. The second report revealed that "at all the big houses, Macmillan, Harper's, Putnam, Henry Holt and others—there was a sedulous watchfulness and study of reviews." It was reported, in contradiction to Walter Page's assertion, that George Brett, the president of The Macmillan Company, made every effort to see the reviews of all the books submitted.[31]

The best evidence that publishers valued editorial notices is the fact that they continued to spend many thousands of dollars annually on review copies. Charles Scribner's Sons distributed 7,058 copies of 52 titles published in 1880 and 1881, an average of 136 for each, especially impressive since the typical edition was less than 2,000 copies.[32] In 1897, George Haven Putnam estimated that between 150 and 300 review copies of novels were ordinarily sent out, 100 to 200 copies of books of "standard literature," and a lesser number of "special works." [33] Since a considerable percentage of the retail buyers indicated they were influenced by reviews, it is fortunate that the policy of the trade was not determined by their frequently expressed disdain for critical comments.

Although the advertising budget of the book trade exceeded $5,000,000 by the turn of the century,[34] publishers professed to consider advertising another one of the unsolvable mysteries of their business. Walter Page wrote in 1905: [35]

> About the advertising of books, nobody knows anything. The most that can be said is that some publishers are making interesting experiments. But nobody has yet worked out a single general principle that is of great value. The publishers frankly confess that they do not know how to advertise books—except a few publishers who have had little experience.

Page was willing to admit that "as a theoretical proposition . . . the publisher who will spend the most money in newspaper advertising will sell the most books." [36] But it was also apparent that selling the most books might result in bankruptcy. Many publishers agreed that each title was apt to effect its own natural distribution unaided by a costly promotion campaign, and that advertising could not profitably expand its sales beyond that point.[37] However, this generality was conditioned by another, which asserted that each book was a problem in itself. At least a few had "elasticity," responding "readily and remuneratively to advertising and pushing." [38] Yet there were degrees of "elasticity," and competition often persuaded publishers to find a flexible market where none existed.

Before the Civil War, the errors were usually made on the side of caution. Advertising was viewed with such suspicion that it was not considered a necessary part of the publisher's function. In many contracts, the author not only paid for any promotion which was undertaken outside the catalogue listing, but was responsible for determining what would be done.[39] During the decades after Appomattox, the attitude of the trade became more positive, but scarcely enthusiastic. The total appropriation for fourteen books published by Charles Scribner's Sons in 1880 was $1,450, to which may be added $420 expended for review copies. The principle of "elasticity" seems not to have been applied, since there was little difference among the budgets assigned for Frances Hodgson Burnett's *Louisiana*, Sidney Lanier's *Science of English Verse*, and T. C. Murray's *Origin and Growth of the Psalms*. Then, too, there was something discouragingly perfunctory about the frequency with which the conveniently round sum of $100 appears in the record.[40]

It was during this same decade that *The New York Times* felt called upon to chastise the book trade for its timidity in advertising.[41] In 1892, the editor of *The Critic* could recall only one "glaring" attempt to advertise a book "sensationally"; some young man had been brash enough to describe Walt Whitman's *Leaves of Grass* as "a daisy—and don't you forget it," a horrifying exhibition of bad taste for which he had been discharged. The legitimate "break" with the "old" method seemed to *The Critic's* observer to consist of ornamental borders on the advertisements of a few adventuresome houses. He added: "*Scribner's Maga-*

zine has gone so far as to use a catch phrase: 'When in doubt, buy Scribner's.' "[42]

Then, on the eve of the Spanish-American War, the atmosphere changed rather abruptly. Advertising appropriations soared and the era of the "boomed book" began. By 1900, most of the large houses spent over $50,000 annually for promotion, and at least one had a budget of $250,000.[43] The reasons for the conversion may be associated partly with the factors which were simultaneously causing a precipitous increase in authors' royalties. "Piracy" had ended, and popular magazines had not only arrived but announced that literature and advertising were hereafter to appear together. Authors' agents had become prominent, and it was logical for them to arrange for their authors to affiliate with houses which would promise a maximum of publicity. Although the publisher's profit could evaporate in buying space in newspapers and magazines, and even on "bill-boards," the writer shared none of this expense and received even a higher royalty under a sliding-scale contract if it stimulated more sales.

A large proportion of this twentieth century advertising was done primarily to please some authors and attract others. Henry Holt was not easily stampeded by this rush, but even he confessed in 1903: [44]

More advertising than we have been doing for some years is unquestionably necessary to keep up our standing with the authors and the trade, the authors and the trade, however, being largely mistaken.

Some writers were so persuaded of the certainty of increased returns that they undertook themselves to finance advertising campaigns when the publisher proved obdurate to their pleas. Walter Page recounted the disheartening story of one of his authors who invested $1,000 for extra publicity, the appearance of which just happened to coincide with the initial decline in the sales of his book—an education too expensive for most writers to secure.[45]

Publishers were not alone in their new effort at book promotion. Retail booksellers often made up small pamphlets describing a few selected titles which they sent directly to their own customers. Some of the publishers encouraged this local publicity by making a special allowance for advertising in their wholesale prices. Henry Holt and Company wrote to a dealer in Syracuse, New York, "We should be glad to send you 250 at 40 & 10% and to allow you $25 for advertising, or 100 at 40 & 5 with $10 for advertising." [46] The large Chicago distributor, A. C. McClurg and Company, usually received a standard discount of 5¢ a copy for its own promotion campaigns.[47] Other publishers, however, were so inclined to deprecate these local efforts that they refused to cooperate. *Publishers' Weekly* reported in 1912 that a large Midwestern dealer with a house organ distributed monthly to over 3,000 customers could not persuade a single New York publisher to bear even a prorated share of the mailing expenses. But, continued the journal, some of these same houses shipped the dealer large quantities of their own catalogues, expensive and worthless to him, without so much as a request.[48]

Whether this apathy to the ventures of enterprising retailers was a result of a general saturation with advertising schemes or came from a qualitative judgment of their value, cannot be surmised. Aside from the question of how much should be spent for publicity, there was the even more difficult problem of the best choice of media and the portion of the public at which advertising should be directed. A nonfiction title designed for a limited audience was advertised as a matter of routine in specialized journals catering to the same interests. But the so-called "general literature," especially the novels, admitted no such easy solution. No one actually knew whether it was better to spend $16.50 for a four-inch advertisement in a New York morning newspaper or $7.00 for comparable space in *The Nation.*[49] Robert Sterling Yard yearned in 1913 for a return to the more dignified and literate publicity of the nineteenth century.[50] But Henry Holt thought that "extensive advertising probably does not pay for itself . . . unless they are of a nature that anybody can read who can eat sausage, and are not apt to be read very freely by people who are timid about sausages." [51] Apparently Holt believed that sausage eaters not only were more numerous, but also had among them more book buyers than appeared on the subscription list of *Atlantic Monthly.*

The one point on which most publishers agreed was that in seizing upon advertising, they had grabbed the tail of a monster which might swallow them. The excessive demands made by authors' agents for their writers were only the first of many legitimate obstacles publishers had to face in adapting modern methods of sales promotion to a business which often seemed unable to accept the help that was offered by them. Intelligent advertising had to be based upon a knowledge of what the public wanted, but no publisher felt himself capable of defining what made a book become popular. In other industries, the value of a "brand-name" gave to publicity a cumulative effect; but the book trade realized that few of its purchases could be attributed to the name of a particular company on the title page. The advertising of each book, insofar as it affected the consumer, was useful only to that book. William Ellsworth laid bare the core of the book advertising problem when he wrote: [52]

> The reader of "Hugh Wynne" doesn't go forth and buy another copy as soon as he has read the first; in fact, that is the last thing he does. He is through with "Hugh Wynne" forever, and he turns to another book, an entirely fresh one, probably born in the brain of another writer and turned out from the factory of another publisher. For he is not even impressed by the publisher's name . . . ; the reader doesn't say, as he lays down "Hugh Wynne", "Give me The Century Company's books or none."

Well might the publisher lament his fate, and cast envious glances at the shoe manufacturer or the distributor of patent medicines. In return for the task of making known dozens of different products each year, he had only the consolation of a limited amount of free publicity in the editorial columns of the newspapers and magazines to whose advertising revenue he reluctantly contributed.

Rather desperately, the trade waited for the tide to turn against large advertising appropriations. In 1905, Walter Page announced with some satisfaction that the "boomed book," its sales inflated at the cost of the publisher's profits, was passing.[53] But on the eve of the First World War, another publisher made the same observation over again, referring back to the era of which Page had written as the beginning of the era of "boomed books." [54] Apparently both statements contained a large element of wishful thinking. Addressing the trade in 1943, Alfred Harcourt could look back upon the days before 1914 as the dawn of advertising rather than its noon.[55]

However, there is also at least partial evidence that the fifteen years before the First World War did witness an early climax in advertising which even today's publishers would think excessive. The unnamed house which spent approximately a quarter of a million dollars in 1905 probably did not have sales exceeding $1,500,000, if the statistics of Harper and Brothers are a good indication of the volume of the largest firms. To allot 17 per cent of the gross proceeds for promotion was considered extravagant in 1913 and would be thought equally so now. On the other hand, the 10 per cent which represented an acceptable budget then would not be questioned by most publishers of today.[56] Whatever differences could be noted would concern more the quality of advertising than its quantity. Yet a more clear-cut knowledge of the psychology of the public and of the need for tailoring promotion to suit the needs of each individual title did not bring to the trade an appreciably greater confidence in its publicity methods. When William Ellsworth asserted that "no one has ever found the sure way to advertise a book," [57] he spoke for the future as well as the past.

These advertising efforts were, of course, primarily designed to get the consumer into the retail store, an institution which the publisher viewed with respect and suspicion. Looked at from a business viewpoint, the suspicion was perhaps more justified. The ultimate effectiveness of publishers' efforts to improve the wholesale structure of their business was dependent on the extent to which it was matched by a development of the bookstores. It is difficult to get reliable statistics concerning the number and quality of these outlets. A comprehensive survey made by the *American Publishers' Circular and Literary Gazette* in 1859 listed 2,090 bookstores in 843 cities and towns, an average of one for 15,000 inhabitants.[58] In 1914, a canvas made for the *American Book Trade Manual* listed 3,501 stores, one outlet for each 28,000 persons. Only 24 of the 801 localities mentioned had populations under 5,000.[59] Although many smaller towns had stores partly devoted to books, it was apparent that the rural areas were inadequately covered. The report made by O. H. Cheney in 1930 showed 4,053 stores, one for each 30,000 inhabitants. Most of these were concentrated in a few large cities. Only 60 per cent of the people living in places with a population between 10,000 and 25,000 were served, and 32 per cent of the American public was without any direct access to a bookstore.[60] These figures offer discouraging testimony not only to the inadequacy of the retail book system, but also to the declining importance of books in the American culture.

Although most publishers were convinced that local retailers were their principal link to the consumer, it is probable that a majority of the books sold in any year before the World War were not purchased from bookstores. Frank Compton estimated that 90 per cent of the book sales of the "Gilded Age" were through other channels.[61] Hubert Hungerford, who entered the trade in the 1890's, described the principal method of book distribution used in that era: [62]

In my bookhood, the predominating plan of selling books was through the army of book agents numbering many thousands who skirmished through every city, town, and hamlet, armed with prospectuses showing various styles of binding and containing persuasive testimonials to back up the carefully memorized sales arguments of the solicitors.

"Subscription books," especially designed for these door-to-door sales, were well known before the Civil War, and a highly organized corps of salesmen was regularly employed in distributing them. Such enterprising individuals as "Parson" Weems, diligently peddling his *Life of George Washington* over the countryside, had given way to companies with a systematic coverage of a particular locality. For example, the *American Literary Gazette and Publishers' Circular* in 1865 carried the advertisement of "Payne and Holden, General Subscription Agency for the West," which announced: [63]

We inform the Publishers of Subscription Books, Engravings, Prints, etc., that we employ a corps of Agents who canvas Ohio, Indiana, Illinois, and other States, and are prepared to push the works of any house if terms are sufficiently liberal.

Although most publishers employed these agencies, the trade as a whole held them in low esteem, judging itself superior to such "peddling" and predicting that this undignified competition with regular bookstores would quickly disappear as the country's urbanization progressed.

By the 1890's subscription selling had reached a yearly volume of over $12,000,000 and *Publishers' Weekly* was forced to the consideration of "whether, after all, this particular line is not more properly a part of the business" than other accepted practices.[64]

Instead of declining in importance, subscription books had proved so profitable that most large houses brought out special titles and established separate departments for this branch of the trade. Although only a few commercial travellers were employed in the wholesaling of books to retail stores, large staffs were organized to compete with the retailers by selling directly to the consumer. The first step had been to hire temporary help to distribute a specific book. The decision of Scribner, Armstrong and Company in 1872 to sell Sir Henry Stanley's *How I Found Livingstone* by the subscription method involved an immediate search for extra salesmen.[65] Thirty-five years later, Charles Scribner's Sons had a "Subscription Department with branch offices in the principal cities and a large number of agents" continually employed to handle whatever books became available.[66]

There are several reasons why the subscription business proved durable. The two factors which made the regular trade financially hazardous, the small size of the average edition and the multiplicity of titles, were seldom present to disturb it. The first printing of most books intended for the bookstores in the "Gilded Age" usually did not exceed 2,500 copies, but a book would not even be considered for the subscription list if the anticipated sales did not justify an initial edition several times as large. Charles Scribner persuaded Thomas Nelson Page to take a reduced royalty on a collected edition of his work distributed by canvassers by citing the $20,000 received by Richard Harding Davis under a similar arrangement for the sale of 50,000 sets of volumes whose bookstore distribution had all but ceased.[67] In 1905, Walter Page could illustrate the profitableness of subscription selling by referring to a publisher who ordinarily did not bring out a book unless he could expect to sell 100,000 copies.[68]

While the nature of regular trade publishing seemed to dictate an extensive list, the subscription branch of the business was built upon the opposite principle. The assumption was not that the popularity of any one title was so much a matter of speculation that many books should be published to guarantee a limited number of successes. Rather, the expectation of success was imposed upon subscription houses. Since only a few titles could be handled at one time by an agent, the subscription house was forced to confine his list and assume that each book would be a success.[69] The greater efficiency of this method of bookselling is apparent at once. Each of the several thousand bookstores on which the publisher relied for trade books could be expected to stock only a fraction of them. But every subscription book was assured of an army of retail salesmen devoted to pushing it. In addition to the special staffs employed by individual publishers, there were distributing firms with as many as 5,000 salesmen, and a host of independent canvassers, estimated in 1894 to total 20,000 in the city of Chicago alone. All these could be called upon by the subscription house. Even when every bookstore in the country carried a trade book on its shelves, that book did not enjoy facilities as ample as those provided by the canvasser's suitcase.[70]

Still another advantage accrued to the publisher of subscription books. It was seldom found necessary to publicize the titles by display advertising in expensive media. Each of the volumes in a collected edition of the works of a famous writer was already well known to the public. For those books which were originally published as subscription volumes, the canvasser acted both as salesman and publicity agent, displaying carefully prepared pamphlets and showing samples of his wares. Critical reviews in the literary journals and newspaper supplements were deemed of such little value that the expense of complimentary copies was largely avoided.[71]

While there was a considerable compulsion within the trade book field to keep costs as low as possible, the purchasers of subscription books were accustomed to large commitments and agents would not even handle a low-priced book. Charles Scribner's list of subscription publications in 1891 included such titles as: *The Cyclopaedia of Music and Musicians* in three volumes, each priced at $25; Bryant's *Popular History of the United States* in four volumes and in a number of different bindings, the prices ranging from $6 to $10.50 per volume; and George Ashdown Andsley's *The Ornamental Arts of Japan,* offered in four parts, $100 for each part.[72] In the early and more suspicious days following the Civil War, agents collected a deposit and a single volume was delivered at stipulated intervals, payment being made in as many installments as there were volumes. However, the subscription business received a large impetus when publishers made the discovery that most people were honest and could be trusted to discharge their obligations even when the entire set of books was delivered at once. Beginning in the 1890's, installment buying assumed in the book business its present characteristics. Some few buyers refused to pay, but losses under this system were actually less than those under the former arrangement.[73] In general, regular retail buying did not lend itself to credit purchases.

One may legitimately ask why, in the face of the evident superiority of subscription selling, publishers continued to conduct so large a part of their business through bookstores. The answer must begin with the understanding that the regular retail trade was less important than it was customarily assumed to be. All of the large houses dealt in subscription books, and considered them the most profitable part of their business. But there were limits to the number of books and the kinds of books which could be sold through canvassers. Single volumes were ordinarily avoided in favor of multi-volume sets. But before the collected works of Rudyard Kipling or Henry James could grace a library, the individual titles had to be offered through the regular trade. Further, the necessity for editions large enough to engage an army of agents eliminated most books from consideration. The trade as a whole required the expensive nourishment which came from countless speculations in small editions.

Even for the individual house, the prospect of conducting a business solely in subscription books was often unattractive. The love of books which led most talented publishers into the trade also obliged them to see this side of the business purely as a marketing device rather than as a service to literature. Many of the titles had no more intrinsic appeal for them than did the showy "gift books," which they gladly discarded in favor of a production schedule making their best works available for the Christmas trade. Instead of viewing subscription books as the soul of their business, they tended to regard them as a subsidy which permitted experimentation with the fine manuscripts provided by younger writers and the occasional volumes of verse adding dignity to their lists and a deficit to their balance sheets. To have denied themselves these extravagances would have been to divest publishing of its most rewarding moments.

Competing with the subscription agent and the retail bookstore alike was the publishers' custom of selling directly to the consumer through the mails. Although statistical evidence is not available, there can be little question that this branch of the business was important at the beginning of the "Gilded Age" and grew steadily up to the eve of the First World War. As early as 1879, *Publishers' Weekly* cautioned the trade about the plight of the bookstores: [74]

> We have received this year, perhaps in greater quantity than ever before—and that is saying a great deal—numerous newspapers and clippings and private letters showing the demoralization of the trade and the impossibility of making any sort of living out of selling books, especially in view of the direct competition of publishers. They are well founded. . . .

A quarter of a century later, the volume of orders received by mail had expanded so greatly as to make it difficult to recall these earlier complaints. Frank Dodd wrote in 1905: [75]

The enormous mail order business which is now being done and which is so rapidly growing all over the country is, of course, a very modern thing. One does not have to go back far to reach the point when it was unknown. I regard this as a most important development of our business life and one which is probably to have far reaching consequences. Indeed, it does not seem impossible that the day will come when the manufacturer and consumer will meet each other directly. The jobber, or middleman between the merchant and manufacturer, has pretty well disappeared. How long is it to be before the retailer will step aside and the manufacturer meet his customer without intervention?

There was, indeed, sufficient difference between mail-order methods in 1865 and 1904 to justify a qualitative distinction, although Dodd underestimated the long-standing quantitative significance of the trade. In place of a perfunctory announcement in advertisements that "books will be sent upon receipt of the price," publishers sought aggressively to place persuasive circulars in the hands of likely book-buyers, even before they had indicated an interest in receiving them. Each house had its carefully selected list of consumers, and to these could be added others rented from the early predecessors of today's "list brokers." Persons who subscribed to magazines were generally considered good prospects, although their response varied considerably from title to title. Consequently, the science of conducting a mail-order business came to include a sampling technique. Only a small portion of the names on a given list would be circularized at first. If the returns from this experiment were satisfactory, a two per cent response being considered adequate, circulars would then be sent to the entire list with the expectancy that the same proportion of sales would result.[76]

This procedure has become standard today; but what is worth observing is that the method was clearly defined before the First World War, and used even more extensively. When Edward H. Dodd, Jr. wrote a history of Dodd, Mead and Company in 1939 he felt obliged to remark that his grandfather's dire prediction of the fate of the bookseller had been incorrect: "Today's jobbers are unusually active and the mail order business has slowed down." [77] At the present time the cost of the mail-order business in books is so high that many publishers economize by paying less than the usual royalty to authors on the resulting sales. On the other hand, this distribution is considered so little to interfere with the regular trade that even the literary agents do not complain about the reduction.[78]

At the close of the half-century following the Civil War book sales were divided roughly into three categories, according to the method used to procure them. Subscription, bookstore, and mail distribution were probably of more nearly equal importance than they had been before or were to be in the future. An analysis of the "direct expenses" of Harper and Brothers for September, 1910, allotted approximately $12,000 for the regular wholesale trade with bookstores, $15,000 for "subscription books" and $9,000 for "direct mail." Were the sales figures available for the same period, they would probably indicate no less equal a division of the total business.[79] However, the prevailing view of trade leaders anticipated that the reliance of the regular trade publisher upon the retail bookstore would increase rather than diminish. Subscription sales were considered a "nuisance" [80] and mail-order distribution an encroachment on the legitimate enterprise of the retailers.[81] *Publishers' Weekly* complained: [82]

If the retail outlets of a trade are to be strong and efficient merchandising outlets for the wholesaler he must give them his sincere and undivided support. The publisher *who goes through the motions of supporting the retail bookseller* while throwing all his enthusiasm and interest into his mail order department need not be surprised if his retail department "does not show returns." Has he any right to complain if dealers "are apathetic"? The wonder, under the circumstances, would be if they were not.

Unfortunately, it was not the bookseller who was apathetic, but the consumer. Subscription and mail-order sales were a symptom of the unprofitableness of the book industry which good intentions toward the retailer could not overcome. Indeed, the dilemma was neatly, although not consciously, posed by those publishers who at the same time urged support of the regular bookstore and confessed to a "radical deficiency of proper distributive machinery." [83] The business in subscription and mail-order books was largely to be separated, like the publication of magazines, from the province of the regular trade publisher. But in its place were to appear the sale of serial, motion-picture, and book-club rights supplying the margin between success and failure. In 1950, as in 1900, bookstore sales provided only a precarious living for retailer and publisher alike.

The Problems of Competition and the Self-Regulation of the Book Trade

chapter 9

The industrial era which followed the Civil War was characterized by competition which had considerable difficulty in restraining itself to profitable limits. Business leaders were caught between a theory that rivalry unrestricted by law was the "life of trade," and the fact that it had caused the death of many commercial enterprises. Neither the railroad "rate wars" of the "Gilded Age" nor the frequent "gluts" of oil in the refining centers testified to the efficiency of unbridled competition, a truth which was quickly acknowledged. If the age of Commodore Vanderbilt and John D. Rockefeller pledged its allegiance to Adam Smith and Herbert Spencer, it invented the "pool" and the "trust" to circumscribe the automatic mechanisms of commerce. When these devices proved either too ineffective or too compulsive, the government was called upon even before the First World War both to limit competition and to insist upon it.

The book trade was typical of other industries in its desperate search for a formula which would permit it to enjoy the benefits of competition without its penalties. Even before the Civil War ended, the problems which were to plague it for the next half-century were clearly evident, chief among them the underselling induced by keen rivalry for the market. Recourse to government regulation was not remotely considered; but leading spokesmen insisted that free enterprise contained within itself the principle of self-control, and presupposed certain rules of business conduct by which all should abide. Addressing a meeting of Philadelphia publishers and booksellers in 1864, Frederick Leypoldt asserted: [1]

> If we take away the principle of a fixed retail price from our business, we destroy it root and branch. . . . It is well known that in every branch of business as well as in bookselling there is a certain point beyond which everything is *not* fair in competition. This point is attained when certain men employ capital and influence to control the market and regulate by their own avarice those prices which should be controlled by the natural laws of supply and demand.

The sense of this exposition, and of the other speeches made at the meeting, was that natural economic law was guided, and should be governed, by a morality generic to it. Price-cutting was considered "dishonorable"; and monopoly was thought attainable only at the sacrifice of the self-restraint demanded by a proper regard for the automatic operation of supply and demand. However contradictory this analysis may be, it was well understood by the audience and lay at the base of every attempt made by the book trade to regulate itself up to 1914.

Like many other business men, publishers were inclined to feel that there was a quality to their trade which made it uniquely vulnerable to excessive competition. "We hold," said *Publishers' Weekly* in 1890, "that the peculiar conditions of the book trade make underselling not legitimate competition, but cut-throatism." [2] There was more than self-pity in this assertion. Publishing shared little in the enormous expansion of markets which many new industries enjoyed; year by year the book trade declined in relative economic importance. While profits multiplied the fortunes of the Armours, the Carnegies, and the Pillsburys, the fate of many leading publishers hung in precarious balance. At the peak of "McKinley prosperity" in 1900, the industry witnessed the disheartening failure of two of its largest and, presumably, its strongest firms—Harper and Brothers and D. Appleton and Company.

Balancing these handicaps were the advantages accruing from the unusually effective cooperation which the producing companies were able to achieve in many aspects of the trade. "Piracy" was substantially limited to a special group of companies outside the circle of regular trade publishers, who themselves confined their competition and increased their expenses by honoring the code of "trade courtesy." Neither was there any large effort, until the 1890's, to compete for native authors by the enticement of larger royalties—a remarkable restraint in view of the overwhelming importance of manuscripts.

These practices tended to channel competition in the direction of price. But price competition was somewhat peculiar in the book trade. Costs did not vary perceptibly from firm to firm, and most retail prices made allowance only for a narrow margin of profit. Consequently, the announced price for any given class of books—novels, travel books, or collections of literary essays—varied little in the trade. Further, since no two titles were identical, direct competition was theoretically minimized. While these conditions did not actually eliminate competition among the publishers, they generated an additional contest among the producer, the wholesaler, and the retailer for the consumer's dollar. If the publisher was compelled by market conditions to offer a discount too large to permit him a profit, he could circumvent not only the wholesaler, but even the bookstore, by offering the book at retail through the mails for a price sufficient to give him a good return, but below which a distributor could sell. However unfair this competition was, it was sufficiently widespread to merit the chastisement of *Publishers' Weekly:* [3]

> The true function of the publisher is that of the wholesaler; and until the American publisher adopts the position of his German colleague, and refuses to sell directly to the customer, he can never hope for healthy conditions in the book trade.

On a different occasion the trade journal referred to another aspect of this internecine war: [4]

> There is probably no trade which has suffered more than the book trade from "competition"—but it is competition of an unusual sort. It is, in the first place, competition of wholesalers with the retailers to whom they sell; it is, in the second place, competition of retailers . . . with wholesalers or other dealers who work chiefly by catalogues or advertisements without local expenses . . . and are able to use the mails.

A settlement would not be obtained in this war between wholesaler and retailer, contended *Publishers' Weekly,* until publishers ceased to compete unfairly in the retail market by underselling their own customers.

This vertical competition interacted with the rivalry among the publishers themselves. Although no two books served precisely the same purpose, the needs of the average buyer were indeterminate enough to be met by a great variety of titles. Novels competed not only with other novels, but also with biographies and histories. Further, since every book could not be carried in any one bookstore, there was considerable competition for the space on the retailers' shelves. Before the days of the travelling salesmen and the large advertising appropriations, the chief inducement offered to the distributors was an extra discount. But when publishers competed by giving lower wholesale prices, they increased the retailer's margin of profit, and invited precisely the same price-cutting which they considered to be the trade's great evil. It was impossible to maintain fixed prices at one level and ignore them at another.

To meet these and other problems, the publishing industry established a series of trade associations which attempted to strengthen the healthy trends of commercial development, and abolish detrimental competitive practices. The first of the many was the American Company of Booksellers, founded in 1801 by members of the trade in New York, Philadelphia, and Boston. The following year the association held the first in a series of annual "literary fairs" designed to increase sales and to stimulate quality in book manufacture through the award of prizes. With the heritage of the gilds behind it, the board of directors assumed more control for this company than any of its successors were to enjoy. The price of all books exhibited was subject to its discretion, and any disputes which arose were arbitrarily settled by the governing body. But the organization proved no better able than the weaker bodies of later years to perpetuate itself for more than a few years.[5] Equally abortive was the first of the special organizations devoted to the sale of schoolbooks. The New York Association of Booksellers, which began its brief existence in 1802, was as much an independent publishing house as a regulatory body. It sought not only to enforce standard discounts and credit terms, but also to establish its own list of school publications to be sold through the stores of its members.[6] This cooperative action was considered the only effective means of meeting the competition of the British texts on which the country primarily depended.

When both of these organizations disintegrated, Henry C. Carey, whose father had been a president of the schoolbook group, tried in 1824 to create a new controlling body among the publishers to sponsor a yearly exhibit of books. His failure turned to success of a kind when a substitute plan, an independent trade sale, attracted such interest that it shortly became a collective enterprise. The trade sales themselves required a considerable degree of cooperation. When publishers again turned to a more formal organization in the 1850's, it was primarily because of the need for regulating them more closely. Known variously as the New York Publishers' Association, the Publishers' Association, and the American Book Publishers' Association, this next attempt at commercial self-government began in 1855 and met its end in the confused days at the beginning of the Civil War. Among its presidents was William H. Appleton. Charles E. Rode, who became secretary in 1856, was also the publisher of the leading trade magazine, the *American Literary Gazette and Publishers' Circular,* which merged its identity with *Publishers' Weekly* in 1872. Although the trade sales were the organization's main interest, considerable effort was made to standardize retail credit policies, and to support George Haven Putnam's fight for an international copyright law.[7]

The early years of the Civil War signalized the beginning of a new era in which the twin problems of irregular discounts and retail price-cutting would be the major concern of reform efforts. Only two years after the demise of the Publishers' Association, and while the war was forcing a general rise in retail prices, the pages of the leading trade journal were filled with complaints of underselling in the peculiar world of books, and with suggestions for a new regulatory body. Retailers were urged to look upon the publishers not as an ally in their fight for stable conditions, but as an opponent. Describing a firm which advertised a retail price of $1.25 and sold at $1.00 directly to the consumer, a correspondent of the *Publishers' Circular* protested: [8]

When a large publishing house of acknowledged standing and respectability in the trade, with extended resources, and having no other motive but a desire to crush all engaged in the retail business, resorts to such a course, it becomes a matter of concern as well as alarm, and should excite the just indignation of all who are in the legitimate pursuit of retail bookselling.

Such a condemnation was more accurate as a measure of the desperate plight of the bookseller than as an analysis of the motivation of the publishers. At least part of the difficulty could be attributed to the fact that the function of the publisher was not clearly defined. The average house combined retailing with its publishing activities; and while it willingly acknowledged the position of the bookstore, it scarcely considered its own sales to the consumer as trespassing. Publishers wished the bookstores to prosper, but they were reluctant to sacrifice to the welfare of the retailer their independence in determining retail prices.

The end of the war intensified rather than lessened the disruptiveness of these conditions. Several years before the Panic of 1873, the trade was wallowing in the trough of a depression and accusations were being exchanged on all sides. The retailer was condemned for his timidity in buying stock, the publisher for making it impossible for him to buy with confidence. Retailers undersold one another, and publishers denounced their competitors for inaugurating a vicious cycle of excessive discounts. In desperation the thoughts of the book trade turned again to an industrial association which would strengthen its ineffectual efforts at self-regulation. The textbook publishers were the first to organize themselves. Meeting in 1870, they established the Publishers' Board of Trade to bring some kind of order out of the unprofitable chaos into which competition had led them. One of the most destructive practices at which the Board immediately struck was the custom of giving a special "introduction" price to a school board in order to secure an adoption. So feverish was the rivalry that this price often amounted to nothing except an uneven barter, the new books being given for an equal number of the old title. *Publishers' Weekly* noted that "some schools, on the pretext of exchange, got their books chronically for nothing; and those not 'so sharp' had to pay the more." [9] The excesses which had been induced can best be illustrated by the maximum discount for "introduction" copies fixed by the reform organization. A 66⅔ per cent discount was to be considered legitimate except in cases where books were actually exchanged for old books in use; the latter were held to have sufficient salvage value to limit the discount to 50 per cent. The other price restrictions were a 40 per cent maximum discount on special quantity purchases made by states and other larger consumers, and 20 per cent as a general maximum discount. The retail price was to be the basis for these computations. The older system of offering reductions from the wholesale price was considered especially pernicious, since that price was minimal and often left no margin for the customary special discounts.[10]

Another great evil in textbook distribution arose from the use of agents, whose aggressive tactics had much to do with the disastrous discount policies. As unwelcome to the publishers as the price wars which they fostered was their frequent recourse to bribery of school boards and individual teachers. The original by-laws provided for the total extinction of these agents, who were the predecessors of the commercial travellers so highly prized in later years. An "arbitration committee," endowed with broad investigatory power, made recommendations in each case of a reported violation which were voted on by the body of the membership.[11]

For several years, the Board of Trade enjoyed a conspicuous success. All of the major textbook publishers participated in it, cutting their agency staffs by a half and raising their discounts to a profitable level. If *Publishers' Weekly* may be believed, the disintegration of the organization in 1877 came about because of public opposition. The Board of Trade was denounced as a monopolistic device for keeping prices artificially high. In the Midwest, the resentment took the form of legislative action designed to circumvent the "ring" by prescribing maximum prices for state procurement. In 1877 Minnesota passed a bill mentioning by name the titles in common use and requiring the state's textbook agent to obtain books of "equal" value for 50 per cent of their retail price.[12] The legend that schoolbook publishers made enormous profits was a persistent one which the trade took some pains to refute. But protests of innocence were not enough to counterbalance the monopolistic appearance of the Board of Trade. At least several houses were willing to sacrifice their organization to the public clamor against it. Even underselling was considered preferable to close legislative control over buying, and the threat of government publishing.

Publishers' Weekly was scarcely willing to acknowledge that the trade was attempting to exploit the public through a monopolistic device. But it lamented that the benefits of reform had not been shared more obviously. Even if the economics of textbook production justified the publishers' attempts to get a larger share of the proceeds, a good public relations policy suggested that the reduction in discounts should be accompanied with some reduction in retail price. But prices did not decline perceptibly during the life of the Board of Trade.[13]

Perhaps even more important to the destruction of the Board than the public criticism directed at it was the internal pressure exerted against its original principles. The decision to abolish all agents was extremely drastic and at odds with the main development in wholesale distribution. Only a year after the original by-laws were passed in 1870, they were amended to admit a maximum of ten agents for each house. "In 1873, the ten became fifteen, and before the Board dissolved, twenty-five."[14] With the return of the agency system, came a renewal of the abuses which had originally prompted the formation of the organization. As the larger houses, led by Ivison, Blakeman, Taylor and Company withdrew from the Board, the structure of regulated discounts disintegrated, bribery was reintroduced, and a fiercely competitive, and generally unprofitable era of textbook selling ensued. The organization was formally dissolved in 1877.[15]

The need of the industry could not be met by attempting an artificial change in the basic system of selling books. But the desired end, which was to introduce into the distributive mechanism a measure of restraint adequate to make the schoolbook business decent and profitable, did not seem attainable. After the failure at collective self-regulation came the attempt of a coalition of firms to achieve stable conditions by monopolizing the field. Previous mention has been made of the community of interest established among Ivison, Blakeman and Company and its principal rivals in the 1880's.[16] Its formidableness is attested to by the withdrawal from the textbook branch of the trade of such former leaders as Charles Scribner's Sons and Harper and Brothers. In keeping with a trend observable in industry as a whole, this loose agreement gave way to a single corporation. It is not too much to say that the American Book Company, formed in 1890, had much the same origin and purposes as Standard Oil of New Jersey. Like other trusts, it encountered the hostility both of the public and its competitors. But its achievements were short of its intentions. The advantages of mere size were not so decisive as to make it impossible for much smaller firms to compete. The consumer was not susceptible to control, and such narrow limits were set on operating economies that the lesser houses could produce as good a product and sell it as cheaply as the American Book Company.

On the eve of the World War, both the threat of monopoly and the curse of underselling had been substantially lessened. As early as 1904, *Publishers' Weekly* could report: [17]

> Schoolbooks are as a matter of fact published today on a system somewhat similar to the net system of the American Publishers' Association—that is to say, with close retail prices from which only a moderate discount is allowed to the trade and in the case of large purchases, as by Boards of Education. The list price—misleadingly called "wholesale", "net" or "introduction" price . . . is in fact the price at which a single copy will be supplied to a teacher.

The journal attributed this fortunate state of affairs and the general excellence of textbooks to "the keenness of private enterprise" spurred on by unrestrained competition.[18] However true this was, it scarcely accounted for the fact that the same competition a quarter of a century before had produced chaos in the market. Neither could the change in atmosphere be explained by a regulatory body, since the unfortunate Board of Trade had no successor. What seems apparent is that a system based on the profit system required an adjustment which would permit some profits. The excessive rivalry of the quarter-century following the Civil War represented a kind of indulgence difficult to stop, but precluded in the long run by the limits placed on capital resources. On the other hand, since the trade was not susceptible to monopoly, competition operated to confine profit margins within a narrow range.

The disruptive years after the Civil War had no less disastrous an effect upon the market in trade books; and like the textbook publishers, the houses dealing in general literature attempted to solve their problems by forming an industrial association. As usual, the first trumpet call for a national organization was sounded by the trade journal, which in 1872 urged that the whole book trade emulate the example of its Philadelphia branch by meeting to consult on common problems.[19] Curiously enough, the first definite steps toward this goal were taken at a meeting of Western booksellers in Cincinnati in 1874. In the following year, the American Book Trade Association took its complete form at a convention held in Put-In Bay, Ohio. The next meeting took place at Niagara Falls, and the last at Philadelphia's centennial celebration in 1876.

Among the several targets of reform, ruinous discounts took first place. Some thirty years later, Frank Dodd facetiously recalled the original intention: [20]

> The basis of that association was an agreement among booksellers and publishers to give no discount, except to ministers, teachers, librarians, and professional men generally and their mothers-in-law. Such an agreement was, of course, soon broken. I remember very well, as one of the committee of the association, going downtown in a coach with Mr. Randolph and Walter Appleton to obtain the signatures of Legatt Brothers, where we had a rough time, and Harper and Brothers, who had up to that time refused to sign their names.

Accompanying this attempt to make the consumer pay the full retail price was a policy of limiting trade discounts to 20 per cent. Since the previous regular discount had been 33⅓ per cent and often rose to 40 per cent or even more, the cure prescribed was too drastic to be administered.[21] Like the Board of Trade, the Book Trade Association attempted so much that it discouraged cooperation with its regulations. And just as the textbook firms had encountered public resentment, so the trade houses were condemned for a selfish attempt to raise prices in the middle of a depression. Frederick Leypoldt found himself a lone voice crying at the last convention for a reduction in retail prices not only to allay public fears, but also to limit the opportunity for price-cutting. The "book butchers" thrived when the regular retailers had a comfortable margin of profit; and only by making the selling of books less profitable could the legitimate distributors be protected.[22]

Contributing to the disruption in both trade discounts and retail prices were the trade sales, which the Book Trade Association made a substantial effort to abolish. The opposition to the sales had centered for several years in *Publishers' Weekly;* and it was its editor, Frederick Leypoldt, who suggested the alternative of a book fair similar to that held annually in Leipzig. The failure in 1876 of two fairs enthusiastically supported by the publishers, and the return of the trade sale to New York in the following year, proved to be more than the fragile reputation of the Book Trade Association could stand. It expired just a few months after the text publishers' Board of Trade.[23]

The 1880's were barren of a general industrial organization, but offered some relief from the depression years. Some measure of prosperity returned to the publishers, lessening the pressure to extend discount competition to suicidal extremes. The trade sales gradually faded because of their basic defects. However, another of the basic problems, whose solution had been held temporarily in abeyance because of more pressing concerns, emerged in this decade to claim the primary attention of the trade. It was indeed futile to attempt to stabilize prices on books when "pirates" were flooding the market with uncopyrighted works at a price so low as to prevent anyone from making money. As early as 1837, Henry Clay had presented the Senate with a bill to protect American authors by preventing the theft of foreign works. A half-century later, the basic copyright law remained unchanged.[24] Even before the Civil War, many American publishers agreed with the writers that "piracy" brought more sorrow than benefit. Ninety-seven publishers and book manufacturers joined George Palmer Putnam in 1843 in petitioning Congress for relief.[25] Mention has been made of the American Book Publishers' Association's efforts in the 1850's to remedy the defects of the copyright law. After Charles Dickens' urgent pleas to an American audience in 1867, an attempt was made to form an International Copyright Organization to agitate for proper legislation and, failing that, to reach some general agreement concerning the voluntary payment of British writers.[26] The practices of "trade courtesy" were thereby strengthened, but a remedy at law was still considered essential. During the 1870's several bills were presented, supported by a majority of the regular publishers, but met with no success.

The opposition was indeed formidable. Beyond the public protest that an international copyright would raise the price of books, serving the interests of a few publishers at a sacrifice of many millions of consumers, there were a number of specific groups determined to defeat it. To the "pirates" could be joined some "respectable" traders like the Harpers and Henry Carey Baird, holding either "an honest if fallacious theory," or convinced that they could hold their own in a ruthlessly competitive market.[27] The distributors of cheap books, including some of the large jobbers, did not want to see their main source of supply dammed up; after the Harpers shifted their views in 1878, the principal opponent was the American News Company.[28]

The opposition outside the industry was even more considerable. Paper-makers, and all the businesses concerned with book manufacture—many of them far more powerful than the book trade—feared that a law giving protection to foreign authors would also multiply the number of foreign books imported.[29]

The fact that many opposed a copyright law did not make its lack more easily endured, nor did it lessen the determination of its advocates to bring their long fight to a successful conclusion. In 1887, the publishers combined their resources for another assault upon Congress. Organizing themselves into the American Publishers' Copyright League, they resolved to exert a continuous pressure through lobbying and propaganda designed to bring before the public and its elected representatives the need for a definitive law.[30] The leaders of the movement were George Haven Putnam, William Worthen Appleton, and Charles Scribner,[31] but the roster of members included all the prominent houses.[32] The intensive effort of several years was capped by the passage of a suitable law in 1891.

It is difficult to estimate the importance of this organization to the final result. Referring to a bill pending in 1888, the treasurer of the League, Charles Scribner, wrote, "We are pushing it with a special man in Washington and at an expense of $40 per day, but *no one* knows whether anything will come of it." [33] During the organization's first year, over $4,000 was spent to speed the cause,[34] but with what effect is not known. The character of the League's officials and the extant private correspondence concerning its activities, do not admit the possibility of anything more sinister than arguments being offered as an inducement to Congressmen. Probably as effective as these contentions was the simple justice of the demands, and the fact that in the final bill, means were found for protecting the manufacturing interests. The protection given to foreign authors was not extended to the original foreign editions, but was limited to books "printed from type set within the limits of the United States, or from plates made therefrom." [35] This clause reflected not only the urgings of binders, papermakers, and metal interests, but also the insistence of the powerful typographical unions.[36]

The effect of the law on the price of books and the profits of publishing was considerable, although probably it did not match the expectations of the supporters or opponents of international copyright. The trade had argued rather consistently that book prices would not be raised appreciably; but it was willing to acknowledge, with *Publishers' Weekly,* that "it is cheaper to steal brooms than to buy them." [37] Henry Holt was not deterred from supporting the principle of international copyright by his knowledge that no law could be drawn "without damaging some interests." [38] Among the victims of 1891 were the "pirate" houses and the people who purchased their products. Many of the series of paper-bound editions which had flooded the country now disappeared, Monro's *Seaside Library* and Harpers' *Franklin Square Library* being two conspicuous examples.[39] Low-cost editions that had been made possible by depriving foreign authors of any returns were swept from the market.

On the other hand, it is questionable that the price for

the regular editions of either American or foreign works increased because of the copyright law. The attitude of the publishers at the time the law was passed was reflected in a letter written by Charles Scribner to an English correspondent, John Murray, Jr.: [40]

> The ruling price for novels here, whether English or American, is 50¢ in paper, and $1.00 or $1.25 in cloth, and we regard it as important that there should be no immediate increase of retail prices on account of the passage of the copyright bill, but that publishers should rely upon the increased profit which would come from the control of the market.

Fifteen years later, the average price for a novel had risen slightly, but the difference can easily be accounted for by increases in advertising appropriations and manufacturing costs. Insofar as copyright was reflected in the price rise, it benefited the writers and not the publishers. However, the law brought other blessings to the trade. Before it was passed, the houses which issued the authorized editions of English writers, paying a royalty before none was legally necessary, suffered considerable losses when pirated editions appeared. Either the competition was met by reducing prices below a point where they could cover costs, or the books were placed in dead inventory to be "remaindered" through the trade sales or at special auction prices. Beyond this negative advantage was the stimulation given to the regular book market by the inability of the public to purchase the works of the best authors in cheap editions.

The other beneficiaries within the trade were the American authors and the book manufacturers. Wrote Charles Scribner: [41]

There can be no doubt that since the passage of the new law there has been a decided increase in the work of type-setting and bookmaking in this country. Of course I can speak most decidedly about the increase in the case of the books of our own house, and I can say as to this that the increase is very considerable. There has been a very considerable number of works made by us in this country which before the passage of the new bill would have been imported either in plates or complete copies. It would be safe in our case to place this number at not less than 10% of the entire number of books published in that time, and I think it would run nearer 15%.

Mention has previously been made of the healthful effect of the law on American authorship. In contrast to the results of the first best-seller poll conducted in 1876, which was based on the assumption that the first score of places should automatically be reserved for British books, a comparative study for the years between 1895 and 1902 revealed that twenty-one of the twenty-seven most successful novels were written by American writers. The law was not wholly responsible, but was undoubtedly an influential factor.[42]

The most extravagant of the opponents of the copyright law had charged that with its passage a book "trust" became inevitable.[43] There is little need to expatiate upon the incorrectness of this prediction. A trust did not arise in general trade publishing; and within a decade, the most likely candidate for membership in the anticipated monopoly, Harper and Brothers, went into bankruptcy.

Although business conditions were considerably improved by international copyright, the problems of irregular discounts and underselling remained. Actually it was the individual retail bookseller, with limited capital and competitors ranging from the American News Company to pushcart peddlers, who was the most pathetic figure in the trade. In his despair he turned, as did the publishers, to regulatory organizations. A roster of book trade associations active in 1876 shows more than a dozen regional and local groups of retailers formed to combat underselling.[44] Their effectiveness was greatly limited by their lack of independence in disciplining members who refused to conform to regulations. A meeting of the New England Booksellers' Association in 1876 devoted considerable attention to the report of its "Arbitration Committee" concerning "the bookseller in this city [Boston] who had persisted in advertising retail books at wholesale prices, and giving presents to his customers in violations of the by-laws." It was noted, rather pathetically, "The committee in this case had prepared a circular, and sent it to every publisher in the United States, requesting them to refuse to sell to said party." [45] The burden of enforcement rested with the publishers, whose interests did not always coincide with that of the dealers. A resolution of the Central Booksellers' Association in the same year illustrates another phase of the retailers' problem: [46]

> Resolved: That a Committee be appointed to prepare a memorial to the American News Company, setting forth the evils that burden the trade from the sale of current books to the bazaars and fancy goods' dealers at rates which foster the system of underselling, and that the memorial be presented to the trade for signatures, and then transmitted to the American News Company.

It would be difficult to conceive of a more futile action.

As the depression decade gave way to the 1880's, the book "bazaars" formed an increasingly large cloud on the retailers' horizon. Although these "bazaars," usually little more than department stores, purchased large quantities of books, the publishers were equally resentful of them because of the discounts they demanded and customarily received. *Publishers' Weekly* reached the limit of vituperation in castigating them in 1882: [47]

The Bazaar, the great parasite of the city, the handmaid of monopoly, the nursery of ignorance and servility, the destroyer of individuality, ambition, independent thought and action, is to-day threatening the future of the aspiring young man in every branch of the trade that is at the mercy of this commercial hydra.

Discounts alone cannot account for the emotional quality of this call to arms. Its tone also reflected a resentment at the commercializing of the book trade, and at the lack of a proper distinction between books and other products sold in the large retail stores. One can almost see the editor cringe as he reproduced the following advertisement of a dry-goods store which appeared in a Los Angeles newspaper in 1885: [48]

Also 1000 volumes of standard novels, printed on extra heavy paper, bound in cloth, and books that sell everywhere for $1 per volume. Our price for next Saturday, 10 cents. These books are now on sale in our muslin underwear department. These books are sold in connection with other goods. . . .

All day Saturday we will sell 4-button gloves at $1, 5-hooks, at $1.25, 7-hooks at $1.50, and 10-hooks at $2, and by paying 25¢ extra you may select any book in the collection

By purchasing 6 pairs Lisle thread hose at 49 cents per pair, you may, by paying 10 cents extra, have the choice of our entire stock of novels, or by paying 25 cents, the choice out of the poetical works. . . .

Many retailers who read this advertisement had entered the book trade and accepted its meagre monetary rewards because they wished to escape an association with "mere merchandise." They experienced a distinct loss in their psychic income as well as in their pocketbooks when books and lisle hose were combined under a single roof. But there is something less than a satisfactory excuse for the antipathy of the rest of the trade. For an ordinarily progressive journal like *Publishers' Weekly* to have so unreservedly condemned a new group of book distributors who were to enlarge the market and stimulate the trade generally, spoke ill for the ability of the industry to adjust itself to a changing world. A love of literature was essential to the book world, but the esthetic pretentions which accompanied that devotion placed it under large handicaps.

However, if the trade was unwilling to welcome a new partner, it furnished him with books and ultimately was willing to acknowledge his place in the industry. With a very short memory but with generous intentions, *Publishers' Weekly* protested in 1909 that it had always seen a legitimate function for the department store and noted with pleasure: [49]

One of the salient and noteworthy features of the resolutions adopted by the recent convention of the American Booksellers' Association was the cordial recognition and welcome of the book department of the department store as an integral part of the bookselling trade.

In less than two decades, the whole industry, even the bedeviled retailers, had gone from denunciation to friendly acceptance. The years between had witnessed such a growth of the book sections of the department stores that there was really no alternative. The largest retail buyers in America were John Wanamaker, with two outlets, and the H. B. Claflin Company, whose expansion was the best index of the change in retail markets. Charles Scribner succinctly described its activities to his London agent in 1914: [50]

Probably you have heard of the failure of H. B. Claflin & Co., whose name is of course known to you as the largest dry goods jobbing house of New York. In order to find outlets for their goods, they had purchased department stores in various cities throughout the country, amounting to 27 branches in all. This led to largely increased financial obligations which they were unable to meet owing to the continued dull business. Unfortunately, they owed us $11,000, half of a special bill sold them six months ago—not general stock but an edition of a set of juvenile books reprinted for them.

It had proved impossible to build a chain of general department stores around their book sections; but the failure of this company was not taken to mean, nor did it portend, that the department stores would surrender their book sections.

The accommodation had not come wholly from the book trade. The department stores had begun by using books as part of promotion schemes, but they ended up with a regular book business which led them to share many of the opinions of the independent retailers. As long as underselling and discounts prevailed in the market they took advantage of them. But when a reform movement was started at the turn of the century, the department stores, no less than the bookstores, were willing to cooperate in the stabilization of prices. The conspicuous exception was R. H. Macy and Company, which defied the best efforts of most of the publishers for several decades.

The first battle of Macy's war was fought with the most effective of the trade's organizations, the American Publishers' Association. The pleasures of international copyright were considerable, but it was difficult to enjoy them in the 1890's, when underselling was no less a problem than it had been twenty years before. The "bazaars" which the trade liked to blame for its ills were less a cause than a symptom of an inability to control discounts which had handicapped the industry before department stores were even noticed.

Fortunately, conditions at the close of the century were more propitious to a settlement of these problems than they had been when they first arose. The rapidly changing conditions of the post-Civil War period provided a poor background for any business reforms. It was not clear what modifications in commercial methods would be effected by the new industrial era. How little its meaning was comprehended by the publishers can be seen in their attempt to abolish travelling salesmen just as the railroad network was assuming its modern dimensions. Other new factors in the book trade, such as the "jobbers" and the great wholesale distributing houses like the American News Company and the Baker and Taylor Company, had not been known in the 1850's. In short, the nation's economy, and even that comparatively stagnant part of it concerned with books, was suffering from "growing pains." But by 1900 the problems of the new era were more familiar ones, many of them unsolved but most of them more clearly defined.

Further, the publishers had proved, at least to themselves, that a trade organization need not end in failure. The Copyright League, founded in 1887, had contributed to the victory of 1891, and it had afterwards remained intact to agitate for further legal improvements. An ally was available in the National Association of Newsdealers, Booksellers, and Stationers. Established in 1885 chiefly for purposes of entertainment, this retailers' body enlarged its vision in 1895 to include a serious consideration of the retailer's business needs. The previously mentioned local organizations, some of which had had a continuous existence since the 1870's eagerly welcomed the new emphasis.[51]

These trade groups proved to be a helpful point of departure for their more effective successors. The mere existence of the Copyright League, as well as its initial success, encouraged the formation of a general regulatory body. Writing to George Haven Putnam in 1897, Charles Scribner remarked: [52]

> Mr. Appleton and I had a conversation the other day with reference to enlarging the powers of the [Copyright] League to include all questions of interest to American publishers such as discounts, etc. . I am heartily in favor of this and hope that at the meeting a suitable resolution may be passed and a committee appointed with power to make the necessary changes.

It did not prove feasible to graft one organization on another. But when the American Publishers' Association was established in 1900, its board of directors was substantially identical with the leading figures of the Copyright League. Frank H. Dodd, Charles Scribner, Craige Lippincott, and George Mifflin were equally vital to both.[53]

The basic objective of the Association was to establish the principle that each copyrighted book have a retail price to be kept uniform throughout the country. The plan which was adopted for attaining this end was modelled on that which the British Publishers' Association put into force in 1897.[54] All books were placed in two categories. The titles in the first group could be handled in any manner their publisher saw fit. The other consisted of "net books" for which the Association provided a number of requirements. If a book was declared "net," it could not be retailed through any outlet at less than the price set by the publisher until a year from publication. A bookstore which violated this regulation was denied the privilege of being supplied with the books of any member of the Association until it showed good faith and was reinstated by formal action.

Although many of the founders, among them George Harvey, William W. Appleton, and Charles Scribner, wanted to make the "net system" mandatory for all categories of copyrighted books, several of the larger houses led by The Macmillan Company successfully insisted that fiction be excluded.[55] To exempt from price control precisely those books which were most in need of it seemed to many a drastic undermining of the Association's major effort. However, this flexibility made possible a gradual adjustment to the "net system" which would otherwise not have been provided. Had all novels been included from the beginning, the public resentment and the protests of the distributors might have been so great as to defeat the plan before it could get started. Further, if a publisher wished to place a novel on a "net" basis, he had the organization's full support.

Even in the first year of the agreement a few publishers were willing to experiment with "net" fiction.[56] But only a small dent was made in the total production up to 1909, when 10 per cent of the season's novels were price-fixed. Thereafter, the increase was rapid. By 1910, the percentage had risen to nearly half; and two years later, when the "net" titles comprised 96 per cent of all fiction, the transition was substantially completed.[57]

The Association's effort to reduce trade discounts was less deliberate. No mention was made in the by-laws of the maximum discounts applicable to "net" books, although it was generally understood that they would be less on these than on other titles. During the first years, this vague agreement was so confusing that it threatened to disrupt the entire system. Henry Holt wrote in 1903: [58]

> So far as the net price system goes, we have found it satisfactory. My only fear regarding it arises from the fact that publishers have been unable to make any agreement among themselves as to the discounts they will give on net books, and are already led by competition to increase the discounts, and with them the temptation for the dealers to break over the system.

However, each season brought the industry closer to the goal of real agreement. A "table of publishers' discounts" compiled in 1910 revealed that every house had about the same schedule for "net copyright books": 25 per cent on a single copy, 30 per cent on five copies; and a maximum of 40 per cent on 250 or more. By contrast, the discounts on "regular books" rose from 40 per cent on a single copy to 50 per cent on quantity purchases.[59]

Unlike their predecessors of the 1870's, the members of the Publishers' Association realized that they could not hope to succeed unless they were willing to share the benefits of the new system. Merely to have maintained prices while reducing trade discounts would have generated hostility not only among the consumers, but among booksellers as well. *Publishers' Weekly* warned against "so transparent a trick," asserting at the same time that the trade was well aware that its truest interests lay in a generous treatment of all.[60]

The Association clung to the principle that standard prices on "net" books should be reduced, and that the system permitted this to be done without sacrifice to legitimate interests. The consumer would benefit directly because of the lower prices. The regular bookseller approved for reasons which are perhaps more difficult to understand. Superficially, the plan seemed to call on him to buy for more and sell for less. However, before the "net" system went into effect, underselling was so prevalent that the established price of a book meant nothing. Even in the most conservatively run shops discounts of at least 25 per cent were often offered to the customer. If these reductions could be eliminated, the retailer would be content to pay the publisher a larger wholesale discount. Further, the department store and the book "butcher," when they bought in quantity lots at larger discounts, would have their advantage destroyed.

Yet the willingness of the bookstores to participate revealed the inner contradiction of the scheme. If both the publisher and the retailer received larger profits, the customer had to pay them. Despite the assurances of the trade, the interests of the public and the retailer were at odds within the plan. If the "net" price was higher than the previous actual price, then the buyer suffered; if it was lower, the bookstore paid the price of a larger return for his supplier. The best hope of the Association was to keep the interests of the two in a precarious balance, and hope that the burden of their reform would be borne by irregular distributors. If there was a further price to be paid, perhaps the financial advantages accruing from a relatively stable market would make the retailer amenable to a narrower margin of profit.

The post-reform price structure is rather difficult to determine. The immediate effect appears to have been to raise the consumers' cost. Charles Scribner, the Association's president, acknowledged as much in a letter written in 1902: "Under the new system the public does pay a somewhat increased price for all the new books except fiction." [61] Eighteen months later, Henry Holt confirmed this observation: [62]

> The only objection made to the system itself, so far as I can see, is that people are not getting their books as cheaply as they did before. The reason is that publishers were selling their books before more cheaply than they could afford to.

Apparently, the increase was not large enough to occasion more than an ineffectual grumble. However, when the "net system" was extended to novels, chiefly after 1909, the publishers moved with considerably more caution. The multiplicity of prices applied to nonfiction to some extent camouflaged the increases for many classes of books. But the range for novels was narrow, and any deviation above the pre-reform price of $1.20 was certain to be noticed. *Publishers' Weekly* took considerable pains in 1912 to refute the charge that the change to "net" fiction had involved a public sacrifice. The statistics which the journal gathered showed that the publishers had reduced the fixed price of novels under the new system to a point where it approximated the actual price under the old. It concluded: [63]

Regarding the actual cost to the public of fiction, generally speaking, there seems to have been scant variation. If we may trust these figures, the novel buyer in 1910 paid, on the average, $1.22 for his book. In the spring of 1911 he paid $1.23; in the fall, $1.20; and this spring $1.23 again—this figure averaging the total number of fiction titles published. This price compares not unfavorably with the $1.20 which was the most common discounted price for the $1.50 novel in the old days. The public, therefore, has little cause to complain of net fiction.

While there is no reason for questioning the accuracy of this analysis, it was nevertheless true that an agreement to maintain prices made the market more responsive to the demands of the trade than it had been before. Fortunately, a large area of competition remained to keep those demands from becoming an illegitimate burden to the book-buying public.

Although the "net system" was proposed by the publishers, it required the wholehearted cooperation of the retail bookstores. As soon as the plan was drawn up, the organizers circularized the retailers for their reaction, suggesting that they form a separate association to deal more effectively with a price maintenance program.[64] The result of this proposal was the formation in 1901 of the American Booksellers' Association, which at its first convention supported the new plan with more enthusiasm than the publishers themselves had shown. It was resolved: [65]

That this, the American Booksellers' Association . . . accept the said net price system, with the distinct understanding that it is the intention of the said American Publishers' Association to include fiction under the net price system as rapidly as possible; and

Furthermore, . . . That . . . we agree not to buy, not to put in stock, nor to offer for sale, after due notification by the Executive Committee, the books of any publisher who declines to support the net price system.

To supervise the new regulations, the Association depended not only upon an investigatory committee, but also upon an enlarged network of local booksellers' societies to whose attention would first be reported any violations.[66] Eight years later, the Booksellers' Association reviewed the plan and again pronounced it good, reiterating its desire to see all books included under it. The chief complaint was directed at the trade discount, which the booksellers wished to see increased to 33⅓ per cent.[67]

Among the retail distributors, it was inevitable that most opposition should come from the department stores, whose book sections had been built upon bargain prices. When the "net system" was started, these outlets were in a transition from their "bazaar" state of development to that of regular book dealer. The new plan for fixed prices presented an opportunity for precipitating that change, but raised the question of whether the trade had sufficient power and an organization strong enough to insist on it.

Most of the department stores fell quickly into line. When Abraham and Strauss capitulated in 1901, the only sizeable opponent was R. H. Macy and Company, sufficiently powerful in itself to threaten the entire scheme.[68] The fight with the latter firm was fought in the markets and in the courts during the entire life of the American Publishers' Association, ending in a victory for the company and at least a technical defeat for the publishers.

The methods by which the Association sought to oppose Macy's efforts to get books after the members refused to sell to it, can best be revealed by quoting at some length a letter from Charles Scribner, written on December 31, 1901, which summarizes a single campaign in one area: [69]

Allow me briefly to go over some recent history, asking you please to remember all the time that the Board, spurred on by the impatience of other department stores, has been directing its best efforts to prevent Macy from getting stock. First we succeeded after great difficulty in closing all sources of supply in this city and then Macy went to Boston and elsewhere to buy. We discovered that Dickerman was supplying him, and Dickerman was cut off though he was loud in protests of ignorance, threats of lawsuit, etc. Then we found that large orders were sent to publishers from Shepard of Providence who had refused to sign our agreement. We asked members to hold supplies pending investigation and asked Shepard to give us assurance that their stocks would not go to Macy. Shepard then admitted that some of his stock would have reached Macy but promised to live up to our agreement. It then appeared that O'Gorman of Providence was directly supplying Macy. We accepted assurances from Shepard and cut off O'Gorman. We then asked the Libby Company, who had previously bought for O'Gorman and who in an advertisement had already attacked the Association as a trust and expressed the intention of beating it, to give assurances that it would not supply O'Gorman or others whose supplies had been stopped. . . . After waiting until Mr. Haywood's reply was received we cut off the Libby Company. We know also that Larrabee (controlled by the Libby Company) was supplying Dickerman who was sending to Macy, and we cut Larrabee off. All this was done by the Board with deliberation and I do not myself see how we could have done differently if acting in earnest.

This statement is supplemented by the somewhat melodramatic testimony offered by Macy's chief buyer, Miss E. L. Kinnear: [70]

When I found that I was boycotted, I set to work to obtain books by other means. I could not buy them in the firm's name, nor in my own name, from the publishers. But I was assisted by relatives and friends and at one time I had eighteen branches buying books and turning them over to me.
I found booksellers as far South as Texas and as far West as Denver, who were in sympathy with me. They would buy books and ship them to Macy's. We had agents of this kind all over the country. . . .

We even went to the extreme of opening book stores in other cities in order to get books. We would stock up these stores and reship to New York. I lived at that time in Chelsea Village, convenient to the old store in Fourteenth Street. Detectives watched my house night and day. They even tried to induce the postman to show them my letters, in order that they might learn where they were mailed.

Meantime, a continual fight was being waged in the courts. The first blow was struck by Macy and Company in 1902 when it brought suit in New York to restrain the Association from enforcing its rules against underselling. The court found against the plaintiff, asserting that there was no violation of the state's antitrust law, the Donnelly Act passed in 1897.[71] Following this preliminary skirmish, an appeal was taken to other courts. The final decision, made by the Court of Appeals in 1908, gave limited victory to each side. It was held that the laws of copyright gave the Association's members the privilege to withhold copyrighted books from the store, but that they had violated the law by including uncopyrighted books in their boycott. Macy and Company was awarded damages of $3,702.98. But meantime the Association had amended its by-laws to satisfy this ruling, and the basic question still remained unanswered.[72]

Charles Scribner took heart from this decision, and anticipated that it might be of some use to him in a countersuit which he started, to force Macy's to maintain the fixed prices of his own "net" publications. He wrote to George Haven Putnam: [73]

I think it is the first time that there has been from the bench a clear cut statement that copyrights enjoyed the same rights as patents. This would seem to make decisions on patents applicable to copyrights. It has a bearing on our suit against Macy to restrain him from cutting prices on copyright books, an injunction in which case was denied by Judge Lacomb—not on the merits of the question but because it had not been established that copyrights enjoyed all the privileges of patents. I think it is a great success that the movement of the Publishers' Association has been substantially upheld.

The future was to show that this optimism was not well founded. After the New York Court of Appeals had awarded Macy and Company damages under state law, the store brought suit in 1909 in the federal courts under the Sherman Act. A series of court actions culminated in a decision handed down on December 1, 1913, by the United States Supreme Court declaring that the laws of copyright did not justify an essential violation of the Sherman Act. Early in 1914, Macy and Company was awarded $140,000 in damages. A few months later, the American Publishers' Association expired.[74]

This was an expensive defeat, and to the amount of the settlement could be added the costs of an eleven-year legal battle. Yet it could be argued reasonably that a larger victory had been won. *Publishers' Weekly* was offering not empty solace but simple facts when it asserted: [75]

Thirteen years ago price cutting was rampant: the trade was disorganized: conditions were verging on the chaotic, and the book business was fast falling into suicidal destruction. The "Macy" cases may have brought knowledge that any attempt to maintain prices by coercion or concerted action of any sort whatsoever is illegal. But they have also brought knowledge that net prices, maintained, not by coercion, but by individual choice, brings trade solidarity, and makes prosperity, if not probable, at least possible. And they have accomplished a further equally general realization that unwarranted "cut prices" are a stupendous merchandising blunder, if not actually immoral or illegal.

Although Macy's trumpeted its contempt for cooperation, most of the trade agreed that the basic principle of the reform should be continued even after the organization which gave rise to it had met its end. Robert Sterling Yard reported as early as 1914: [76]

The combination . . . went out of existence; but the retail trade, including the vast majority of the largest and soundest department stores in the country, no longer troubles itself about those cut-rate shops. They may cut all they please and charge their losses to advertising; but they no longer affect the main current of the country's book business.

The cry of "monopoly" had greeted every effort made by the trade to regulate prices and discount policies for a half-century. Now, at last, that complaint had become official. However, it would be incorrect to equate either the American Publishers' Association or any of its predecessors with ordinary trust practices. For example, none of these trade organizations made any effort to control the prices which individual publishers placed on books. Neither did they desire to agree on a standard royalty for their authors.[77] They did not wish to compel either the individual publisher or the individual bookseller to subscribe to their plan of action. As president of the Publishers' Association, Charles Scribner wrote an emphatic protest to the Booksellers' Association when it sought to have its members boycott the Smith and Street Company for not joining the publishers' group: [78]

The publishers do not confine their sales to members of your Association and we do not ask you to purchase books from those publishers only who belong to our Association. It is of course very natural that booksellers would be disposed to favor publishers who issue their books under the most acceptable conditions, but we do not desire to compel any publisher to join our Association. As you know, our Association is a very representative one and almost all the well known publishers have thought it to their interest to become members of it, but the question of joining or withdrawal should be left to their own judgment and I strongly disapprove of any effort to force them into our Association.

Since it had almost no control over printing, the Association could not dictate what books were published, at what price they were offered to the public, or in what quantity. The three most important classes of books—novels, subscription books of all kinds, and textbooks—were not necessarily subject to the agreement, and only one of the three—fiction—was even eligible for the "net system."

Instead, the members of the Association attempted merely to insist that the prices which they had individually chosen for their own publications be maintained. It is worth observing that Louis D. Brandeis, whose opposition to monopoly was a matter of conspicuous record, strongly supported the right of the manufacturer to set a single price for his product. He argued not only that a fixed price was justified by economic need but also that it was a good defense against the monopolistic device of juggling prices to meet a variety of competitive situations.[79] The Fair Trade laws of recent years demonstrate that the public welfare has been identified with precisely the same principle for which the American Book Publishers' Association was founded.

When a "trust" movement actually appeared through the formation of the American Book Company in 1890, it incurred the trade's immediate hostility. This opposition was not material to the destruction of whatever control the company initially exercised; the business was simply impervious to monopoly.

However, in 1914 it was the law and not the peculiarities of the book trade which determined the Court's decision. There was no question that the book industry had tried to enforce by collective action a given set of prices; there was ample evidence that the Association had restrained the trade with R. H. Macy and Company. But in fairness to the intentions, if not to the actions, of the American Publishers' Association, it does not seem inappropriate to let the trade's spokesman, *Publishers' Weekly* have the last word: [80]

> Let us for once have our say on this misapplied word "trust" ever flung at us when it is simply a question of fair dealing; let us say that this clamor against the so-called "book trust" is nothing but the baldest jingoism, intended to deceive people and to excuse crooked business.

Written in 1902, these angry sentences did less than justice to the trade's ability to accept the final decision. When the award for damages was made in 1914, the journal donned a dignity as appropriate to the occasion as to the industry it represented: "The American Publishers' Association lost, fairly and squarely, in the highest court in the land. It remained only to pay the piper—and the piper's toll has now been levied." [81]

Conclusions

chapter 10

The hopes of the publishers for making the "worst business in the world" a better one were built upon two reforms: an international copyright law and an agreement to regulate retail prices and trade discounts. The achievement of both of these goals proved that too much had been expected of them. They admitted the possibility of prosperity, but they did not guarantee even that publishing would be as profitable and as stable as the economy as a whole. On the eve of the First World War, after a half-century of effort, the trade pronounced its remedies a failure and turned to other measures of reform.

Yet publishers had reason to fear that their new program, whatever it might be, would be no more successful than the old. After the Civil War, the publishing function had been gradually clarified, but the question of how that function could best be discharged was considered to be wrapped in a number of impenetrable mysteries. In the 1850's, it had not been definitely established even that a regular publisher should be prepared to perform extensive editorial services for his manuscripts. The burden of financing manufacture was often divided with the author, who might also be called upon to pay for any publicity beyond a perfunctory listing in an unattractive catalogue. Distribution was considered less a science than a chore which could be left to the whim of the retailer as he perused that same catalogue or stood near the auctioneer's bench at the trade sale.

By 1914, the publisher had acknowledged his duty to edit, to finance, to publicize, and to sell aggressively the books on which he placed his imprint. Large staffs of readers and trained editors were assembled, but who was to say with any confidence what made a book good or a good book popular? The trade confessed that it did not know. It judged manuscripts submitted to it in the light of their commercial desirability, showed more than a minimum tolerance for unorthodox authors and spectacular subject matter, and even entered the domain of the writers in an effort to anticipate public demands. But it accepted as inevitable the dictum that most of its decisions would end in failure. George Haven Putnam could write without fear of serious contradiction, "The history of publishing is a record of erroneous judgments." [1]

But there was an agreement that an effort should be made to increase the popularity of at least some books by means of extensive publicity—a decision which not only entailed considerable expense but created another area of uncertainty. The growth of advertising compounded the mystery of popularity rather than solved it; widely publicized books often failed and obscure ones sometimes sold in large quantities.

With a curious mixture of antipathy and enthusiasm, the

trade turned in the 1860's to applying the tools of the new industrial era to the distribution of books. Salesmen mounted trains for the extreme reaches of a gradually expanding market. The trade sales withered and died unmourned, while the American News Company announced the strength of the middleman in an increasingly complex economy. But this new machinery rested upon a slender base; the retail bookstore was counted on to cap the structure of distribution, but it failed to keep pace with the rapid changes of a swiftly moving era. When modern techniques of retail merchandizing produced a new kind of outlet, the department store, the trade tried to reject it, then approved when it conformed to the older pattern. At the close of the era, the largest retail buyer of books, R. H. Macy and Company, was also the one whose presence was most regretted by the trade. Although the reasons for its unpopularity were generally understood, publishers do not appear to have considered what positive lessons could be learned from the store's success in selling their product.

However, they were willing to acknowledge, in deed if not in word, that the ordinary retailer did not give them sufficient contact with the market. While vigorously asserting their essential reliance on the regular bookstore, they made large efforts to compete with the bookstore for the consumer's dollar. The publisher's business in mail-order and subscription books far exceeded the sales through stores. In different ways, each of these methods employed the lessons of the new era. Successful selling by mail utilized modern techniques of writing promotional material and determining to what people it should be sent; the marketing of subscription books provided the most fruitful field for the use of a highly trained corps of salesmen working from branch offices.

Despite these successes, the end of the era found the publishers recording still another failure and posing another mystery. Book distribution was considered painfully inadequate, but no one could suggest a remedy. To the historical observer, a possible solution seemed available which the trade never considered seriously. Whatever the problems of distribution, they were enormously complicated by the tremendous number of titles which flooded the markets in small, necessarily expensive editions. A distinction must be made between the social usefulness of this practice, which cannot be denied, and its appropriateness to the commercial needs of an industry which seems chronically to have been ill.

The typical publisher had two answers to the charge that he was creating large obstacles to his prosperity by swamping the market with publications. He argued legitimately that his own books were merely a fraction of the total; by reducing his list fifty per cent, he could effect only an imperceptible decrease in the total number of books in the market. The problem was one for the trade as a whole to solve rather than the individual company. Yet an enforced restriction would have involved more restraint of trade and a more sinister form of "trust" activity than was ever attempted. It is a tribute to the decency of the publishers, if not to their business sense, that they never even contemplated such a program.

The publisher's second argument rests on shakier

ground. The undeniably difficult task of predicting the sales of any given book led to the questionable view that all publications were equally speculative. A certain percentage were bound to fail and only a small fraction, computed at 20 per cent in more optimistic moments, would yield a profit. This theory can be partly refuted by the actions of the publishers themselves in the opening years of the twentieth century. The initial print orders, the royalty rates, the advertising budgets of books varied enormously, and necessarily implied that decisions had been made concerning their individual markets.

It must be acknowledged that if the publishers had concentrated only upon those titles about which they were optimistic, the structure of the business would have been changed considerably. The quantity approach to constructing a list made provision for a large permanent staff of editors and production managers whose presence created a high fixed overhead. But it was because of this overhead that the sights of the business were set so low. Many books were published with no better hope than that they would meet the costs of their manufacture and contribute a small share of the expenses of running a huge establishment. But their cost was actually much greater than the amount of money taken to produce finished copies and pay editors' salaries. To this could be added the sales lost on other books because of their publication. The catalogues became longer, their formidable bulk discouraging careful attention to the titles which were supposed to do more than serve merely as "fillers." Advertising budgets were expanded to include books which could not be advertised.

Salesmen had to spread their efforts over a larger area, and waste precious moments trying to persuade retailers to experiment with books of limited appeal. The retailer himself was caught in the flood, often depriving himself of quantity discounts to take a more generous sampling of books which would stay on his shelves until he "remaindered" them on special bargain counters.

The subscription business supplied a good illustration of the results of a smaller number of titles. A huge sales organization was combined with a very limited editorial staff. It also indicated the nature of books which might result from the application of subscription techniques in the field of trade books. Books which had to be sold in large quantities were not necessarily good books. Indeed, the assumption, too often proved, that there were more people with bad taste than with good, produced a number of subscription titles in which their publishers took little pride. Finally, it should be remembered that a large part of the subscription list was parasitic, consisting of books already tested through the bookstores.

The business in trade books was necessarily more speculative. A greater number of titles had to be published, and the huge numbers characteristic of subscription editions could not be printed except in exceptional circumstances. But if the example was less than perfect, it was at least valuable. If original editions could not reach 100,000, trade publishers might profitably have limited their choices to titles whose minimum sales expectations were, for instance, three times as large as would be necessary to return the original costs. The fact that the effectiveness of subscription salesmen was greatest when they worked with a short list did not prove that commercial travellers should be limited to a dozen titles; but it did suggest that they might be more effective if they did not have several hundred.

That the subscription business combined a large sales force with a huge volume of sales was a lesson difficult to apply. The endless multiplication of commercial travellers was not feasible. But an increased emphasis on the sales, as opposed to the editorial, aspect of publishing had long been indicated. The negative attitude which most publishers took towards experimentation in the means of distribution is at direct odds with their willingness to gamble on editorial decisions. But the problem of selling books went beyond the conditions of business; it touched the personal philosophy of all the great publishers in the "Gilded Age." They were not merchandizers but business men of letters, who preferred to share in the creation of literature rather than in its dissemination.

It may be questioned whether, as Walter Page and William Ellsworth asserted, the talents of these men were sufficiently general to make them successes in other lines of business. But within the field of publishing, a compelling devotion to literature was an advantage as well as a handicap. The sensitivity which enabled the capable publisher to work with authors and see the virtues and defects of a great variety of manuscripts might not have been of much use in the steel industry, but it produced better books. The fact that the publisher received rewards from his business activity which had nothing to do with its profits materially influenced his conduct of that business. If the publisher lost sales because of his reluctance to be a merchandizer, he accomplished as an editor and as a producer of literary products what a mere merchandizer would not have had the vision to achieve.

Probably it is unreasonable to expect to find in one man these two sets of abilities. Perhaps great editors are made by the same qualities which preclude conspicuous achievements in salesmanship. At any rate, the records of publishing in the "Gilded Age" show an unequal development in these two basic parts of the business; more good books were published than could be sold in commercially satisfactory quantities. Publishers cultivated close relations with their authors but shunned the market place.

In a sparkling memoir called the *Garrulities of an Octogenarian Editor,* Henry Holt recalled an experience which reveals much of the peculiar quality of publishing in the "Gilded Age." It was during the decade of the 1890's, when America faced the greatest depression she had yet endured, that a number of publishers met for a monthly dinner at the Aldine Club. An especially memorable meeting celebrated the coming wedding of one of the company, George Haven Putnam. A huge loving cup was given to the prospective bridegroom, and on it were five panels with these inscriptions: [2]

With love of Appleton *With love of Harper*
With love of Scribner *With love of Holt*
For love of Putnam

One wonders what Jay Gould would have thought had he been privileged to be present.

Notes

cc is used as an abbreviation for carbon copy

CHAPTER 1. THE PHILOSOPHY OF PUBLISHING

1. *The Publishers' Weekly* (hereafter referred to as *P.W.*), October 7, 1911, Vol. 80, No. 2070, p. 1403.
2. *P.W.*, August 29, 1896, Vol. 50, No. 1283, p. 278.
3. *P.W.*, October 2, 1897, Vol. 52, No. 1340, p. 582.
4. William Miller, *The Book Industry*. New York, Columbia University Press, 1949, p. 3.
5. Walter H. Page, *A Publisher's Confession*. Garden City, Doubleday, Page and Company (1905, 1912), 1923, pp. 13–14.
6. William W. Ellsworth, *A Golden Age of Authors*. Boston, Houghton, Mifflin Company, 1919, p. 13.
7. Walter H. Page, *op. cit.*, p. 13.
8. *Ibid.*, p. 170.
9. The New York *Evening Post*, July 21, 1908, quoted in *P.W.*, August 1, 1908, Vol. 74, No. 1905, p. 276.
10. Walter H. Page, *op. cit.*, pp. 74–75.
11. *Ibid.*, p. 172.
12. *P.W.*, November 13, 1897, Vol. 52, No. 1346, p. 794.
13. *P.W.*, December 2, 1905, Vol. 68, No. 1766, p. 1692; February 23, 1907, Vol. 71, No. 1830, p. 766.
14. *P.W.*, February 12, 1910, Vol. 77, No. 1985, p. 930.
15. *P.W.*, September 28, 1901, Vol. 60, No. 1548, p. 589.
16. Grant Overton, *Portrait of a Publisher; and the First Hundred Years of the House of Appleton, 1825–1925*. New York, D. Appleton and Company, 1925, pp. 4–5.
17. Edward H. Dodd, Jr., *The First Hundred Years*. New York, Dodd, Mead and Co., 1939, p. 5.
18. Roger Burlingame, *Of Making Many Books*. New York, Charles Scribner's Sons, 1946, pp. 74–76.

19. George Haven Putnam, "The Founder of the House of Putnam," in *P.W.*, October 12, 1912, Vol. 82, No. 2123, p. 1247.
20. Joseph Henry Harper, *The House of Harper*. New York, Harper and Bros., 1912, pp. 20, 26.
21. Moses Dodd's *Catalogue for 1839*.
22. George Haven Putnam, *Memories of a Publisher*. New York, G. P. Putnam's Sons, 1915, pp. 44–46.
23. Joseph Henry Harper, *op. cit.*, pp. 37–46.
24. cc Letter J. Blair Scribner to Charles Welford, October 12, 1875.
25. *P.W.*, June 16, 1894, Vol. 45, No. 1168, p. 886.
26. *P.W.*, October 28, 1899, Vol. 56, No. 1448, pp. 782–84.
27. *P.W.*, July 15, 1876, Vol. 10, No. 235, p. 149.
28. Henry Holt, quoted in *P.W.*, February 12, 1910, Vol. 77, No. 1985, p. 929.
29. *The Book Buyer,* February 15, 1872, Vol. 5, No. 5, p. 16.
30. *P.W.*, January 25, 1879, Vol. 15, No. 367, pp. 74–75.
31. George H. Doran, *Chronicles of Barabbas, 1884–1934*. New York, Harcourt, Brace and Company, 1935, p. 78.
32. George Haven Putnam, *Memories of a Publisher,* p. v.
33. *P.W.*, March 21, 1896, Vol. 49, No. 1260, p. 552.
34. See below, chapter 3, for discussion.
35. cc Letter Henry Holt to Carolyn Wells, July 18, 1903.
36. Walter H. Page, *op. cit.*, p. 179.

CHAPTER 2. THE BUSINESS OF PUBLISHING

1. Reported in *P.W.*, July 22, 1876, Vol. 10, No. 236, p. 175.
2. *P.W.*, January 18, 1890, Vol. 38, No. 938, p. 45.
3. *P.W.*, June 20, 1896, Vol. 49, No. 1273, p. 1008.
4. *P.W.*, September 23, 1911, Vol. 80, No. 2068, p. 1066.
5. *P.W.*, May 9, 1914, Vol. 85, No. 2205, p. 1541.
6. *P.W.*, October 10, 1910, Vol. 78, No. 2019, p. 1392.
7. Census materials have been taken from the Censuses of Manufactures compiled between 1860 and 1910, and from the special report on *Printing and Publishing* prepared by the Bureau of the Census in 1914.
8. See, for example, the editorial titled, "The Publisher in Com-

petition with the Bookseller," in *P.W.*, January 21, 1893, Vol. 43, No. 1095, p. 58.

9. cc Letter J. Blair Scribner to Charles Welford, December 18, 1877.

10. cc Letter Charles Scribner to James B. Pinker, October 31, 1905.

11. cc Letter Henry Holt to Edward Kellogg Baird, March 4, 1913.

12. *P.W.*, November 8, 1913, Vol. 84, No. 2179, p. 1515.

13. cc Letter Charles Scribner's Sons to Professor Francis Bowen, November 14, 1879.

14. Cited by the *American Publishers' Circular and Literary Gazette,* March 16, 1861, Vol. 7, No. 11, p. 101.

15. *P.W.*, January 9, 1886, Vol. 29, No. 728, p. 49. *The American Literary Gazette and Publishers' Circular* expressed the view in its issue of March 2, 1867 (p. 242) that Lippincott's was "the most extensive book house in the United States."

16. *American Literary Gazette and Publishers' Circular,* April 15, 1864, Vol. 2, No. 12, p. 406.

17. Appendix to *P.W.*, Vol. 59, 1901.

18. *P.W.*, January 25, 1913, Vol. 83, No. 2138, pp. 302–316.

19. *Census of Manufactures: 1914, Printing and Publishing,* 1918, Washington, Government Printing Office, p. 152.

20. MS, "Harper and Brothers Summary of Business, October 1, 1900–March 1, 1915."

21. This estimate is based upon information in the *Census of 1914,* showing the total value of books produced to be $56,000,000.

22. MS, "Recapitulation of Sales for 1912."

23. Based upon MSS memoranda in the archives of Henry Holt and Co.

24. cc Letter Charles Scribner to Mrs. E. A. Abbey, February 6, 1904.

25. Charles Morgan, *The House of Macmillan,* 1944, New York, The Macmillan Company, pp. 163–164.

26. Joseph Henry Harper, *op. cit.*, p. 650.

27. *P.W.*, September 29, 1900, Vol. 58, No. 1496, p. 674a.

28. *P.W.*, March 24, 1900, Vol. 57, No. 1469, pp. 628–629; June 23, 1900, Vol. 57, No. 1482, p. 1221; August 18, 1900, Vol.

58, No. 1490, p. 383; June 11, 1904, Vol. 65, No. 1689, p. 1490; cc Letter Charles Scribner to L. W. Bangs, August 6, 1901.

29. Frank Luther Mott, *Golden Multitudes.* New York, The Macmillan Company, 1947, Appendix A.

30. Although statistics on best sellers are still debated, there is no doubt that they were even more unreliable prior to 1895. Beginning in that year, trade publications such as *The Bookman* and *Publishers' Weekly* endeavored to gather reliable figures. A convenient consensus of these early polls is contained in Alice Payne Hackett's *Fifty Years of Best Sellers,* published in 1945 by the R. R. Bowker Company, which is also the owner of *Publishers' Weekly.* The above computations are based on Miss Hackett's study.

31. *P.W.*, November 8, 1902, Vol. 62, No. 1606, p. 969.

32. *P.W.*, April 6, 1878, Vol. 13, No. 325, p. 378.

33. *P.W.*, April 16, 1881, Vol. 19, No. 483, pp. 433–34.

34. Alfred Harcourt, "Publishing Since 1900," in *The Bowker Lectures on Book Publishing,* First Series. New York, The Typophiles, 1943, p. 63.

35. *P.W.*, October 26, 1901, Vol. 60, No. 1552, p. 885.

36. *P.W.*, November 8, 1913, Vol. 84, No. 2179, p. 1515.

37. Quoted in *P.W.*, April 30, 1887, Vol. 31, No. 796, p. 587.

38. William Miller, *op. cit.*, p. 73.

39. MSS Ledger in the archives of Charles Scribner's Sons.

40. Quoted in *P.W.*, December 12, 1885, Vol. 28, No. 724, p. 919.

41. O. H. Cheney, *Economic Survey of the Book Industry, 1930–1931.* New York, National Association of Book Publishers, 1931, p. 85.

42. *P.W.*, January 13, 1877, Vol. 11, No. 261, p. 37.

43. cc Letter Charles Scribner to Charles Welford, March 31, 1882.

44. *P.W.*, January 20, 1900, Vol. 57, No. 1460, p. 57.

45. *P.W.*, May 14, 1904, Vol. 65, No. 1685, p. 1287.

46. O. H. Cheney, *op. cit.*, p. 87.

47. Quoted in *P.W.*, October 26, 1901, Vol. 60, No. 1552, p. 885.

48. cc Letter Henry Holt to R. A. Bennet, November 19, 1907.

49. This idea was repeated often enough to be a cliché of the business. For an example of its use, see *P.W.*, April 24, 1886, Vol. 29, No. 743, p. 542.

50. *P.W.*, November 8, 1913, Vol. 84, No. 2179, p. 1515.

51. cc Letter Charles Scribner to Charles Welford, January 31, 1881.

52. cc Letter Charles Scribner to Charles Welford, August 4, 1880.

53. Conversation with editor who prefers to remain anonymous, August 18, 1950.

54. *P.W.*, April 18, 1885, Vol. 27, No. 690, p. 469.

55. *P.W.*, June 21, 1890, Vol. 38, No. 960, p. 823.

56. *Ibid.*

57. Walter H. Page, *A Publisher's Confession,* p. 109.

58. *P.W.*, April 26, 1913, Vol. 83, No. 2151, p. 1493.

59. R. L. Duffus, "Printing and Publishing," in *Encyclopedia of the Social Sciences,* Vol. 12, New York, The Macmillan Company, 1934, pp. 413–414.

60. Alfred Harcourt, *op. cit.*, p. 71.

61. Frank Luther Mott, *op. cit.*, Appendix A.

62. Robert Sterling Yard, *The Publisher.* Boston, Houghton Mifflin Company, 1913, p. 10.

63. MS, Harper and Brothers "Summary of Business, October 1, 1900 to March 1, 1915."

64. Walter H. Page, *op. cit.*, p. 54.

65. See, for example, *American Literary Gazette and Publishers' Circular,* January 2, 1871, Vol. 16, No. 5, p. 80.

66. cc Letter Charles Scribner to Charles Welford, September 28, 1883.

67. cc Letter Charles Scribner to H. H. Boysen, April 15, 1879.

68. MSS. Agreement, October 6, 1885.

69. cc Letter Charles Scribner's Sons to Maurice Thompson, February 18, 1880.

70. cc Letter Charles Scribner's Sons to Maurice Thompson, June 25, 1878.

71. Quoted in *P.W.*, October 16, 1897, Vol. 52, No. 16, p. 646.

72. *P.W.*, January 31, 1891, Vol. 39, No. 992, p. 238.

73. Quoted in *P.W.*, April 16, 1910, Vol. 78, No. 1994, p. 1705.

74. See, for example, a letter dated December 29, 1896 to Frank Dodd from the English poet and essayist, Austin Dobson, in which the latter refuses to undertake a projected biography because the

effort would be greater and the returns smaller than that required for a series of "Vignettes" planned for magazine publication.

75. Advertisement appearing in *American Publishers' Circular and Literary Gazette,* April 2, 1859, Vol. V, No. 14, p. 163.

76. See, for example, the report of a $5,000 bribe offered to a member of the Washington State Board of Education in *P.W.*, June 14, 1890, Vol. 37, No. 959, p. 793.

77. See below, Chapter 8, for discussion.

78. *P.W.*, July 26, 1879, Vol. 16, Nos. 392–393, pp. 85–86.

79. cc Letter Charles Scribner to Charles Welford, June 8, 1883.

80. *Ibid.*

81. cc Letter Charles Scribner to L. W. Bangs, June 13, 1890.

82. *P.W.*, April 26, 1890, Vol. 37, No. 952, p. 557.

83. Quoted in *P.W.*, June 20, 1891, Vol. 39, No. 1012, p. 864.

84. *P.W.*, February 13, 1909, Vol. 75, No. 1933, p. 824.

85. *P.W.*, July 16, 1892, Vol. 42, No. 3, p. 107.

86. *P.W.*, July 26, 1913, Vol. 84, No. 2164, p. 170.

CHAPTER 3. THE ANTAGONISMS AND FRIENDSHIPS OF PUBLISHING

1. William Ellsworth, *op. cit.*, p. 185.

2. Quoted in *P.W.*, April 9, 1887, Vol. 31, No. 793, p. 513.

3. cc Letter Henry Holt to Professor Bright, April 8, 1892.

4. G[eorge] H[aven] P[utnam] and J. B[ishop] P[utnam], *Authors and Publishers.* New York, G. P. Putnam's Sons, 1897, p. 201.

5. George Haven Putnam, quoted in *P.W.*, September 5, 1891, Vol. 40, No. 1023, p. 288.

6. William W. Ellsworth, *op. cit.*, p. 201.

7. cc Letter Henry Holt to Prof. G. T. Dippold, April 12, 1889.

8. cc Letter Henry Holt to Hackett, July 9, 1903.

9. Walter H. Page, *op. cit.*, p. 20.

10. *P.W.*, March 19, 1887, Vol. 31, No. 790, p. 394.

11. *P.W.*, April 9, 1887, Vol. 31, No. 793, pp. 511–514.

12. *P.W.*, July 29, 1893, Vol. 44, No. 1112, p. 156.

13. *P.W.*, February 22, 1896, Vol. 49, No. 1256, p. 358.

14. *P.W.*, July 5, 1901, Vol. 60, No. 1536, p. 14.

15. *P.W.*, April 12, 1913, Vol. 83, No. 2149, pp. 1351–1354.

16. *P.W.*, April 9, 1889, Vol. 35, No. 793, pp. 211–212.

17. Walter H. Page, *op. cit.*, p. 110.

18. cc Letter Charles Scribner to Charles Baxter, September 24, 1894.

19. Walter H. Page, *op. cit.*, pp. 110–111.

20. See the remarks of George Haven Putnam, quoted in *P.W.*, September 5, 1891, Vol. 40, No. 1023, p. 289.

21. *P.W.*, August 22, 1896, Vol. 50, No. 1282, p. 260.

22. G. H. P[utnam] and J. B[ishop] P[utnam], *op. cit.*, pp. 158–159.

23. cc Letter Henry Holt to E. A. Dithmar, "Saturday Review," *New York Times*, September 14, 1903.

24. Walter H. Page, *op. cit.*, p. 67.

25. Walter H. Page, *op. cit.*, p. 56.

26. Conversation with Charles Scribner III, August 12, 1949.

27. *P.W.*, March 11, 1911, Vol. 79, No. 2040, p. 1208.

28. Typescript of speech prepared by Frank Dodd for delivery at the Booksellers' Association Dinner in June, 1905.

29. cc Letter Henry Holt to Miss Alger, October 23, 1880.

30. cc Letter Charles Scribner to H. O. Houghton, November 1, 1883.

31. Letter William Dean Howells to Frank H. Dodd, September 12, 1900.

32. G. H. P[utnam] and J. B[ishop] P[utnam], *op. cit.*, p. 72.

33. cc Letter Henry Holt to J. O'H. Cosgrave, July 3, 1903.

34. cc Letter Charles Scribner to Messrs. Roberts Brothers, September 26, 1893.

35. Typescript of address by Frank H. Dodd to the Booksellers' Association, June, 1905.

36. Walter H. Page, *op. cit.*, pp. 66–67.

37. cc Letter Henry Holt to Mrs. Dolores M. Bacon, September 13, 1907.

38. Letter from Henry C. Lea published in *American Literary Gazette and Publishers' Circular*, May 15, 1867, Vol. IX, No. 1, p. 36.

39. Raymond Howard Shove, *Cheap Book Production in the United States, 1870–1891*. University of Illinois Library, Urbana, 1937, pp. vi–vii.

40. Henry Walcott Boynton, *Annals of American Bookselling, 1638–1850*. New York, John Wiley and Sons, Inc., 1932, pp. 185–186.

41. Boynton, *op. cit.*, p. 186. *American Literary Gazette and Publishers' Circular*, April 15, 1867, Vol. VIII, No. 12, pp. 348–349.

42. *American Publishers' Circular and Literary Gazette*, May 12, 1860, Vol. VI, No. 14, p. 246.

43. *American Publishers' Circular and Literary Gazette*, May 15, 1863, Vol. I, No. 2, p. 98.

44. *P.W.*, February 25, 1893, Vol. 43, No. 1100, p. 360.

45. cc Letter Scribner, Armstrong and Co. to Messrs. Roberts Brothers, March 31, 1876.

46. cc Letter Scribner, Armstrong and Company to Messrs. J. B. Lippincott, January 17, 1877. See also Scribner to Putnam, October 10, 1876; Scribner to Lippincott, January 1, 1877 and March 26, 1877.

47. cc Letter Henry Holt to Henry Altemus, October 9, 1890.

48. *P.W.*, March 19, 1881, Vol. 19, No. 479, p. 364.

49. The files of Charles Scribner's Sons contain extensive information concerning this dispute. The best record of Scribner's viewpoint is in a series of letters written by Charles Scribner to Charles Welford, his partner in London, between February 15, 1881, and May 3, 1882. For the Harper position, there is a series of four letters addressed by the firm to Scribner's in February, 1881, and an eight-page pamphlet summarizing the case against Scribner and Froude.

50. cc Letter Henry Holt to George Haven Putnam, April 20, 1880.

51. cc Letter Charles Scribner to Charles Welford, July 6, 1881. Letter J. Henry Harper to Henry Holt, April 16, 1877.

52. cc Letter Charles Scribner to George Haven Putnam, May 19, 1882.

53. cc Letter Charles Scribner's Sons to Professor William Ihne, September 24, 1879.

54. Letter Charles Scribner's Sons to DeWitt C. Dent, February 16, 1893.

55. cc Letter Charles Scribner to L. W. Bangs, July 1, 1891.

56. cc Letter Scribner, Armstrong and Co. to Messrs. Harper and Brothers, November 30, 1877. cc Letter Scribner, Armstrong and Co. to Messrs. Henry Holt and Company, December 10, 1877.

57. cc Letter Charles Scribner to Charles Welford, August 19, 1879.

58. cc Letter Charles Scribner to Charles Welford, November 1, 1881.

59. cc Letter Charles Scribner to Charles Welford, July 13, 1881.

60. cc Letters Charles Scribner to Charles Welford, January 8, 1884 and September 26, 1884.

61. *P.W.*, February 25, 1893, Vol. 43, No. 1100, p. 360.

62. cc Letter Charles Scribner to Charles Welford, March 10, 1882.

63. *P.W.*, July 26, 1884, Vol. 26, No. 652, pp. 131–132.

64. cc Charles Scribner's Sons to Max O'Rell, April 1, 1884.

65. cc Letter Charles Scribner to Robert Louis Stevenson, October 27, 1887.

66. cc Letter Charles Scribner to John Murray, Jr., April 10, 1891.

67. MSS Ledger of Funds Received from and for Foreign Publications. [Charles Scribner's Sons.]

68. MSS Royalty Account [Harper and Brothers].

69. Robert Sterling Yard, *op. cit.*, pp. 171 & 175.

70. William W. Ellsworth, *op. cit.*, p. 106.

71. Quoted in *P.W.*, August 13, 1910, Vol. 78, No. 2011, p. 726.

72. cc Letter Henry Holt to A. P. Watt, July 30, 1890.

73. cc Letter Charles Scribner to Stephen Townsend, August 28, 1899.

74. cc Letter Charles Scribner to L. W. Bangs, July 13, 1893.

75. G. H. P[utnam] and J. B. P[utnam], *op. cit.*, pp. 124–125.

76. William Ellsworth, *op. cit.*, p. 106.

77. Robert Sterling Yard, *op. cit.*, 1913, p. 172.

78. William Ellsworth, *op. cit.*, p. 107.

CHAPTER 4. CONTRACTS BETWEEN AUTHORS AND PUBLISHERS

1. Robert Sterling Yard, *op. cit.*, p. 29.

2. Quoted in *P.W.*, June 23, 1888, Vol. 33, No. 856, p. 963.

3. Robert Sterling Yard, *op. cit.*, p. 179.

4. *American Publishers' Circular and Literary Gazette,* January 1, 1864, Vol. 2, No. 5, p. 171.

5. The preceding paragraphs are based upon manuscripts in the archives of Dodd, Mead and Company, the successor to Moses W. Dodd.

6. cc Letter Henry Holt to Professor Simon Newcomb, April 9, 1880.

7. Letter E. H. Babbitt to Henry Holt, November 28, 1910.

8. cc Letter Henry Holt to Professor H. Newell Martin, April 20, 1880.

9. See, for example, the arbitration clause in the contract signed by Harper and Brother on August 1, 1901, for George Ade's *Fifty Modern Fables.*

10. See, for example, cc Letter Charles Scribner to Henry Holt, November 8, 1880.

11. G[eorge] H[aven] P[utnam] and J. B[ishop] P[utnam], *op. cit.*, pp. 160–61.

12. *P.W.*, March 13, 1915, Vol. 88, No. 2249, pp. 791–92, contains an interesting article on arbitration by the textbook publisher, Frederick A. Stokes.

13. G[eorge] H[aven] P[utnam] and J. B[ishop] P[utnam], *op. cit.*, pp. 74–79.

14. Walter Page, *op. cit.*, pp. 102, 107, 109.

15. cc Letter Charles Scribner's Sons to Prof. John D. Davis, March 8, 1894.

16. cc Letter Holt and Co. to Mr. M. Ramsey, July 24, 1893.

17. *The Book Buyer*, November, 1888, Vol. 5, No. 10, p. 388.

18. cc Cables Charles Scribner's Sons to Frances Hodgson Burnett, January 5, 1888 and January 12, 1888.

19. cc Letters Charles Scribner to Mrs. Helen Hunt, February 26, 1879 and March 15, 1879.

20. cc Letter Henry Holt to Mme. L. Ailliot, October 10, 1880.

21. See, for example, cc form sent to Arlo Bates, dated April 25, 1885.

22. See, for example, MS contract dated July 14, 1899 with Tappan Adney for a manuscript entitled *Gold, Fire and Frost.*

23. cc Letter Henry Holt to Joseph Blethen September 4, 1903.

24. MS Royalty Ledger, 1900–15.

25. The preceding pages are based primarily upon the manuscript "Royalty Ledgers" of Harper and Brothers. There are four volumes of these, each volume containing about 800 pages, which present the terms of contracts in a form useful to this survey.

26. Robert Sterling Yard, *op. cit.*, p. 176.

27. cc Letter Charles Scribner to Mrs. James Russell Parsons, Jr., September 21, 1898.
28. MSS "Royalty Ledger," 1900–1903.
29. MSS Ledgers "Royalty Accounts" 1881–89; 1888–94.
30. cc Letter Charles Scribner to Richard T. Ely, September 6, 1898.
31. MSS Ledgers "Royalty Accounts," 1888–1915.
32. *P.W.*, April 24, 1886, Vol. 29, No. 743, p. 542. Robert Yard, *op. cit.*, pp. 11–13.
33. Robert Sterling Yard, *op. cit.*, p. 14.
34. Henry Walcott Boynton, *op. cit.*, pp. 147–48.
35. cc Letter Charles Scribner to Dr. Swan M. Burnett, February 9, 1881.
36. *P.W.*, April 20, 1876, Vol. 9, No. 227, p. 633.
37. cc Charles Scribner's Sons to Victor H. Olmstead, U. S. Department of Labor, March 31, 1900.
38. Robert Sterling Yard, *op. cit.*, p. 14.

CHAPTER 5. PRIVATE PUBLISHING AND PUBLIC SPEECH

1. Letter Albert Jonas to Scribner, Armstrong and Company, August 18, 1877.
2. *The Book Buyer*, April 1887, Vol. 4, No. 3, p. 115.
3. Alfred Harcourt, *op. cit.*, pp. 71–72.
4. cc Letter Henry Holt to Dr. Lyman C. Newell, February 20, 1900.
5. cc Letter Charles Scribner to Col. Charles W. Larned, February 3, 1899.
6. Frederick S. Crofts, "Textbooks are Not Absolutely Dead Things," in *The Bowker Lectures on Book Publishing*, First Series. New York, The Typophiles, 1943, p. 98.
7. Frederick S. Crofts, *op. cit.*, p. 91.
8. cc Letter Charles Scribner to Charles Welford, November 12, 1880.
9. cc J. Blair Scribner to Charles Welford, July 24, 1877.
10. cc Letter Charles Scribner to Kingsley, November 11, 1919.
11. cc Letter Henry Holt to F. M. Holland, May 7, 1884.
12. cc Letter Charles Scribner to L. W. Bangs, August 9, 1886.

13. *P.W.*, October 21, 1899, Vol. 56, No. 1447, p. 742.

14. *P.W.*, July 27, 1889, Vol. 36, No. 913, p. 117.

15. *The Book Buyer*, November 15, 1872, Vol. 6, No. 2, p. 12.

16. Catalogue of Harper and Brothers for 1872.

17. Morris L. Ernst and William Seagle, *To the Pure.* New York, Viking Press, 1928, pp. 10–11.

18. Letter John Hassard to Messrs. Scribner, October 13, 1887.

19. cc Letter Charles Scribner to Gertrude Atherton, October 10, 1887.

20. cc Letter Henry Holt to Robert A. Bennet, July 16, 1903.

21. *P.W.*, March 8, 1890, Vol. 37, No. 945, p. 353.

22. *P.W.*, September 6, 1890, Vol. 38, No. 971, p. 271.

23. cc Letter Charles Scribner to L. W. Bangs, February 8, 1911.

24. cc Letter Charles Scribner to L. W. Bangs, July 19, 1906.

25. Quoted in the *New York Times Book Review*, September 26, 1948, p. 8.

26. Harold Underwood Faulkner, *The Quest for Social Justice, 1898–1914.* New York, The Macmillan Company, 1931, p. 265.

27. Frederick A. Stokes, "A Publisher's Random Notes, 1880–1935," in *The Bowker Lectures on Book Publishing*, First Series, pp. 11–12.

28. "Obituary" of Edward Youmans in *P.W.*, January 22, 1887, Vol. 31, No. 782, pp. 92–93.

29. *P.W.*, September 1, 1877, Vol. 12, No. 294, p. 209.

30. cc Letter Charles Scribner to James Anthony Froude, March 3, 1880.

31. *P.W.*, October 19, 1889, Vol. 34, No. 925, p. 579.

32. cc Letter Henry Holt to Edward Kellogg Baird, March 4, 1913.

33. Gustavus Myers, "Preface to the 1936 Edition," *History of the Great American Fortunes*, New York, the Modern Library, pp. 19–20.

34. Harold Faulkner, *op. cit.*, p. 265.

35. Mark Sullivan, *Our Times*, Vol. II, New York, Charles Scribner's Sons, 1927, p. 471; Alice Payne Hackett, *op. cit.*, p. 22.

36. cc Letter Charles Scribner to L. W. Bangs, March 10, 1910.

37. *P.W.*, December 29, 1888, Vol. 34, No. 883, p. 985.

38. Dr. Joseph Dorfman, author of *Thorstein Veblen and His*

America, has seen correspondence indicating that Scribner believed Veblen's work would be welcomed by the business community, a fact which makes the publication of *The Theory of Business Enterprise* less suitable as evidence of the breadth of Scribner's publishing views.

39. Unless otherwise indicated, the information concerning the publishers of these books has been taken from the Catalogue of the Library of Congress.

40. Quoted in *The New York Times Book Review,* September 26, 1948, p. 8.

41. Morris L. Ernst and William Seagle, *To the Pure.* New York, the Viking Press, 1928, p. 150.

42. Morris L. Ernst and Alexander Lindley, *Hold Our Tongue.* New York, William Morrow and Company, 1932, p. 309.

43. Morris L. Ernst, *The First Freedom.* New York, The Macmillan Company, 1946, pp. 17–18.

44. Morris L. Ernst and William Seagle, *op. cit.,* p. 39.

45. *Ibid.,* p. 76.

46. *Ibid.,* p. 75.

47. Morris L. Ernst and Alexander Lindley, *The Censor Marches On.* New York, Doubleday, Doran and Company, 1940, p. 26.

48. Morris L. Ernst and William Seagle, *op. cit.,* p. 100.

49. Morris L. Ernst, *op. cit.,* p. 18.

50. Morris L. Ernst and William Seagle, *op. cit.,* p. 1.

51. Morris L. Ernst, *op. cit.,* p. 18.

52. *P.W.,* June 7, 1902, Vol. 61, No. 1584, p. 1321.

53. *P.W.,* February 6, 1892, Vol. 41, No. 1045, p. 290.

54. *P.W.,* July 30, 1910, Vol. 76, No. 2009, p. 597.

55. Morris L. Ernst and Alexander Lindley, *op. cit.,* p. 9.

56. Morris L. Ernst and William Seagle, *op. cit.,* p. 36.

57. *P.W.,* June 30, 1894, Vol. 45, No. 1170, p. 942.

58. See, for example, Morris L. Ernst and William Seagle, *To the Pure,* pp. 167–168; and Morris L. Ernst and Alexander Lindley, *The Censor Marches On,* pp. 218–219.

59. Frederick Crofts, *op. cit.,* p. 91.

CHAPTER 6. THE CREATIVENESS OF PUBLISHING

1. G[eorge] H[aven] P[utnam] and J. B[ishop] P[utnam], *op. cit.*, pp. 6–7.
2. Walter Page, *op. cit.*, p. 104.
3. Henry Holt, quoted in *P.W.*, April 16, 1910, Vol. 77, No. 1994, p. 1705.
4. *Ibid.*
5. Henry Boynton, *op. cit.*, p. 185.
6. Walter Page, *op. cit.*, pp. 83–89.
7. Quoted in *Saturday Review of Literature*, May 12, 1945, p. 4.
8. See, for example, cc Letter Charles Scribner to Hazzard, May 13, 1887 and cc Letter Henry Holt to Montgomery Schuyler, April 14, 1903.
9. Modern publishers whom the present writer has served in the capacity of "reader" attribute it to both.
10. See, for example, cc Letters Henry Holt to Dr. J. G. Brinton, December 11, 1890; to A. P. C. Griffin, June 29, 1891; to Professor G. H. Palmer, January 16, 1892.
11. cc Letter Charles Scribner to Professor George B. Stevens, September 19, 1893.
12. See, for example, cc Letters Henry Holt to Edwin De Leon, June 25, 1891; to Professor Wood, July 2, 1891; to Miss F. C. [illegible], October 26, 1880; to J. O. Cosgrave, July 3, 1903.
13. Walter H. Page, *op. cit.*, p. 86.
14. Quoted in *P.W.*, August 13, 1892, Vol. 42, No. 1072, p. 231.
15. Quoted in *P.W.*, October 15, 1892, Vol. 42, No. 1081, p. 632.
16. William Ellsworth, *op. cit.*, pp. 186–187.
17. G[eorge] H[aven] P[utnam] and J. B[ishop] P[utnam], *op. cit.*, p. 108.
18. cc Letters Charles Scribner to Professor George T. Fisher, March 5, 1890 and to Charles Welford, April 9, 1880.
19. cc Letter Henry Holt to Dr. S. Weir Mitchell, February 1, 1878.
20. See for example letters to Holt from T. R. Lounsbury, January 16, 1878, Henry A. Beers, March 18, 1879, Daniel Coit Gilman, February 18, 1878.

21. Frederick Stokes, *op. cit.*, pp. 99–100.

22. cc Letter Charles Scribner's Sons to General A. W. Greely, March 21, 1893.

23. William Ellsworth, *op. cit.*, pp. 259–267.

24. cc Letter Charles Scribner's Sons to John Muir [October 17 or 18, 1878].

25. cc Letter Charles Scribner to Professor George Adam Smith, March 9, 1899.

26. See, for example, Letter C. E. Bessey to Henry Holt, May 8, 1878.

27. cc Letter Henry Holt to Professor T. D. Goodwell, January 30, 1903.

28. *P.W.*, April 1, 1876, Vol. 9, No. 220, p. 431.

29. *Ibid.*, p. 437.

30. *Ibid.*, p. 431.

31. cc Letter Charles Scribner to Thomas Nelson Page, March 8, 1898.

32. Letter Charles Scribner to Messrs. Gebbie and Co., July 16, 1902.

33. cc Letter Charles Scribner to Charles Welford, April 15, 1881.

34. cc Letter Henry Holt to Professor Trent, December 16, 1903.

35. cc Letter Henry Holt to George Waring, April 12, 1880.

36. cc Letter Henry Holt to J. Cosgrave, July 3, 1903.

37. cc Letter Charles Scribner to Donald Mitchell, Janaury 12, 1893.

38. cc Letter Henry Holt to Miss Macfarlane, November 21, 1884.

39. Morris L. Ernst and William Seagle, *op. cit.*, p. 46.

40. cc Letters Charles Scribner's Sons to Rev. Washington Gladden, December 14, 1897, and Charles Scribner to L. W. Bangs, December 6, 1904.

41. See, for example, cc Letter Henry Holt to W. D. Hyde, April 4, 1892.

42. cc Letter Henry Holt and Company to William E. Bailey, July 3, 1884.

43. cc Letter Henry Holt to Mrs. Dolores M. Bacon, January 10, 1906.

44. cc Letter Henry Holt to Mrs. Bosch, November 12, 1902.

45. cc Letter Henry Holt to Mrs. Dolores Bacon, December 20, 1907.

46. cc Letter Edward L. Burlingame to Robert Louis Stevenson, June 20, 1890.

47. cc Letter Henry Holt to General Adam Badeau, January 26, 1885.

CHAPTER 7. THE MACHINERY OF WHOLESALE DISTRIBUTION

1. *P.W.*, April 26, 1913, Vol. 83, No. 2151, p. 1493.

2. *American Literary Gazette and Publishers' Circular,* January 1, 1864, Vol. 2, No. 5, p. 176.

3. *P.W.*, June 5, 1886, Vol. 29, No. 749, p. 738; Frank E. Compton, "Subscription Books," in *The Bowker Lectures on Book Publishing,* First Series. New York, The Typophiles, 1943, pp. 127–129.

4. Henry C. Carey, quoted in *American Publishers' Circular and Literary Gazette,* June 1, 1863, Vol. 1, No. 3, pp. 130–131.

5. *American Publishers' Circular and Literary Gazette,* June 18, 1859, Vol. 5, No. 25, p. 294; and July 23, 1859, Vol. 5, No. 30, p. 357.

6. *American Publishers' Circular and Literary Gazette,* April 16, 1859, Vol. 5, No. 16, p. 186.

7. *American Literary Gazette and Publishers' Circular,* April 16, 1866, Vol. 6, No. 12, p. 332.

8. The story of the trade sales is scattered through the issues of the *American Publishers' Circular and Literary Gazette* and *Publishers' Weekly* over a period of forty years. It is impossible to cite one or several articles which explain it, since every reference presupposes a considerable knowledge on the part of the reader. Such limited knowledge as can be gained must be built up from many incidental bits of information which only an extensive reading of these trade journals can bring to light. The most exact reference which can be made is to the issues published between 1855 and 1875 during the months of April and September, when the sales were held.

9. *American Publishers' Circular and Literary Gazette,* September 24, 1859, Vol. 5, No. 39, p. 473.

10. *American Literary Gazette and Publishers' Circular*, September 1, 1869, Vol. 13, No. 9, p. 249.
11. Frank Compton, *op. cit.*, pp. 130–131.
12. *Ibid.*
13. Frank Compton, *op. cit.*, p. 132.
14. *P.W.*, September 16, 1876, Vol. 10, No. 244, p. 456.
15. *P.W.*, February 5, 1876, Vol. 9, No. 212, p. 167.
16. *Ibid.*
17. See *P.W.*, September 16, 1876, Vol. 10, No. 244, p. 458 for a list of the participants.
18. *P.W.*, April 8, 1876, Vol. 9, No. 221, p. 475.
19. *P.W.*, September 30, 1876, Vol. 10, No. 246, pp. 567–568.
20. cc Letter J. Blair Scribner to Charles Welford, January 16, 1877.
21. *P.W.*, January 20, 1877, Vol. 11, No. 262, p. 60.
22. *P.W.*, April 7, 1877, Vol. 11, No. 273, pp. 396–397; and September 29, 1877, Vol. 12, No. 294, p. 365.
23. Quoted in *P.W.*, July 29, 1882, Vol. 22, No. 550, p. 135.
24. Quoted in *P.W.*, March 11, 1882, Vol. 21, No. 530, p. 257.
25. *P.W.*, April 19, 1884, Vol. 25, No. 638, p. 479.
26. *P.W.*, May 3, 1884, Vol. 25, No. 640, p. 530.
27. *P.W.*, April 23, 1887, Vol. 31, No. 791, p. 562.
28. *P.W.*, September 10, 1887, Vol. 32, No. 815, p. 263.
29. *P.W.*, April 12, 1890, Vol. 38, No. 950, p. 509.
30. *American Publishers' Circular and Literary Gazette*, November 5, 1850, Vol. 5, No. 45, p. 554.
31. Frederick Stokes, *op. cit.*, pp. 18–19. I am indebted to Mr. Chris Gerhardt, who was employed by Bangs and Company from 1884 to 1903, for an understanding of the activities of that company. Mr. Oscar Weglin, who entered the book trade in New York in 1893, has been similarly helpful in explaining to me the workings of the "parcel" and "trade" sales.
32. Typescript of an Address by Frank Dodd to the Booksellers' Association, June, 1905.
33. MSS Agreements of February 3, 1877 and January 10, 1879 between Dodd, Mead and Company and J. F. Smith.
34. Letter Houghton, Mifflin and Company to Dodd, Mead and Company, September 8, 1882.

35. *American Publishers' Circular and Literary Gazette,* February, 1862, Vol. 8, No. 2, p. 19.

36. *P.W.*, February 18, 1882, Vol. 21, No. 527, p. 182.

37. *American Publishers' Circular and Literary Gazette,* September 15, 1864, Vol. 3, No. 10, p. 340.

38. *P.W.*, June 26, 1909, Vol. 75, No. 1952, pp. 2057–2058; cc Letter Charles Scribner to H. O. Houghton, November 1, 1893.

39. cc Letter Charles Scribner to Mrs. Edward Wharton, November 10, 1905.

40. William Ellsworth, *op. cit.,* p. 174.

41. cc Letter Charles Scribner to Mrs. Stephen Townsend, June 4, 1901.

42. *P.W.*, March 17, 1877, Vol. 11, No. 270, p. 292.

43. *P.W.*, March 17, 1877, Vol. 11, No. 270, p. 292.

44. See, for example, MS Agreement between Dodd, Mead and Company and Samuel Carson, "Manufacturers' Agent" of San Francisco, May 26, 1880.

45. Edward H. Dodd, Jr., *op. cit.,* p. 28.

46. cc Letter Henry Holt to Professor Jabez Brooks, November 18, 1884.

47. cc Letter E. N. Bristol to Robert M. King, June 9, 1902.

48. *P.W.*, January 6, 1906, Vol. 67, No. 1771, pp. 14–15.

49. *P.W.*, January 2, 1897, Vol. 51, No. 1301, p. 6.

50. *P.W.*, February 29, 1908, Vol. 73, No. 1883, p. 950.

51. *P.W.*, February 26, 1910, Vol. 77, No. 1987, p. 1045.

52. *P.W.*, February 21, 1914, Vol. 85, No. 2194, p. 634.

53. *P.W.*, February 21, 1914, Vol. 85, No. 2194, pp. 629–630.

54. cc Letter Henry Holt to F. S. Hackett, July 9, 1903.

55. *P.W.*, January 16, 1909, Vol. 75, No. 1929, p. 79.

56. *P.W.*, April 26, 1913, Vol. 83, No. 2151, p. 1493.

CHAPTER 8. THE ASSAULT ON THE CONSUMER

1. cc Letter Henry Holt to F. S. Hackett, July 9, 1903.

2. Walter H. Page, *op. cit.,* pp. 91–92.

3. cc Letter Charles Scribner to L. W. Bangs, April 29, 1895.

4. Quoted in *P.W.*, December 12, 1885, Vol. 28, No. 724, p. 919.

5. Robert Sterling Yard, *op. cit.,* pp. 50–54.

6. Quoted in *P.W.*, November 16, 1901, Vol. 60, No. 1555, pp. 1041–1042.

7. *Ibid.*

8. Quoted in *P.W.*, June 20, 1903, Vol. 63, No. 1638, p. 1419.

9. O. H. Cheney, *Supplementary Report of the Economic Survey of the Book Industry for Bookbinding Executives.* New York, Employing Bookbinders of America, 1932, p. 11. MS "Recapitulation of Sales" [for 1912, Henry Holt and Company].

10. See above, Chapter 2.

11. cc Letter Henry Holt to J. J. Lalor, February 6, 1878.

12. *P.W.*, July 30, 1898, Vol. 54, No. 1383, p. 152.

13. *The Book Buyer,* December 16, 1867, Vol. 1, No. 3, p. 1.

14. *P.W.*, February 19, 1910, Vol. 77, No. 1986, p. 976.

15. Ralph Thompson, *American Literary Annuals and Gift Books, 1825–1865.* New York, The H. W. Wilson Company, 1936, p. 1.

16. cc Letter Charles Scribner to Charles Welford, August 2, 1881.

17. *P.W.*, December 10, 1910, Vol. 78, No. 2028, p. 2338.

18. *American Literary Gazette and Publishers' Circular,* January 1, 1864, Vol. 2, No. 5, p. 173.

19. cc Letter Scribner, Armstrong and Company to the *New York Daily Bulletin,* December 7, 1875.

20. cc Letter Charles Scribner to Thomas Nelson Page, May 5, 1903.

21. Walter Page, *op. cit.,* pp. 35–36.

22. G[eorge] H[aven] P[utnam] and J. B[ishop] P[utnam], *op. cit.,* p. 171.

23. Robert Sterling Yard, *op. cit.,* pp. 79–80.

24. Frederick Stokes, *op. cit.,* p. 21.

25. *P.W.*, September 28, 1912, Vol. 82, No. 2121, p. 964.

26. *P.W.*, August 30, 1902, Vol. 62, No. 1596, p. 299; January 14, 1911, Vol. 79, No. 2033, pp. 47–48.

27. Quoted in *The Book Buyer,* October, 1900, Vol. 21, No. 3, p. 183.

28. G[eorge] H[aven] P[utnam] and J. B[ishop] P[utnam], *op. cit.,* p. 171.

29. cc Letter Charles Scribner to Hamilton W. Mabie, May 28, 1900.

30. MS Letter Edward Abbot to Henry Holt and Company, March 20, 1878.

31. *P.W.*, August 30, 1902, Vol. 62, No. 1596, pp. 299–300; January 6, 1912, Vol. 81, No. 2083, pp. 8–10.

32. MS Ledger, "Production Statistics," 1880–1882.

33. G[eorge] H[aven] P[utnam] and J. B[ishop] P[utnam], *op. cit.*, p. 178.

34. *P.W.*, October 5, 1901, Vol. 58, No. 1549, p. 763.

35. Walter H. Page, *op. cit.*, p. 115.

36. *Ibid.*, p. 95.

37. *Ibid.*, pp. 38–39; Robert Sterling Yard, *op. cit.*, p. 29.

38. G[eorge] H[aven] P[utnam] and J. B[ishop] P[utnam], *op. cit.*, p. 174.

39. The Dodd, Mead and Company collection of early manuscript agreements contains several illustrations of this. See, for example, the contract signed June 3, 1853 with D. M. and S. W. Whitney for *Open Communion.*

40. MS Ledger, "Production Statistics," 1880–1882.

41. Quoted in *P.W.*, April 18, 1885, Vol. 28, No. 690, pp. 469–470.

42. Quoted in *P.W.*, August 20, 1892, Vol. 42, No. 1073, pp. 252–253.

43. Walter H. Page, *op. cit.*, pp. 18, 118–119.

44. cc Letter Henry Holt to F. S. Hackett, September 16, 1903.

45. Walter H. Page, *op. cit.*, p. 51.

46. cc Letter Henry Holt and Company to C. E. Wolcott, July 23, 1903.

47. cc Letter Henry Holt to F. S. Hackett, September 4, 1903.

48. *P.W.*, August 31, 1912, Vol. 82, No. 2117, p. 569.

49. G[eorge] H[aven] P[utnam] and J. B[ishop] P[utnam], *op. cit.*, pp. 168–169.

50. Robert Sterling Yard, *op. cit.*, pp. 59–62.

51. cc Letter Henry Holt to F. S. Hackett, September 16, 1903.

52. William Ellsworth, *op. cit.*, pp. 168–169.

53. Walter H. Page, *op. cit.*, p. 18.

54. Robert Sterling Yard, *op. cit.*, pp. 16–17.

55. Alfred Harcourt, *op. cit.*, pp. 61–62.
56. Robert Sterling Yard, *op. cit.*, pp. 65–66.
57. William Ellsworth, *op. cit.*, p. 168.
58. *American Publishers' Circular anl Literary Gazette,* August 6, 1859, Vol. 5, No. 32, p. 386; September 10, 1859, Vol. 5, No. 37, pp. 452–54; March 24, 1860, Vol. 6, No. 12, pp. 142–44.
59. *American Book Trade Manual, 1915.* New York, R. R. Bowker Co., 1915, pp. 243–327.
60. O. H. Cheney, *op. cit.*, p. 238.
61. Frank Compton, *op. cit.*, pp. 130–133.
62. Hubert Hungerford, *How Publishers Win.* Washington, D.C., Ransdell Inc., 1931, p. 281.
63. *American Literary Gazette and Publishers' Circular,* July 1, 1865, Vol. 5, No. 5, p. 113.
64. *P.W.*, January 27, 1894, Vol. 45, No. 1148, p. 191; March 26, 1898, Vol. 53, No. 1365, p. 583.
65. cc Letter Blair Scribner to Charles Welford, September 10, 1872.
66. cc Letter Charles Scribner to Messrs. Smith, Elder and Co., September 16, 1897.
67. cc Letter Charles Scribner to Thomas Nelson Page, June 21, 1905.
68. Walter Page, *op. cit.*, pp. 148–150.
69. cc Letter Charles Scribner to F. W. Hewes, January 16, 1906.
70. *P.W.*, January 27, 1894, Vol. 45, No. 1148, p. 191.
71. cc Letter Scribner, Armstrong and Company to George W. Childs, May 18, 1876.
72. "List of Subscription Publications, Charles Scribner's Sons, February 22, 1891."
73. Robert Sterling Yard, *op. cit.*, pp. 100–101.
74. *P.W.*, January 18, 1879, Vol. 15, No. 366, p. 48.
75. Typescript of Address by Frank Dodd to the Booksellers Association, June, 1905.
76. Robert Sterling Yard, *op. cit.*, pp. 126–129.
77. Edward H. Dodd, Jr., *op. cit.*, p. 30.
78. The author is indebted for this information concerning present practices to the director of the mail-order department of a large house who prefers to remain anonymous.

79. MS, "Analysis of Expenses, September 30, 1910," Harper and Brothers.

80. Walter H. Page, *op. cit.*, p. 122.

81. cc Letter Charles Scribner to J. W. Nichols, January 12, 1905.

82. *P.W.*, August 24, 1912, Vol. 82, No. 2116, p. 407.

83. Walter H. Page, *op. cit.*, pp. 122–124.

CHAPTER 9. THE PROBLEMS OF COMPETITION AND THE SELF-REGULATION OF THE BOOK TRADE

1. Quoted in *American Literary Gazette and Publishers' Circular,* February 1, 1864, Vol. 2, No. 7, pp. 238–239.

2. *P.W.*, April 19, 1890, Vol. 38, No. 951, p. 529.

3. *P.W.*, March 6, 1909, Vol. 75, No. 1936, p. 1044.

4. *P.W.*, March 10, 1888, Vol. 33, No. 841, p. 470.

5. *P.W.*, June 6, 1896, Vol. 49, No. 1271, pp. 951–952.

6. *P.W.*, June 13, 1896, Vol. 49, No. 1272, p. 985.

7. *P.W.*, August 4, 1900, Vol. 58, No. 1488, pp. 326–327; *American Publishers Circular and Literary Gazette,* August 1, 1863, Vol. 1, No. 7, p. 258; *American Literary Gazette and Publishers' Circular,* March 1, 1865, Vol. 4, No. 9, p. 238. *P.W.*, June 13, 1896, Vol. 49, No. 1272, pp. 985–96.

8. Quoted in *American Literary Gazette and Publishers' Circular,* December 1, 1863, Vol. 2, No. 3, p. 80.

9. *P.W.*, March 3, 1877, Vol. 9, No. 268, p. 244.

10. From the "Minutes of the Regular Quarterly Meeting of the Publishers' Board of Trade," quoted in *The Publishers' and Stationers' Weekly Trade Circular,* April 11, 1872, Vol. 1, No. 13, pp. 325–327; *P.W.*, January 15, 1881, Vol. 19, No. 470, pp. 48–49.

11. From the "Minutes of the Regular Quarterly Meeting of the Publishers' Board of Trade," quoted in *The Publishers' and Stationers' Weekly Trade Circular,* April 11, 1872, Vol. 1, No. 13, pp. 325–327; *P.W.*, January 15, 1881, Vol. 19, No. 470, pp. 48–49; *American Literary Gazette and Publishers' Circular,* May 7, 1871, Vol. 17, No. 10, p. 3.

12. *P.W.*, February 27, 1877, Vol. 11, No. 267, pp. 225–226.

13. *P.W.*, January 15, 1881, Vol. 19, No. 470, pp. 48–49.

14. *Ibid.*

15. *P.W.*, March 31, 1877, Vol. 11, No. 272, p. 374.
16. See above, Chapter 2.
17. *P.W.*, July 23, 1904, Vol. 66, No. 1695, pp. 177–178.
18. *P.W.*, July 26, 1913, Vol. 84, No. 2164, p. 153.
19. *The Publishers' and Stationers' Weekly Trade Circular,* March 28, 1872, Vol. 1, No. 11, p. 268.
20. Address of Frank Dodd to the Booksellers' Association, June, 1905.
21. cc Letter Scribner, Armstrong and Company to Professor Francis Bowen, June 17, 1876.
22. *P.W.*, April 5, 1884, Vol. 25, No. 636, pp. 438–439.
23. *Ibid.*
24. *P.W.*, June 6, 1891, Vol. 39, No. 1010, p. 788.
25. *P.W.*, October 17, 1885, Vol. 28, No. 716, p. 547.
26. *American Literary Gazette and Publishers' Circular,* March 2, 1868, Vol. 10, No. 9, p. 240; *P.W.*, October 17, 1885, Vol. 28, No. 716, p. 547.
27. Henry Boynton, *op. cit.*, p. 179.
28. *P.W.*, March 3, 1888, Vol. 33, No. 840, p. 448.
29. Henry Boynton, *op. cit.*, p. 179.
30. *P.W.*, January 31, 1888, Vol. 33, No. 834, pp. 66–67.
31. Frederick A. Stokes, *op. cit.*, pp. 3–4.
32. *P.W.*, January 31, 1888, Vol. 33, No. 834, pp. 67–68.
33. cc Letter Charles Scribner to L. W. Bangs, December 4, 1888.
34. cc Letter Charles Scribner to George Haven Putnam, January 31, 1889.
35. *P.W.*, March 7, 1891, Vol. 39, No. 997, pp. 364–368.
36. *P.W.*, January 9, 1904, Vol. 65, No. 1667, p. 35.
37. *P.W.*, January 4, 1879, Vol. 15, No. 364, p. 8.
38. cc Letter Henry Holt to Eugene L. Didier, October 29, 1878.
39. Frederick Stokes, *op. cit.*, p. 25.
40. cc Letter Charles Scribner to John Murray, Jr., March 27, 1891.
41. cc Letter Charles Scribner to J. C. Kennedy, November 16, 1892.
42. *P.W.*, June 27, 1903, Vol. 63, No. 1639, p. 1451.
43. *P.W.*, February 15, 1890, Vol. 37, No. 942, p. 274.
44. *P.W.*, June 1, 1876, Vol. 10, No. 233, pp. 8–9.

45. Quoted in *P.W.*, February 26, 1876, Vol. 9, No. 215, p. 255.
46. *Ibid.*
47. *P.W.*, June 17, 1882, Vol. 21, No. 544, pp. 642–643.
48. Quoted in *P.W.*, June 27, 1885, Vol. 27, No. 700, p. 732.
49. *P.W.*, May 22, 1909, Vol. 75, No. 1947, p. 1714.
50. cc Letter Charles Scribner to L. W. Bangs, July 14, 1914.
51. *P.W.*, October 3, 1896, Vol. 50, No. 1288, p. 592.
52. cc Letter Charles Scribner to George Haven Putnam, October 13, 1897.
53. *P.W.*, December 22, 1900, Vol. 58, No. 1508, p. 1734.
54. *P.W.*, July 17, 1897, Vol. 52, No. 1329, pp. 120–122.
55. cc Letters Charles Scribner to George H. Mifflin, December 14, 1900 and February 8, 1901.
56. *P.W.*, March 2, 1901, Vol. 59, No. 1518, p. 613.
57. *P.W.*, May 11, 1912, Vol. 81, No. 2101, p. 1547.
58. cc Letter Henry Holt to E. A. Dithmar, September 14, 1903.
59. *P.W.*, May 14, 1910, Vol. 77, No. 1998, pp. 1957–1958.
60. *P.W.*, October 12, 1901, Vol. 60, No. 1550, p. 312.
61. cc Letter Charles Scribner to J. W. Nichols, January 3, 1902.
62. cc Letter Henry Holt to E. A. Dithmar, September 14, 1903.
63. *P.W.*, May 11, 1912, Vol. 81, No. 2101, p. 1547.
64. *P.W.*, October 13, 1900, Vol. 58, No. 1498, p. 917.
65. Quoted in *P.W.*, August 3, 1901, Vol. 60, No. 1540, p. 216.
66. *P.W.*, December 21, 1901, Vol. 60, No. 1560, p. 1409.
67. *P.W.*, May 15, 1909, Vol. 75, No. 1946, p. 1654, 1672.
68. cc Letter Charles Scribner to George P. Brett, November 7, 1901.
69. cc Letter Charles Scribner to John M. Brown, December 31, 1901.
70. *P.W.*, December 13, 1913, Vol. 84, No. 2184, p. 2078.
71. *P.W.*, December 13, 1902, Vol. 62, No. 1611, p. 1427; January 17, 1903, Vol. 63, No. 1616, pp. 66–72.
72. *P.W.*, March 5, 1904, Vol. 65, No. 1675, pp. 752–759; August 17, 1907, Vol. 72, No. 1853, p. 380; October 16, 1909, Vol. 76 No. 1968, p. 1079.
73. cc Letter Charles Scribner to George Haven Putnam, February 29, 1904.
74. *P.W.*, December 6, 1913, Vol. 84, No. 2183, pp. 1933–1937;

July 4, 1914, Vol. 86, No. 2213, pp. 7–8; November 7, 1914, Vol. 86, No. 2231, pp. 1433–1434.

75. *P.W.*, July 4, 1914, Vol. 86, No. 2213, p. 7.

76. Robert Sterling Yard, *op. cit.*, p. 19.

77. cc Letter Charles Scribner to George L. Leonard, May 19, 1903.

78. cc Letter Charles Scribner to J. W. Nicholas, The American Booksellers' Association, August 8, 1902.

79. Quoted in *P.W.*, January 16, 1915, Vol. 87, No. 2241, p. 138.

80. *P.W.*, August 16, 1902, Vol. 57, No. 1594, p. 247.

81. *P.W.*, July 4, 1914, Vol. 86, No. 2213, p. 7.

CHAPTER 10. CONCLUSIONS

1. G[eorge] H[aven] P[utnam] and J. B[ishop] P[utnam], *op. cit.*, p. 188.

2. Henry Holt, *Garrulities of an Octogenarian Editor*. Boston, Houghton Mifflin Company, 1923, p. 211.

Bibliography

A. MANUSCRIPTS

1. *Charles Scribner's Sons Collection*

The largest part of this collection consists of letter-books containing copies of the outgoing correspondence of the company's chief officials. There are seven volumes with about 4,300 letters written by J. Blair Scribner between 1869 and 1879. Some twenty-five volumes containing about 23,000 letters written between 1878 and 1906 have been retained of the correspondence of Charles Scribner. Among these the most valuable are four volumes of letters to the firm's English representatives, Charles Welford and L. W. Bangs, between 1878 and 1893. These letters summarize business trends and comment on general trade problems.

Except for the years from 1875 to 1879, the only incoming correspondence which has been retained is the letters of the authors, and even these files are incomplete. At the request of the company, these incoming letters were not examined.

Supplementing this correspondence are miscellaneous business and production records, among them the following:

"Abstract of Copyright Contracts" [1852–1894]
"Abstract of Copyright Contracts" [1898–1906]
"Copyright a/cs from July, 1861 to July 1874"
[Ledger of Import and Export Contracts, 1899–1906]
"Manuscript Record" [1873–1883]
"Plate Book" [1874]
"List of Subscription Publications, February, 1891"
"Book on Inventory of Scribner's Magazine, 1905–1915"
"Record Book of Plate Costs, 1873–79"
"Record Book of Plate Costs, 1897–1900"
"Record Book of Plate Costs, 1900–03"

Taken as a whole, the Scribner archives are the most extensive in the industry for the period between the Civil War and 1914.

2. *Henry Holt and Company Collection*

This collection consists almost entirely of the letter-books of outgoing correspondence. There are about 200 of these volumes, each with approximately 500 letters. At least a third of the letters are so faded as to be unreadable. Of the remainder, more than three-quarters relate to such routine matters as the acknowledgment of orders and specific inquiries concerning the firm's publications. The most valuable portion is the correspondence of Henry Holt himself, which comprises not fewer than 8,000 letters written between 1878 and 1904.

The remainder of the collection contains several rather unenlightening account books of the 1860's, about 1,000 letters received in 1876 and 1877, and fragments of financial records, of which the most valuable pertain to 1912.

3. *Harper and Brothers Collection*

This collection is especially useful for its information concerning authors' contracts. Extracts of the terms are listed in a series of "Royalty Ledgers," the earliest of which is for 1881. However, the ledgers for the periods 1900–03 and 1912–15 give the essential details of 1,600 contracts signed over a period of more than fifty years, the earliest in 1848. To these summaries may be added copies of the full text of several hundred contracts negotiated between 1885 and 1914, which are filed with the correspondence concerning them.

The archives include also a number of miscellaneous business records, especially significant for the years after the firm was reorganized under Colonel George Harvey in 1900. An unusually complete file of the firm's catalogues rounds out the most valuable portion of the collection.

4. *Dodd, Mead and Company Collection*

This collection is also especially notable for the light it throws on relations with authors. Included in it are twenty-nine contracts signed between 1849 and 1855. The most helpful of the manuscripts after the Civil War are some fragmentary financial records, among them a few annual statements, and a number of documents relating to the firm's capital structure. Several agreements signed with commercial travellers and special representatives reveal the new methods of distribution. The firm published a series of undated pamphlets which summarize its growth from 1839, and explain its internal organization in the last quarter of the nineteenth century.

B. TRADE JOURNALS

No history of book publishing could be written without the assistance of *Publishers' Weekly* and its predecessors. This widely respected journal began in 1873 as a result of the consolidation of the two leading trade organs of the day. *The American Publishers' Circular and Literary Gazette,* sometimes called the *American Literary Gazette and Publishers' Circular,* was founded in 1855 and published continually until it was purchased by Frederick Leypoldt in 1872. Leypoldt then merged it with *The Publishers' and Stationers' Weekly Trade Circular,* which he himself had established in 1869.

From its first issue, *Publishers' Weekly* enjoyed a well-merited respect, which it has never lost. It is especially valuable to the historian for its editorial comments on trade conditions, and for its report on the meetings of the trade's many associations, whose minutes it often reproduced *verbatim.* It solicited lengthy analyses from trade leaders, conducted polls and interviews, and reproduced pertinent articles culled from numerous and otherwise unavailable sources. Compared to *Publishers' Weekly,* other trade magazines such as the *Bookman* and the *Book Buyer* have an incidental importance for this study, and have been used only incidentally.

C. SECONDARY MATERIALS

Clarence E. Allen, *Publishers' Accounts.* London, Gee and Company, 1897.

Frederick Lewis Allen, *Paul Revere Reynolds.* New York [Privately Printed], 1944.

James S. Bain, *A Bookseller Looks Back.* London, Macmillan and Company, Ltd., 1940.

The Bowker Lectures on Book Publishing, First Series. New York, The Typophiles, 1943.

The Bowker Lectures on Book Publishing, Second Series. New York, The Typophiles, 1945.

Henry Walcott Boynton, *Annals of American Bookselling, 1638–1850.* New York, John Wiley and Sons, Inc., 1932.

Roger Burlingame, *Of Making Many Books.* New York, Charles Scribner's Sons, 1946.

[Anon.] *A Century of Book Publishing, 1848–1948.* New York, D. Van Nostrand Company, Inc., 1948.

O. H. Cheney, *Economic Survey of the Book Industry, 1930–1931.* New York, National Association of Book Publishers, 1931.

O. H. Cheney, *Supplementary Report of the Economic Survey of the Book Industry for Bookbinding Executives.* New York, Employing Bookbinders of America, 1932.

Frank E. Compton, "Subscription Books," in *The Bowker Lectures on Book Publishing,* First Series. New York, The Typophiles, 1943.

[ed.] G. D. Crain, Jr., *Teacher of Business, the Publishing Philosophy of James H. McGraw.* Chicago, Advertising Publications, Inc., 1944.

Frederick S. Crofts, "Textbooks Are Not Absolutely Dead Things," in *The Bowker Lectures on Book Publishing,* First Series. New York, The Typophiles, 1943.

Edward H. Dodd, Jr., *The First Hundred Years.* New York, Dodd, Mead and Company, 1939.

George H. Doran, *Chronicles of Barabbas, 1884–1934.* New York, Harcourt, Brace and Company, 1935.

William H. Ellsworth, *A Golden Age of Authors.* Boston, Houghton Mifflin Company, 1919.

Morris L. Ernst, *The First Freedom,* New York, The Macmillan Company, 1946.

Morris L. Ernst and Alexander Lindley, *The Censor Marches On.* New York, Doubleday, Doran and Company, 1940.

Morris L. Ernst and Alexander Lindley, *Hold Our Tongue.* New York, William Morrow and Company, 1932.

Morris L. Ernst and William Seagle, *To the Pure.* New York, Viking Press, 1928.

Harold Underwood Faulkner, *The Quest for Social Justice, 1898–1914.* New York, The Macmillan Company, 1931.

Alice Payne Hackett, *Fifty Years of Best Sellers.* New York, R. R. Bowker Company, 1945.

Francis Whiting Halsey, *Our Literary Deluge.* New York, Doubleday, Page and Company, 1902.

Alfred Harcourt, "Publishing Since 1900," in *The Bowker Lectures on Book Publishing,* First Series. New York, The Typophiles, 1943.

Joseph H. Harper, *The House of Harper.* New York, Harper and Brothers, 1912.

Henry Holt, *Garrulities of an Octogenarian Editor.* Boston, Houghton Mifflin Company, 1923.

[Anon.] *Henry Holt.* New York, James T. White and Company, 1944.

[Anon.] *The House of Appleton-Century.* New York, D. Appleton–Century Company, 1936.

Hubert Hungerford, *How Publishers Win.* Washington, D.C., Ransdell, Inc., 1931.

Hellmut Lehmann-Haupt *et. al., The Book in America.* New York, R. R. Bowker Company, 1939.

William Miller, *The Book Industry.* New York, Columbia University Press, 1949.

Charles Morgan, *The House of Macmillan.* New York, The Macmillan Company, 1944.

Frank Luther Mott, *Golden Multitudes.* New York, The Macmillan Company, 1947.

Gustavus Myers, "Preface to the 1936 Edition," *History of the Great American Fortunes.* New York, The Modern Library.

Grant Overton, *Portrait of a Publisher; and the First Hundred Years of the House of Appleton, 1825–1925.* New York, D. Appleton and Company, 1925.

Walter H. Page, *A Publisher's Confession.* Garden City, Doubleday, Page and Company (1905, 1912), 1923.

John Barnes Pratt, *Personal Recollections; Sixty Years of Book Publishing.* New York, A. S. Barnes and Company, 1942.

George Haven Putnam, *Memories of a Publisher.* New York, G. P. Putnam's Sons, 1915.

George Haven Putnam and J. Bishop Putnam, *Authors and Publishers.* New York, G. P. Putnam's Sons, 1897.

Raymond Howard Shove, *Cheap Book Production in the United States, 1870–1891.* Urbana, University of Illinois Library, 1937.

Frederick A. Stokes, "A Publisher's Random Notes, 1880–1935," in *The Bowker Lectures on Book Publishing,* First Series.

Walter T. Spencer, *Forty Years in My Bookshop.* Boston, Houghton Mifflin Company, 1923.

Mark Sullivan, *Our Times,* Vol. II. New York, Charles Scribner's Sons, 1927.

Ralph Thompson, *American Literary Annuals and Gift Books, 1825–1865.* New York, The H. W. Wilson Company, 1936.

United States Bureau of the Census:

Manufactures of the United States in 1860. Washington, Government Printing Office, 1865.

Report of the Manufactures of the United States at the Tenth Census, June 1, 1880. Washington, Government Printing Office, 1883.

Report on Manufactures and Industries in the United States at the Eleventh Census: 1890. Washington, Government Printing Office, 1895.

Census Reports. Twelfth Census of the United States. Taken in the year 1900. Manufactures. Washington, Government Printing Office, 1902.

Census of Manufactures: 1905. Printing and Publishing. Washington, Government Printing Office, 1907.

Census of Manufactures: 1914. Printing and Publishing. Washington, Government Printing Office, 1918.

Sir Stanley Unwin, *The Truth About Publishing.* London, George Allen and Unwin, Ltd. (1926), 1946.

Ann Watkins, "Literature for Sale," in *The Bowker Lectures on Book Publishing,* Second Series. New York, The Typophiles, 1945.

Robert Sterling Yard, *The Publisher.* Boston, Houghton Mifflin Company, 1913.

INDEX